Shine like a Glow-Worm

Shine like a Glow-Worm

A. W. TAYLOR

SERENDIPITY

First published in 2002 by
Serendipity
Suite 530
37 Store Street
Bloomsbury
London

British Library Cataloguing-in-Publication data
A catalogue record for this book is available from the British Library

ISBN 1-84394-016-7

Printed and bound in the UK by Alden Digital, Oxford

To Ivy
My Love and my Life

Acknowledgements

I WISH TO THANK MY WIFE, Ivy, who understands me perfectly. Her infinite patience and encouragement shone out like a lighthouse beacon whenever I was despondent. She would ignore my unbearable and irritable moods, and persuade me to keep going; I could not do without her.

My very good army pal Terry Herbert with whom I was reunited after almost fifty years, helped me with my photographs and many reminders of our days in Berlin. Both he and his wife Gerda have entertained us at their home many times; I am grateful for their continuing friendship.

I also thank the curator of the National Rifle Association's Museum who helped me when I was researching and provided me with the information I required.

Finally my brothers and sisters whose reminiscences of family life when we were all young helped me stir up my own thoughts and memories of the thirties.

Preface

THE DITTY THAT FOLLOWS is one that my mother always wrote in her children's autograph books. The principle is self evident, and was her way of instilling certain facts of life. Not everyone becomes famous or rich, and the chances of doing so for poor working-class families in the 1930s were remote indeed. If we learnt and understood this, then we could take the knocks and disappointments in life in our stride without suffering the neurosis and unhappiness that follow from too high an expectation. Fate has decreed that we all have a place in society; great or small, we have to accept it.

Shine like a glow-worm.

Do what you can,
Be what you are,
Shine like a Glow-worm
If you can't like a star.

Work like a pulley
If you can't like a crane,
And be a wheel greaser
If you can't drive the train.

Part One

Parental grandparents. John Henry and Sarah (standing).
Left: Father. Centre: Sarah's mother, Great-Gran Carver, Aunt Edith and Sarah's twins.

Chapter One

I SUPPOSE MY STORY REALLY STARTS toward the end of 1918. The Great War had just ended, and George Taylor, a signaller in the Somerset Light Infantry, was returning home to the small country town of Midsomer Norton in Somerset, after four years of war, mostly spent on active service in the trenches. He was very glad to be back.

Before he had left home to fight for his country, Mrs Uphill, and unknown to George at the time, his future mother in law, had waylaid him on the street where they both lived, and with an eye to searching out possible future husbands for her daughters, had suggested that perhaps George might like to correspond with Ethel, her eldest daughter, whilst he was away in the army. George knew Ethel of course, they had been at school together; they were about the same age, and she was a pleasant and comely enough girl, so he agreed and they did indeed write to each other whilst he was away in France.

On his return, George and Ethel met and continued a form of courtship, but she was somewhat reluctant to cement the relationship, and George, getting more and more frustrated, eventually presented her with an ultimatum, namely that she should make up her mind and marry him, or he would be leaving England to seek a new life in America, where he had been offered work by two of his great-uncles who had emigrated some years before and had prospered there, having acquired ownership of a coal mine.

The outcome of this ultimatum was that Ethel decided that marriage was probably better than working in Service, and so accepted the proposal. They were married in the Registry Office at Long Ashton, Bristol in March 1919. In relating details of the wedding many years later, Ethel my mother told me that the only family members attending were her parents, and those of George. The whole party had travelled by train, and her main recollections were of both sets of parents making frequent stops at pubs on the way home from the station in order to celebrate the occasion. Needless to say, only the bride and groom were still sober by the time they arrived back home. There was no honeymoon, and normal work resumed the next day.

My maternal grandfather had a firm Victorian outlook. He was passionately fond of horses, and with his friend, an ex-Farrier Sergeant, now a peacetime blacksmith by trade and who shared this love, travelled around all the local horse fairs dealing in horses; they had a talent for buying unbroken horses, breaking them in and selling them again, quite a profitable sideline. My recollections of Granddad included his annual

My maternal grandparents, Charles and Eliza Uphill.

visits to Wincanton races, where he would make small wagers on his fancied horses and invariably finish the day well in pocket. Not that he was a gambler, but he was a very good judge of horses and won most of the bets he placed. He always said that gambling was a mug's game.

In his earlier years, Granddad had been employed at the local coal mine where he worked on the surface with a circular saw cutting up pit props and other timber required for the underground workmen. An unfortunate accident occurred one day, and the saw amputated the thumb and the first three fingers of his right hand leaving only the little finger and half the palm. He wore a special glove that Grandma had knitted to cover and keep warm the mutilated hand.

Granddad was awarded two hundred and fifty pounds compensation for the injury, or alternatively employment for life. He would have chosen the money, a small fortune in those days, but Grandma, who had a family of five to feed, made him choose the employment for life. She had known hard times, and had the foresight to know that the regular weekly income far outweighed the glitter of the lump sum which she knew well would not have lasted very long. That decision was to have a bearing on her grandchildren yet unborn, because many years later during the industrial unrest and severe unemployment of the thirties with very little money about, Gran often turned up at our house carrying a large saucepan of nourishing stew full of doughboys and other good things, a welcome dinner indeed and a great help to my parents who had a family of five children of their own by this time. Gran was a godsend and helped our family a great deal when I was young; that she was able to do so was because of her very wise decision after Granddad's accident.

Sometime before this happened, Grandma was frequently in difficulties trying to make ends meet and sometimes was a bit short of the rent money. The landlord, a local business man, was very hard on those that couldn't pay their rent, and would threaten to have the family evicted if they did not pay up. One week he was absolutely insistent on being paid, and Grandma was forced to sell her sewing machine to get together enough money to pay the rent. She was distraught, the machine was her only means of making clothes for her family, and she cursed the landlord.

Whether it was coincidence or the curse I can't say, but the landlord's wife gave birth to a mongoloid son some time later, and for the rest of her life, Grandma held him up as an example of God's punishment on the landlord for his cruelty to her when she was in desperate need.

I happened to be one of Gran's favourites, and not many days went

My aunts, with Mother.
Left to right: Olive, Emma, Ethel (mother), Rose.

by without me visiting her house. I seemed to have the knack of arriving there just as Granddad got in from work and was about to have his dinner. I was allowed a drink from his cider mug, and he would spear a potato with his fork and give it to me. I ran a lot of errands for Granny and was usually rewarded with a piece of fruit cake, and sometimes a halfpenny, quite a handsome amount in the thirties; one could buy two ounces of sweets, or two sherbets, or four gob-stoppers, or even a yard of liquorice, dependant on one's fancy that day. Of course it was a rare enough occasion, but all the more enjoyable because of that.

As well as my mother, there were four other children in Gran's family. Mother was the eldest, then came Aunt Rose, Aunt Emm, Aunt Olive, and Uncle Bill. We never saw much of him because he was a Regular soldier and had spent many years in India between the wars. He was very popular and had a happy jovial personality. All our aunts were wonderful: Aunt Rose because we spent many wonderful summer holidays with her; Aunt Emm because she was exceedingly kind to everyone who knew her, she never forgot a birthday or Christmas present; and Aunt Olive with whom we always spent Christmas or Boxing Day. She was always very jolly and guaranteed to liven up any gathering.

1. Grandad Taylor; 2. Uncle Ernest; 3. Aunt Gertie; 4. Joch; 5. Dad; 6. Mum; 7. Joyce.

Dad's family was quite different. His mother had a hard unrelenting life of toil and trouble; I can visualise her now with a man's cap on her head turned back to front, working in the garden picking apples or digging. She was a hive of activity and never still. She had borne sixteen children, not an uncommon number at the turn of the century and long before the time of family planning, and like the misfortune that dogged most working-class families at that time, lost two thirds of her children at birth or soon thereafter. My father was the eldest of six that survived to adulthood. They were Uncle Ernest, Aunt Edith, Uncle Percy, Aunt Violet and Uncle Fred. They were all very friendly to us but we were not as close to them as we were to Mother's family whom we saw more or less on a daily basis.

Father left school at the age of twelve, barely able to read and write, and was immediately sent down the coal mine to earn his living working alongside his father. His job, like that of most boys at those times, was to haul the putt with a Gus and chain; this was the method used to move stone and coal in confined spaces. The Gus was a rope that encircled the waist and to which was attached a chain that passed down the front of the body and between the legs. This chain was attached to the putt, a box-like structure, by means of hooks and was hauled by the boy on his hands and knees just like an animal out to where the roadway was higher and wider, sometimes a distance of forty to fifty yards.

Here the coal or stone was loaded into larger tubs, and a number of tubs formed a train which was hauled by pony along a track to the shaft bottom where the tubs were in their turn wound up the pit shaft to the surface eight at a time in the cage.

The reader should know that many of the coal seams in the Somerset coalfields were very narrow, most of them averaging two to three feet thick; indeed some were not more than twenty inches. The miners had to lie on their sides picking out the coal by hand. More often than not, water would be running freely through the coal face, and if the men were not wet through from that, they surely would be from sweating in the hot and humid atmosphere even though most wore just trousers or shorts. It was a hard life, and the men worked long hours. Their sons were initiated into the hard physical labour of the miner's life, it was normal and expected of them, and they knew no other way. The poor pay meant they were often hungry. They worked at a job probably unequalled for hard work and bad conditions, and their bodies carried the marks of the Gus and chain to the grave. Thank God such conditions no longer exist.

It is not surprising, then, that Granddad with his workmates came up the pit shaft at the end of the shift and went straight to the pub, black as they were and in their working clothes. It was common knowledge that he could put away eighteen pints of ale without difficulty. A lot of body fluid had been sweated out underground and that had to be replaced, besides which, drinking ale was one of the few pleasures open to the working man. The only trouble was that Granddad often drank away his wages, and there was nothing left for Granny to keep house on. It was no use her complaining because Granddad would beat her unmercifully, for which he was extremely sorry after he had sobered up.

Granny overcame this problem by doing what most other wives did in similar situations: she met her husband at the pithead when he had finished his shift on pay days, and took charge of the wages whilst Granddad was still sober and before he got to the pub. He in turn bought his ale on the slate and paid for it whenever he could beat Granny to the pub.

When the miners eventually arrived home, wives and daughters went into the busy routine of pouring buckets and kettles of hot water into tin baths that were placed in front of the kitchen fire for the men to bathe in. Stripped off, the miner's body is pale and scarred; an injury caused by coal leaves a scar which is blue and peculiar to workers in that industry. Some of the older miners always left a small patch on the back unwashed, as it was believed that washing the whole of the back would weaken one.

Father and Mother: George Henry Taylor and Ethel.

Chapter Two

WORLD WAR ONE changed things for Father who saw it as a golden opportunity to get away from the dreadful drudgery of the pit, so, increasing his age by two years and a bit, and heeding the call that Kitchener and his country needed him, he took the King's shilling and joined the army for the duration of the war. He was rapidly trained and serving in the trenches before his sixteenth birthday. Enough has been written about that terrible period of history, but Father served four years, was wounded four times and awarded the Military Medal for Gallantry in the Field.

When asked how he won his MM, Father would tell us how it was during the British retreat in the Mons battle. He and a friend came across a deserted officers' mess still intact with liquor stocks; obviously the former occupants had left in a great hurry and not had time to pack up, even weapons and ammunition had been left behind.

It was clear that Father and his pal could not let all that drink fall into enemy hands and so they did their very best to dispose of as much as it as possible. Having drunk themselves into near oblivion, the two of them set up a Lewis gun and caused havoc amongst the pursuing German cavalry, holding up their advance quite effectively. The whole scene had been witnessed by a senior ranking French officer who reported the heroic action, hence the award. Father's memory was a bit hazed over at this point, but he thought that after he and his friend ran out of ammunition, they left the scene and ran like hell.

Father had learned a great deal about life and death by the time he returned home from the war after seeing the misery of his mother and life at home. He knew that the demon drink was mainly responsible for the poverty and heartache, and he resolved to have a better life if it was at all possible. After his marriage, he continued working as a miner. Now a man, and on an equal footing with his brother and father, he worked hard to get established and provide a home for his new wife and family.

It was the custom for the miners to work in a team of three, and the senior partner would collect the wages for them all. This was of course

Granddad who was supposed to pay the other two members their money every week, but Granddad, being who he was, could scarcely find the money to pay his sons, and my mother often complained bitterly that Father had been short changed by the odd two or three shillings. The way of life that his mother had to endure must have had a profound effect on Father, and I never ever saw him drink throughout his entire life except for an occasional nip at Christmas or some other very special occasion.

Mum and Dad had borrowed one hundred and ninety pounds from an uncle to buy a three bedroomed terrace house, and then they both worked like mad to pay the loan off. The last payment was due the same week as the General Strike was called in 1927, and they argued between themselves about what should be done. Father felt that they should retain the money for food; there was a family of four children to keep now, Mother said it was more important to have the roof over their head: they might starve, but at least the home would be paid for. Being a devout Christian, she felt that the Lord would provide and keep body and soul together. Her point of view prevailed, but there were times ahead when she had doubts about the wisdom of her decision.

Mum's first job after leaving school at the tender age of thirteen was as a housemaid, in service it was called. It entailed cleaning and polishing, cleaning out and making up fires, waiting on table, polishing silver, kitchen work and the one thousand and one other tasks that were the lot of a maid working in a middle-class Edwardian household. Her first employer was a very religious chapel going person who neither smoked nor drank. He had a small printing business which expanded into a very large company by the end of the Second World War, partly because of the proprietor's hard working thrifty ways, but mostly because the firm went over to war work and made huge profits from it.

The working day started at five a.m. and the cleaning out and lighting of fires as well as the general tidying of rooms was expected to be completed by the time the family arose at seven a.m. For breakfast, duties of one kind or another continued throughout the day except for meal breaks until nine p.m, at which time the staff had to retire to bed, except of course for the Butler and Cook. Mum was allowed half a day off each week, and had to attend Church twice on Sundays. One full day each month was also given off work so that the staff could visit their families, but they were required to be back at their place of work in time to retire at nine.

Chapter Two

Early one Sunday morning, Mum was black-leading the fireplace, a job that should have been completed the day before, and one that was never allowed to be done on the Sabbath, when her employer came in and caught her red-handed. He was quite serious when he ticked her off for doing the Devil's work on the Sabbath, and was in no doubt that if Ethel did not mend her ways, she would surely come to a very bad and sticky end.

Mother worked for several families in service, but she really loved working for a farming family, where she performed all the normal household duties and was also able to work with the animals, so she became a dairymaid, milking and making butter and cheese. Her employer was a Mr Holler and the farm was quite large, but it was a place where in spite of all the hard work, she was very happy, and treated as a member of the family. It was from this job that she married Father in 1919.

Both Mum and Dad were very hard working and thrifty people but had opposing characters. Mother was kind, Father was stern; she was very warm hearted and generous, he was cold and seemingly unfeeling. On the very rare occasions that we received pocket money it was from Mum, and although we were punished by her for any misdemeanour, it was more of a persuasive talking to. From Dad we could expect a severe beating. I have to say that the younger children did not get the beatings that I received, often for nothing, but I imagine that as times got better Father was under less pressure as he became financially more secure as the years progressed. Mother was always gentle, Father was always rough and uncompromising. I had known him to be generous and kind, but it was a rare occurrence as far as I was concerned. On reflection, it was probably his very severe upbringing that made him hard; he had never known kindness as a child, only hardship, and the forming of his character stems from those early times in his life. He became hard and tough and stubborn, impervious to the feelings of others.

Whatever the situation, Father was always right; he could and would shout and rave and browbeat, putting his own viewpoint over, and never listening to others, even though quite reasonable arguments might be expounded. The children of course had nothing to say, and Mother in her superior wisdom, would cease to argue whilst Father, thinking he'd had won the battle, would gradually calm down with occasional mutterings of how some people were stupid and could not see sense and suchlike. As the years went by, Mother never argued with Father at all, taking the view that peace at any price was preferable to the upset.

During the early years of my life my main recollections are of Father always working, and except for one or two short periods of his life which events I will relate later, he continued to make work his god for the remainder of his life; certainly I know of no other man that has worked physically longer or harder than he. As well as his regular work in the mine, he had a meat business, a fish business and an ice-cream business at differing times; he also took on part time work on the farm, and always took advantage of the farmer's need for extra hands at harvest and haymaking times.

He started selling pork from door to door. The meat was obtained by slaughtering his own pigs and purchasing others wholesale, cutting the meat into joints and delivering to order. He built up quite a good round, and the income was a welcome supplement to his income. There were always two pigs in the sty at the bottom of our garden, bought in as weaners, which were fattened up to slaughter weight. In earlier years Father did that job himself, but after a change in the law slaughtering had to be done by a butcher.

The theatrics that took place at these times were a sight to behold and listen to. Everyone with any knowledge of pigs knows that they can not be driven anywhere, and yet when Father intended to do something, it was bloody well going to be done come hell or high water. The pigs had to be moved from the sty at the bottom of the garden up a path the length of the garden, alongside the house, down the front path to the road and into the van where they were loaded to be taken off to the slaughterhouse. Their squealing could be heard half a mile away, and with Father grasping the pig's ear with one hand and its tail with the other, the poor creatures were cajoled, driven, pulled, half carried and pushed all the way to the van. The next time we saw them, they were sides of pork and bacon, and bladders of lard hanging on hooks in the back kitchen. Father eventually left the meat trade and moved into fish distribution. He still kept pigs at the bottom of the garden, but these were for the sole use of his now rapidly expanding family.

To assist him in the new fish business, father had purchased a 1000 c.c. American motorcycle known as an Indian; to this he had attached a large box sidecar with a lift up lid. They were used quite a lot by small tradesmen in the thirties, and Father, keeping up with the times, thought he could profit by owning one. He would order his wet fish from the

Chapter Two

Father's bike.
Left to right: Grandad Uphill, Joan, Author, Mother with Ivy, Granny Uphill, Jean, Father.

docks, and it would arrive packed in boxes of ice at the local railway station at 5.30 a.m. Father would collect it and deliver to his customers at breakfast time. Getting fresh fish to his clients so early was a bonus that was greatly appreciated, and the business flourished and trade increased.

Dad's reputation as a hard, skilled and fearless worker in the pit grew and became common knowledge when he became involved in an accident when working with Granddad. Though he had learned his trade as a coal breaker, a name given to those coal face workers who actually mined the coal, he had also become specialised in Branching, which was also Granddad's trade; this was a job that had more to do with rock mining. The work entailed blasting roads through the solid rock to get at and work the new coal seams.

Geological faults were frequently found underground, and in many cases the coal seam would either disappear in a jumble of rock, or maybe it would end in a wall of granite. A skilled brancher had to use his knowledge and experience to judge in what direction and at what level the lost coal seam lay so that it could be found and coal production start again with the minimum of delay. Sometimes the seam would be lost for ever, but a skilled brancher was worth a lot of money to the pit owner because he could quickly locate the level and direction of the lost coal seam. Granddad and Father were the best, and their services were frequently called on to do just that.

Branchers also blasted out and made haulage roads which had to be high and wide enough for pit ponies to be able to haul a train of eight or more tubs running on rails out to the shaft bottom. They also were required to make safe those areas of the mine that had become unstable: the rock tunnels were constantly altering as the earth's crust moved and settled, falls of roof constantly required attention; the work of maintaining the pit and keeping it in a working condition also fell to the brancher.

And so Granddad and his two sons became expert. They discovered a new coal seam; it was named The Big Vein and Granddad received a handsome reward. Of course the mine owner profited to a much greater extent from the discovery, but the workers were content with their lot, the new road they had driven through to the new seam had been named Taylor's road after Granddad, and though he had received and drunk away the lion's share of the two hundred pounds awarded them for the discovery, Father had been well pleased with his share of the money.

One day, two of them had been working near the new coal seam. For some reason only Granddad and Father were there, Uncle Ernest had not turned in for work that day, when suddenly the roof caved in and collapsed without warning, both men were completely buried. Coal mines in the thirties did not have a very good safety record. Everyone knew that roof props had to be used at specific intervals but they cost money and owners were more interested in profit than in safety.

The miners themselves, though obviously recognising the danger, knew that time spent on cutting and placing roof props, meant less time in hewing coal, and as the men were only paid for the amount of coal actually arriving at the pithead and for nothing else, one can imagine that they often cut corners and took risks. It was one such time when the accident happened, Father knew that a roof prop was needed for safety, but they both thought it could be left for a little while. One gets into a rhythm of manual work, and to break that rhythm is very time wasting; to stop shovelling at that moment would have been a nuisance, and so the prop was left.

The pressures exerted on the void when rock and coal is removed can be tremendous, and if the roof is faulty or loose, then that pressure will bring about a collapse in the roof at that particular spot. It might only be a small fall involving just a few hundredweight of rock, or it could be many thousands of tons. They had lady luck with them on this particular day because only about five tons fell. That was still bad enough because the area was confined and the fall nearly filled the working area.

Granddad was completely buried, and Father almost completely, being young and in his prime, and fortunately not seriously injured, he quickly managed to extricate himself. He suffered cuts and bruises himself but was unaware of the state of Granddad who had completely disappeared under a pile of rubble and dust. Father tore away at the rock, and managed to clear sufficient space around Granddad's head to enable him to breathe which he was scarcely doing. They were both in complete darkness, their carbide lamps having been extinguished by the air blast created as the roof collapsed, but he found and relit his lamp, and ignoring his own hurts, worked like a demon to free Granddad who was unconscious. The sweat poured from his body, the dust filling and swirling in that confined air space choked him. They were alone in that dark and desolate place.

Eventually, clearing sufficient rubble, he pulled his father clear and laid him out as flat as he could. Granddad's body was crushed and bleeding, both legs were disjointed and broken and sticking out at a peculiar angle, and Father, who had seen many injuries in the trenches during the war, knew that things were serious. He needed to get help quickly, and the nearest help was at the shaft bottom nearly two miles away. The majority of roads in the mine were designed to allow room for a pony and tubs to pass through them and were only about five feet high, and this was not high enough to hoist and carry a man on one's back and remain upright. It would have been impossible to carry an inert body whilst bent double.

But there was a tub nearby. The two of them preparatory to opening up the new found Big Vein coal seam had laid about half a mile of rail for their own use to dispose of unwanted rubble.

Father put Granddad in the tub and pushed him out as far as he could toward the shaft bottom. Making Granddad as comfortable as he could, Father left him and hurried on out to get help.

Arriving back at the shaft bottom, he found the under-manager of the colliery, Nick Carter, a phlegmatic man whose interests lay in the same general direction as that of the owners, mainly because the amount of coal produced by the mine was a determining factor in the calculation of his own salary. Father hurriedly explained to Nick what had happened and quite naturally expected an immediate response from him. Nick, very loath to remove men working on more profitable employment, dallied and dallied, hesitating because not only he would have to use men to get Granddad out, but he would also have to stop hauling coal in order to get the injured man up the shaft to the pithead thereby losing some valuable coal production.

Father became more and more exasperated. He was worried and concerned for Granddad lying injured and alone, and he did not know how serious the injuries were, and he finally exploded in a burst of frustration and anger. A small group of miners had gathered around by this time, interested in the outcome of the confrontation; both men stood their ground, each defiant of the other, and the atmosphere heating up to boiling pitch.

It was not very long before the shift would be over, and Nick was hoping to wait until then, when the men could get the injured man out in their own time and not that of the management. The haulage of coal had to stop anyway for the shift change-over. He also took the view that his authority was being questioned and undermined, whilst Father thought that the stupid old sod had no regard for the seriousness of the situation, or for the welfare of the men working under him.

'What's the matter George?' Nick said, 'Afraid of the sight of a drop of blood?' Father turned white with temper, and stung by the sneering remark retorted, 'Nick, I have seen thousands of men die, and more blood than you ever will. And what is more, I could cut your bloody head off and then sew it back on again with a needle and cotton, without turning a hair, but that is my father back there, and I don't know how serious his injuries are.'

Bitter remark followed bitter retort, and Father, now almost driven to despair, threatened to knock Nick's bloody head off if he did not order some help to get Granddad out of the pit, and Nick, realising that Father might have carried out his threat, reluctantly sent a stretcher and men to get the injured man out. It was not that Father had any particular love for Granddad, but the bond of working comradeship was there, and after all, the stronger bond of flesh and blood.

The injuries that Granddad received were indeed serious and he was never able to work underground again. A lesser man would probably not have survived; although no vital organs had been badly damaged, the spine had suffered injury and both legs had been fractured, one of them in several places. It was to be a very long time before he was up and about again, and he had to make use of two walking sticks at first; he was eventually able to discard one of them, but was forced to use the other for the rest of his life.

That he survived at all was due to some good luck and his extreme toughness. Such was his outlook though that he fretted to get back to work, and injuries that would have incapacitated most men, were treated as minor irritations by him. My mother told me about the explosion that occurred at the mine in 1913. Eighteen men had been killed. Granddad who had also been working at the mine that night was one of the survivors. He had virtually crawled home that night after the explosion and should have been in hospital, but he reported back for work the very next morning just as he normally did. Work was a god, and all important; it did not even cross his mind that he should take a day off.

For his services to the pit, Granddad received employment for life, and worked until his retirement in the Blacksmith's shop on the surface. He walked the one and a half miles each way to and from work for the whole of his life.

To Father then, quite naturally, fell the honour and distinction of being the best brancher in the area, as his own father had been. He could and would do all the jobs that others refused; he was a skilled and fearless worker. Often working in dangerous areas, he had the same outlook as his father before him. Work was money and not to be refuted.

As a boy, it was my job to carry Father's food and drink to the pithead whenever he had to work late to finish a job. Mother would prepare hot food and drink, and I had to be at the pithead at a certain time so that Father could meet me, bolt his food and drink down and rush back to his work as quickly as possible. Even at home, he was always in a hurry; dinner not only had to be on the table at a certain time, but it also had to be at the right temperature, neither too hot nor too cold, which would allow Father to eat it without delay and not have to wait for it to cool down.

Mother got this off to a fine art, and the family were used to Father rushing in, eating his dinner, and rushing out again with hardly a word spoken.

Once, I remember, Father had a particularly dangerous job to do: the cage at Old Mills Colliery had caught on a projection some way down the shaft, and the steel winding cable had wrapped itself around the cage. The whole caboodle had become a tangled mass of cable; it was coiled and jammed into what seemed an impossible mess. It left an almost demented manager who could not get anyone to sort it out. After all, there were easier ways of committing suicide.

Father was approached, and for a price, took the job on. He was lowered by means of a rope down the shaft, and in his own indomitable style, proceeded to sort the jam out. The great steel cable, the thickness of a man's wrist, and made of individual strands of wire twisted together, had to be cut by hand. There were no machine tools in existence that could do the job, Using a hacksaw, Father cut away at the cable a little at a time until he managed to clear it away, then connect a new cable to the cage, then clear the obstruction. It was a very hazardous operation which he carried out on his own. The only help he got was from men at the top of the shaft to whom he relayed instructions for tools and equipment to be lowered down the shaft to him, I remember that it took four days and three nights to complete the job, and he hardly stopped during the whole of that time, and I relayed food and drink to him at regular intervals.

When one thinks about what could have happened: the obstruction holding the cage might easily have given way at any time, and had it done so, it would certainly have killed anyone working in the shaft in that vicinity, and the tangled mass of cable would have cut to ribbons anyone there. Father gave no thought to the danger; it was work, he was being well paid to do it, and it was just another job.

Chapter Three

MOTHER TOO WAS WORKING VERY HARD. As well as having to cook and do all the housework, she would take in washing, and frequently shampoo and dry a large carpet, pulling it up and down the grass afterwards to bring up the pile. This job would take a whole day to complete, and her reward was one shilling. She was also a very good cook, and despite the family's very low income in the early days, she would produce low cost but nourishing food for the family. Times were difficult; Father brought home about thirty shillings a week at that time, and unlike his own father, who was the main custodian of all finances, would put his wage packet unopened on the table every pay day, and Mother would take charge of the finances. She bought Father's cigarettes, but the balance of the money was spent on the essentials for the family and home.

Mother made all the clothes for her children, although we got many hand-me-downs from various sources. She performed miracles in keeping the kids clothed and fed, and she was usually very cheerful, but I do remember seeing her crying one day. I learned later that she had been in despair, and did not have anything to make dinner with; she had no money left. For the children the times did not seem bad. I suppose we thought that our way of life was normal. We did not know that we were poor, and the seriousness of the times were not fully understood by us. As far as we were concerned we had full bellies; we did not have caviar, but we would not have known what that was anyway. We were happy, and enjoyed the only life we knew. There were ten children in the family altogether, and Mother brought us all up to respect others, and being a good church-going Christian, made us attend church and Sunday school four times every Sunday. She was a staunch member of the British Legion, and attended the Mother's Union meetings regularly.

The firstborn came into the world in 1920. She was a lovely baby girl, and from all accounts was bright and intelligent. She was named Joyce, and was much wanted and loved. It was however the beginning of trouble and heartache for my parents, for at the early age of two, she was struck down with the dreaded infantile paralysis, later known as polio.

My sister and youngest children in approximately 1934. The eldest brother is not present, two younger children were not yet born, author is centre.

The after-effects of this disease severely affected her spine which became deformed and mis-shapen rather like the letter S. Most of her early years were spent in hospital, and she underwent many operations in attempts to straighten her spine, none of which were successful, and she was displayed to medical students as a typical case history of that disease. Despite these numerous operations and varied treatments over many years, she never recovered from the illness, and was left deformed, and with a scar running the length of her back.

One can only suppose that medical knowledge on this particular disease was very limited at the time. I know that quite a number of eminent surgeons and consultants were very interested and involved in my sister's case, but it was all to no avail and she finally left hospital in her teens, my parents having been informed that there was nothing more that medical science could do for her. Her body was by now so deformed that she was unable to stand for any length of time and only able to walk very short distances. Despite the handicap, she was always very cheerful and happy. She had a loving personality, and though at times she suffered considerable pain, I never heard her complain once.

Mother managed to find employment for Joyce at the Standard Cheque Book Co. It was sedentary, and something she became proficient at, so she could earn her living. As she grew older her condition worsened and she was unable to move around; eventually she was confined to a wheelchair for the last few years of her life. I often used to torment and tease her, something she took in good part most of the time, but I well remember on one occasion I tormented her to distraction and she threw a kitchen knife at me which cut my arm and left me scarred for life. It was richly deserved and I did not bear any grudges.

It was my job to push her around town in her bathchair. It was one of the old fashioned willow basket chairs with two large wheels at the back and a smaller wheel at the front to which was attached the steering arm controlled by the patient. I provided the motive power, and Joyce steered with the handle. When we came to a downhill slope, I would run round to the front of the chair, sit at my sister's feet and get a free ride to the bottom of the slope. Fortunately, there were no serious mishaps, Quite unlike what happened to a local elderly lady of the same family name as us, but not related in any way. She had a son called Claude who pushed his mother around in an identical bathchair.

Now Claude was not particularly bright, in fact I often heard him described as tuppence short of a bob, but he was very devoted to his mother and she to him. They spent their lives together, with Claude pushing his mother far and wide around the district, travelling many miles on their journeys. They were a regular part of the daily scene and activity of the town.

One day, just a few miles from town, and at the top of a steep hill called Nettle bridge, Claude accidentally lost his hold on the wheelchair and his mother with rapidly increasing momentum hurtled at ever increasing speed down the hill with Claude in hot pursuit. He never had a snowball's chance in hell of ever catching up. It is amazing how the old lady managed to keep control of the chair for as long as she did, as the hill had several bends in it. She must have been in her seventies and had probably never travelled in excess of two or three miles an hour in her life before this particular occasion. But here she was doing what must have been at least sixty miles an hour.

She negotiated most of the hill, but unfortunately the sharp curve at the bottom proved too much for her and the vehicle. She shot across the road and was roughly deposited in the ditch at the side. She suffered a broken arm and various bruises, but got away rather lightly in view of what could have been far more serious consequences. Needless to say, I don't think Claude was allowed to take that particular route ever again.

I never did ever come as close as that to losing control of my sister's chair, but we did have fun at times. As the years passed, Joyce became increasingly incapacitated, and eventually the severe pressure on her heart, exerted by the curvature of her spine against it, resulted in her premature death at the age of twenty. Scarcely remembered by the younger members of the family, she was much loved and sorely missed by the older children, my parents and her many friends.

The second child of the family was a boy; he was named Eric and was born in 1922. He became my parents' pride and joy because although he had only an elementary education, he grew up to be very clever, an exemplary student, always neat and tidy in appearance and his school work and homework were always immaculate. Many years later after Eric's death in his middle age, his old school teacher came across some of his text and exercise books and returned them to my elderly parents. They were, he told them, remarkable examples of first-class work and showed exceptional quality and intellect in a boy of such tender years.

Eric's first job was as a store warehouseman in a local grocery shop called Harvey. His workmates upended him into a large flour tub by way of initiation when he first started work, and he arrived back home powdered white from head to foot. Some months later, Mother found a hair in her flour; she was convinced that it came from Eric and had been deposited at the time of his ducking in the flour barrel.

He was far too clever to remain for long in the grocery trade, and when the opportunity came, got employment in the Electricity company, a cut above the average type of work normally available to the working classes in the area, although electricity had been around for some considerable time, only the gentry had it connected to their houses; most of the working classes had gas lighting, and quite a large number were still using oil lamps.

Having obtained knowledge and skill in his new trade, Eric persuaded Father to go modern and have the house wired for electricity. My mother's sight was failing, aggravated by the constant sewing, patching and mending in the very poor gaslight. We used to laugh at her trying time after time to thread a needle and constantly missing the eye with the thread, as the look of concentration on her face, and her patient sighing when she failed yet again, caused us great amusement. But now the brilliance of the electric light made life much more pleasant. It used to be gloomy, but now it was as if sunlight could be produced at the touch of a switch.

Eric did all the work himself and my father was so very proud that not only was his house the first one in the road to have electricity, but it had been made possible through the efforts of his own clever son, and at cost price too, some twenty pounds: a lot of money then, but prestige-wise, a very good investment.

I know that Mother had been opposed at first. She was a little afraid of electricity, she knew nothing about it, she could not understand it, and probably thought it would blow the house up, or else some other dreadful catastrophe would occur; however she was eventually persuaded to accept progress and after it had been installed, agreed with some reservations that it was a great improvement. Certainly it was easier to thread her needles and see the close work of her sewing than it was in gaslight, and I think that she too was secretly pleased with the new fangled modern lighting after a while.

My parents were also proud because Eric had a trade that was not connected in any way with the pit. That was a wonderful thing and a break with tradition. Certainly my mother lived in constant fear for Father's safety, as accidents underground were quite commonplace and Father's body often showed the marks of minor injuries that could have been serious ones. She half expected bad news whenever he was working on some particularly dangerous job. He was proud and confident in his own skills, but he always hoped and often said that no son of his would work in the pit if it could be avoided. He could not forget his own early days as a young boy; the Gus and chain were indelibly stamped on his memory.

The family image was greatly enhanced because of Eric's new job, as it was a time when most miners' sons followed their fathers down the pit. Eric regularly attended evening classes at the college in Bristol, and his quick ability for learning helped him advance rapidly up the ladder, as improving his knowledge and skills produced proficiency in his chosen trade.

My second sister Joan was born in 1925 and became the eldest able-bodied girl. On her eventually fell the customary duties of a miner's daughter. Like the others in the family, she had a fairly happy and carefree childhood marred only by having a cyst at the base of her spine which had to be surgically removed when she was a quite small but which caused her no further trouble thereafter. She also pushed a small button up one of her nostrils when she was just two years old, which too had to be removed by surgery. But there were no after effects or further escapades after that.

As she grew older she had to take on more responsibility. It was her lot to have to bear the brunt of the domestic work, helping Mother to cook, clean and sew. She also had to prepare the hot water for Father to bathe in after work, also to clear up and perform the many chores that had to be done. As Mother was regularly confined producing the next brother or sister, Joan became the second mother to the younger ones and was well able to run the house during the ten days or so that Mother was in her bed at these times.

I was born in 1927, the second son, not as bright as my elder brother: I managed to scrape through school, just. I hated most of it, but when threatened, caned and punished enough I could apply my mind and do about average in the subjects I liked, but these were not many. I just could not get away from school quickly enough and was usually first through the door. I was a rebel and preferred the outdoor life. In later years, my sisters thought that I regularly played truant from school, but in fact I only did that twice. My Aunt Emm recognised my adventurous spirit, and it was only from her that I received books full of adventure stories on my birthdays, or perhaps at Christmas time. These I read and re-read with great relish, imagining myself as the principal character, roving the world, climbing mountains, sailing the oceans, visiting far off mysterious and exotic lands, and doing in my imagination all the wonderful things that a young boy dreams about.

My sister Jean was born next in 1929. She became the first member of the family to pass the eleven plus examination at junior school, thereby winning herself a place at the secondary school. Not too many pupils of the working classes ever achieved this distinction because it was who your family was, and how high up the social scale they were that dictated who would get the privilege. Academic ability was only a secondary consideration in the choice. I remember many pupils going to the secondary school who were right duffers, but because Daddy was in business, his little cherubs were able to make the grade.

Father's views on the subject of education for girls were firmly ensconced in his mind. Any girl who attended secondary school would require school uniforms, and he would also have to buy sports equipment and other things considered to be essential for children attending that establishment. This he considered was a waste of time and money; education for girls was quite unnecessary since they only got married and finished up running the home; there was just no point in them having more than the basic education because they would never need or use it. And so Jean remained at the elementary school until the age of fourteen, the normal leaving age.

This however did not prevent her from getting on in the world, and after a spell of work at a local factory, she went into the nursing profession, and worked her way up to Theatre Sister, living and working in various hospitals until she got married.

From her teens on, Jean had the ability to wrap Father round her little finger, as the saying goes. The other children were unable to influence any of his decisions, but Jean could wheedle her way into Dad's good books, and persuade him to grant whatever favour she was seeking at the time. She could do no wrong in his eyes, and she retained the ability to charm him all of his life.

Ivy, my fourth sister was born two years after Jean. She completed the female side of the family. Her childhood was marred by an unfortunate accident when she was quite young, about four or five years of age. It was the custom after Sunday dinner, to go for a long walk. I had been put in charge of three or four younger children, and we were all walking up Clapton Hill on a lovely summer's day, I remember that there were some of us on each side of the road, and we were all picking flowers, I heard a motor bike coming and shouted across the road for the children to remain in the side close to the hedge.

Ivy became confused and started to run across the road to me just as the motor bike came round the corner. She was struck in the face by the handlebar which smashed her nose, making a complete mess of it. At the time, it looked as if she might be badly disfigured, but the injury healed very well. Her nose was a little bit flatter than normal, but she had by no means been made ugly by the incident. The doctor promised her a new nose when she grew up, but she never did bother, and as time passed the whole thing was forgotten. She was very much like Mother in nature, warm, considerate, and with loving caring ways.

Jean and Ivy seemed to have an interest in going on the stage; they were always practising chorus line dancing and kick ups. Ivy was very supple and could bend backwards and make her feet touch her head, but their ambitions never amounted to anything, and as time passed they lost interest in the dancing.

The last four members of the family arrived in rapid succession, and were all boys, the first of them being Robert. He was quiet, neat and tidy. He amazed the family by revealing a wonderful talent for art; his drawings and painting showed great detail and a natural aptitude. The local school headmaster begged my parents not to let his talent go to waste, and they were persuaded to enrol him in the Bath Art School.

The next child was David, also a clever boy at school, who was the first one in the family to pass his eleven plus examination and then actually to attend the Secondary school. He was good at most subjects, but was a sportsman at heart; he loved cricket especially. Calamity struck at him when he was quite young, when a Bristol bus knocked him down and crushed his foot. The doctors wanted to amputate it but Mother would not agree and it eventually healed. He managed quite well with it thereafter, and did not let it bother him too much, but the foot was very badly deformed and frequently caused him pain. It was also quite expensive having to buy the special boot he needed to have made for it.

Graham, the next brother, did not do well at school, but after leaving, he started attending night classes and completed a number of correspondence courses over several years; by this means he became a highly qualified engineer, and surprised everyone.

The reader might think that the list is never ending, but Richard, the next born, was also the last member of the family. Being the baby he was a little spoilt as all the youngest members of families usually are. It seemed that these two youngest boys were always wrestling and fighting each other, usually on the floor and of course always in fun. They were inseparable pals as children, but of course grew apart as time and marriages forced a separation on them in later years.

Chapter Four

FROM THE FOREGOING one can see that we were quite a large family, Mum and Dad and ten children, a round dozen altogether and a conglomeration of mixed personalities, yet with a bond of unity that seems to exist only in large families. It seems to me that they get along together far better than small ones. Our regular family gatherings which were usually weddings or funerals were always happy occasions with Mother delighted to have everyone around her. As another brother or sister got married and produced children, there were ever increasing reasons for a family get-together.

Times improved during the 39–45 war. Dad did war work, his pay was much better, and life was more comfortable for the younger children. The hardships suffered by the older members were not repeated as the general standard of living improved.

The fact that the house always seemed to be full of kids was quite a natural thing. As well as the older ones, it seemed to me that there was one baby crawling, another suckling, and yet another on the way. My sisters said that they did not know how Mother managed, but manage she did and very well too. One of the local shopkeepers had a disgruntled wife who was known to make the comment that the Taylors were at home breeding like rabbits. Mother got to hear about it, and swore that she would never enter the shop again. She never did, that particular shop lost a great deal of custom over the years by making that remark, and Mother's honour was eventually satisfied when that same shop was forced to close when a local family were taken ill with food poisoning attributed to eating produce obtained there.

Despite our poor circumstances, certain basic principles were adhered to. It was a disgrace to owe money, so nothing was ever bought on credit, everything was paid for in cash, and if there was insufficient money then we went without. Father was always striving for the little luxuries in life however and we were one of the first families in the street to own a Cat's whisker. I was allowed to stay up late one night to listen to the Tommy Farr-Joe Lewis fight from America. All the men from neighbouring houses were in the kitchen. The headphones of the wireless were placed in two pudding basins to help amplify the sound, and there had to be absolute silence from everyone present because it was only just possible to hear the commentator amongst the crackle, whistling, and static emanating from the set. Everyone was disappointed that Tommy lost the fight.

We later had a proper radio set which was powered by an accumulator, wet batteries that had to be replaced every few days. I often had the job of taking the old one to the shop for a replacement. The music was loud whilst the power remained high, but as it faded, so did the volume, and the sound would gradually fade until one could no longer hear it, and the battery would have to be changed again. Strict silence had to be observed at news time, and any noise made by the children during the six or nine p.m. news would be rewarded with a clout from Father. Our special treat on Saturday evenings was to be allowed to listen to 'In Town Tonight' and the music hall acts. Father would buy some toffees, and we would listen to the various artistes. Mother would tell us about them and once made the statement that one famous violinist was so good that he could make his violin talk. I listened and waited in vain hoping to hear him make the violin talk, and I was quite a bit older before I understood her meaning.

Another occasional treat for the family was when Father decided to take us all out for a spin in the country. He still had his motorcycle to which he affixed a double adult sidecar. I do not remember where we went, but I vividly recall the capers we got up to in loading up for the journey, and the painful uncomfortable seating arrangements that my sister Joan and I had to put up with on these outings. Down in the nose of the sidecar, sitting on a small stool in the darkness, sat Jean, Mother was in the front seat of the sidecar with the two youngest babies on her lap, Joyce sat in the rear seat of the sidecar with yet another toddler on her lap, and Joan and I were put in the dickey seat, not a real seat at all, just a cavity large enough to hold a suitcase which was its real purpose. We sat with our knees tucked up almost to our chins facing each other. On the motorcycle of course was Father with his cap turned back to front so that the peak lay behind his neck, a pair of cheap goggles on, and finally, riding pillion, was Eric.

Now if one totals that lot up one finds that the total complement was ten persons; the two youngest children not yet born. Father would drive round the countryside at top speed, still in a hurry as always, and attempting to visit all the beauty spots around. Of course there was the unending chore of stops for toilets and lemonade in that order, and we occasionally got crisps, but it was the hassle of loading and unloading that I shall never forget. I could never quite understand why we never stopped at one of the many Free Houses we passed on the way. After all, it seemed silly if everything they offered was free and we did not take advantage of it. Father pulled my leg about it later, but he did not explain what it meant at the time. Father accidentally mounted a grass bank once and turned the outfit over depositing the family on the road. Luckily no one was hurt, and no damage was done to the combination, so we all remounted and went on our way. We would gaily wave to all and sundry as we speeded along, hair blowing in the wind, and we arrived back home tired but happy.

It was I believe in 1934 that Father launched into business properly. Through my Uncle Bill, Father learned of an Italian family who had a fruit business; they also made rather good ice cream and Father became convinced that there was a future in making and selling it. It was a very good decision because the only mobile ice cream vendors at the time were the Walls tricycles which had 'Stop me and buy one' painted on the large box in which they stored the frozen ice cream and lollies and various other products that they sold. It must have been very hard work pedalling these cumbersome trikes around and apart from a very few shops, these tricycles were only seen in towns and built up areas, and never in small villages.

Father rightly thought that if he could take the ice cream to the customer, it would be good for business, and give him an edge over possible rivals, so he bought the equipment, purchased the ingredients, arranged a supply of fresh milk from a local farmer who was also a relative, and started manufacturing.

In theory, the manufacturing process of producing ice cream is simple and straightforward, but the practical side of it had to come in somewhere and that was the snag. A stainless steel drum was placed inside a larger wooden barrel, a metal pin on the bottom of the drum fitted into a cup at the bottom of the barrel to keep it in a central position, and in the two inch space between the drum and the barrel a large quantity of chopped ice pieces about the size of golf balls was rammed tightly down around the drum which was now encased in ice. Preserving salt and sacking was jammed on top of the ice to keep the lot firm, and it would remain intact for several hours before it started to melt down.

Into the drum went the required ingredients in correct measure and according to the secret formula, milk, powder, sugar and flavouring, and it had to have the correct percentage of butterfat. A special mixing blade was then inserted into the drum and a tight fitting cover with a special cog arrangement sealed the whole lot in. A handle was attached to the cog, and after about two hours' vigorous turning, and if things went well, the result was two gallons of delicious ice cream. The process was repeated until sufficient had been made to suit Father's requirements for that day. The ice cream was packed into stainless steel drums which were in turn packed in ice as previously described, ready to be loaded into the vehicle.

Poor Mother. She must have turned that handle for hours and hours, and woe betide everyone if the ice cream was not ready for Father to load up. He dashed in from work at the pit, bathed and changed, had his meal, loaded up and off he went. On very hot days, holidays or weekends, a lot of ice cream was needed and the machine would be in constant use all day. Father would sell out, race home and load up the next batch, and drive off immediately. The whole process was repeated until daylight would fade, and the demand cease.

Naturally, Mother could not keep up this hectic pace under such pressure on her own, so it often became the lot of the older children to take turns in helping out. The arguments and noisy discussions that took place at such times were a regular occurrence and each one of us would try to avoid the tedious work. 'Whose turn is it on the handle?' Mother would call. I would argue that it was my sister Joan's turn. 'No, it's your turn,' she would say, and the bedlam would continue until one or the other of us was forced to put our shoulder to the wheel to keep the never-ending production line going.

We also had the job of chopping the ice up into suitable pieces. Father bought it from a local butcher as and when he needed it. It came in blocks measuring 18 × 9 × 6 inches thick and we used a pick head to chop it up. It was a cold job and bits of ice would fly into our faces, down inside our clothes and everywhere else too. It was an awful job for children, and Mother had to do most of it because we children would disappear from sight if we could.

Father looked quite smart in his white coat and apron. He still wore his old tweed cap, normal head dress for working chaps. He had changed his Indian motorcycle for a BSA, but the sidecar, once used for fish, had been given a face lift and was gaily painted in cream and yellow with hand painted signs all over it proclaiming to the world that Taylor's ice cream was pure and delicious, as indeed it was; Mother insisting that if the business were to succeed, only the highest standards and the best quality were good enough.

Daily making the round of all the local villages and beauty spots, Father soon became well known and popular and built up a good custom. What he lacked in business acumen he made up for in zeal. He would arrive at his pitch in each village and loudly ring a hand bell to let his customers know that he was there and ready for business. Occasionally, one of the children would travel with him, purely for the opportunity of being allowed to ring the bell. As time passed, business gradually improved; the motorcycle combination was changed for a small van, and Dad bought a small petrol engine to do the work of making the ice cream. There was still much hard work involved, of course, but the tedium of turning the handle by hand was now gone. The onset of the Second World War in 1939 finally put paid to the business. Shortages of essential ingredients severely handicapped production, so Father got a job doing war work, and that was the end of the ice-cream business.

Chapter Five

Our day started quite early. We were usually wakened between seven and eight o'clock and it took quite a while for everyone to wash and dress and have our breakfast. It was usually porridge made in a large black saucepan, to which was added milk and sugar. This was washed down with cocoa which Mother poured from a large half gallon enamelled jug, and which had been made prior to the breakfast stampede. We all huddled round the fire on cold winter mornings, and one of my sisters still complained that I hogged the fire and the smaller children did not get their fair share of warmth but I honestly do not remember that.

When it was time for school, we were all lined up in order of age and seniority, and each child opened their mouths in turn and received a large spoonful of Virol with cod liver oil, followed by a boiled sweet to take the nasty taste away. Mother firmly believed that this daily treatment warded off colds and flu. She used many other old fashioned remedies too, she swore by them, and whenever anyone of the family fell ill, out would come the camphor oil for rubbing chests, senna pods or syrup of figs for opening the bowels, socks around the throat for colds and sore throats, inhaling the steam from boiling water and eucalyptus leaning over a bowl with a towel over the head, and numerous other remedies: whatever the illness, Mother had a remedy for it. By and large though we were a disgustingly healthy lot really, and seldom ill. It was a great tribute to Mother who kept her family healthy during times when mortality in children from diphtheria and other diseases were commonplace.

Our main meal was midday dinner. We had simple plain cooking, stews and roasts made from the cheaper cuts of meat. We frequently had roast rabbit usually provided by Aunt Rose who worked on the farm and had easy access to abundant game which had been shot or trapped by her husband Uncle Fred. Mother had quite a job making that rabbit go round; the trouble was that everyone wanted a back leg because there was more meat on that, so there was always an argument and a clamour as to who was to get what. Mother had a brilliant solution that always seemed to work: she would turn the rabbit round on the dish twice, and over once, then state that she was going to cut off another back leg. She continued in this vein until everyone who wanted one got their back leg. We did not realise at the time that Mother couldn't cut five or six back legs from one rabbit; we were too young, and she was too clever, and we were all too confused by her adroitness to properly understand. At any rate we all were satisfied with our back leg, and Mother repeated the trick on many occasions.

There was one exception in the demand for back legs. My sister Jean was the only one who requested and always received the rabbit's head; this she would dissect and neatly extract the brains of which she was very fond. We all thought the it was disgusting, but she argued that eating brains made one clever.

Tea consisted of bread and margarine and home-made jam, or dripping or lard, and the daily routine of Mother continuously cutting bread non stop sometimes for as many as three loaves before appetites were sated. There were also cakes or tarts or pie which Mother had made during her less busy moments. The exception to the foregoing was Sundays, when breakfast would be a fried one. Dinner was usually stuffed ox heart and vegetables followed by fruit tart and custard or some other dessert made fresh that day.

Mother did most of her baking on Sundays, and my sisters were all instructed in the art of cooking at these times. They were allowed to prepare and bake their very own cakes and tarts, and I must say that they all turned out to be fine cooks.

One day I remember my brother Eric arrived home from work and was given a poached egg on toast for his tea. I complained to Mother that I should have had one for my tea too. She sharply reprimanded me, and said that when I went out to work, I would be entitled to a poached egg also. I just mention this because eggs were considered to be a luxury and one had to be contributing to the family income before becoming eligible for an egg.

Chicken was also considered to be a delicacy, and the only time we ate that was at Christmas. We never saw turkey, but Father killed a cockerel for our Christmas dinner. It was one of the highlights of the year, and I look back with fond memories to those times. On Christmas morning we opened our presents and went to church.

The Salvation Army Band always played carols and hymns in our road on Christmas mornings; this added very much to the festive spirit.

Whilst all the children were hanging up their stockings on, Christmas Eve, Father would be making great play of hanging up his trousers, the legs of which were tied at the bottom. Father Christmas would be able to put far more goodies in his trousers than could be fitted into a little stocking. On the following morning, Father's trousers would be filled with coal, whereas our stockings would be filled with nuts and fruit and sweets and other small goodies. Father made a great fuss about it, complaining bitterly about not getting the same as us, and teaching everyone that it did not pay to be greedy. We always spent Christmas or Boxing Day at Aunt Olive's house; she lived about two miles away and the day was alternated every year. All the children had wonderful times. She produced lots of food, the Christmas tree was filled with chocolate goodies, we sang songs, played games and returned home very late completely worn out by all the excitement. It was also around this time that the British Legion held an annual party for members and their families. That too was very enjoyable because we played games and pulled crackers. We received a present, and did all the things kids enjoy and we always eagerly looked forward to the next party.

The only other highlight of the year was the annual Sunday school party. There was a tea, followed by the presentation of prizes, always a book, the quality of which was dependent on the number of Sunday school attendances the previous year. Of course there were other occasional treats during the year, but the ones I have mentioned were regular occurrences and eagerly awaited by us all.

With such a large family, there had to be a routine so that the domestic running of the house was smooth. Mother was very fussy about cleanliness, and the kitchen table top was scrubbed daily, and also the stone flagged floors. One sister would be employed on that job whilst another dusted and polished, and yet another made beds and cleaned the bedrooms. There was always a pile of washing and ironing to be done, food to prepare and cook, and a multitude of other jobs waiting to be done. Mother always said there was no excuse for dirt, she maintained that soap and water were cheap enough, and she ensured that the children were clean and the house a credit to her.

Looking back I do remember that although no one could say that we were dirty kids, our clothing gave us away as being from a poor family. Mother hand-made shirts and trousers for the boys, and dresses for the girls, but patches were commonplace on my trousers, woollens and socks were full of redone darns and coats were handed down from elder to younger until they were no longer fit to wear. One jacket that I had originated at one of my aunts after two cousins had outgrown it. My elder brother had worn it as long as he was able, but inevitably it came to me. I was quite proud to wear it because, regardless of the number of previous owners, my mother pointed out that it was very good quality, Harris tweed no less, it never wore out and I was lucky to have it. I did of course grow out of it in time and it was handed on down to the next one it fitted. Being second or third hand before we got it anyway, it had a very long and varied career, and a succession of owners ad infinitum.

Stockings too were always in need of darning. It is not surprising really in my case because my feet were shod with miner's work boots. They were thick heavy leather, and the soles were covered with hob nails, standard footwear for most miner's sons. They had to withstand stone kicking, tree climbing, football, water, weather and a host of other destructive activities.

As a boy, most of my young life was spent out of doors. I was a member of the brickyard gang, a group of local lads with an adventurous spirit. Our leader was Nutty Chivers, who was the eldest; only quite small but extremely tough, he took the lead in all our escapades. We dug a cave in a bank of the hill on the edge of Chilcompton Woods, and we would sit in the cave in the evenings, light our smoking candles and hold endless discussions, mostly about rival gangs, and our future plans for their destruction.

We also built a cabin in the woods and built a stockade around it. Norman Swain, our adjutant who was generally accepted to be the brains of the gang, drew up the rules and a list of weapons that were to be used in the event of an attack on our stronghold by outsiders. It was a source of great amusement to my parents when this list fell out of my pocket one day and was discovered by them. The part which read 'Cudgels for short range, and bows and arrows for long range' caused great hilarity among my elders and great embarrassment to me for a long time. Ah, but they were wonderful times for me, and I spent many happy hours playing in those woods, only returning home for meals or to sleep during school holidays.

There were times when our stronghold was attacked by rival gangs. It was never captured though. We had a large supply of wood chumps stored inside the stockade, built up by dint of much hard work in more peaceable times. With these we would repel all and sundry by hurling them from the safety of our stockade. It was a very brave lad indeed who could approach within twenty yards of our fence because he would be met by a dozen or so wood chumps, flying at him from all directions, a very dangerous position for him to be in. We were the 'Kings of our castle' and not to be trifled with.

As the family increased in size over the years, it became necessary for something to be done to increase living space. The house was a three bed terrace, but downstairs only consisted of a front drawing room, and a living room and kitchen combined. There was no bathroom, and the toilet was outside in the back yard.

Father, always willing to tackle any problem, decided to add an extension which would enlarge the living room and kitchen, and also include an indoor bathroom and toilet. This work entailed knocking down one wall and building several others, adding new windows, doors and a roof.

Father was a hard and swift worker but he was certainly no builder, and it was only with a great deal of trial and error that the job was eventually finished. The dirt, mess, and upheaval created by this project made Mother wonder whether the improvement was worth all the work and worry it had caused, but Father had made up his mind that the job had to be done, and Mother as usual submitted to Father's dominant personality.

All able-bodied members of the family were called upon to fetch and carry and help in whatever was demanded during the building operations, and one or two of my uncles arrived to assist Father in the heavier and more difficult part of the jobs. When it was finished, the whole family could now sit at the enlarged table, with most of the younger children sitting on a purpose built bench against the back wall and the other three sides of the table being used for the remainder of the family. The bench included room for Tiger our dog who always sat up at the table with the children also.

Tiger had a firm place in our hearts. He was a mongrel of who knows what ancestry, who came at no cost from a farmer, and it was the general consensus of opinion that he had some Alsatian in him. He was big and bore some resemblance to that breed as far as his body went, but his head and ears were something else. All the kids thought he must be part greyhound because of his speed, but no one really knew, least of all his previous owner. He had a wonderful nature, and loved and guarded all the children. He would growl to warn, and even attack anyone who raised their voice against them, and that included Father. He sat up at the table at breakfast time between the children and ate milk and cornflakes or porridge just as a member of the family which of course he was. He was always playing with the children, and would hear my whistle several hundred yards away; he would come charging down the road at a furious pace, and would end up hurling himself at my chest, almost knocking me over in his exuberance and excitement.

Once I remember that he was inadvertently shut indoors and the children were playing outside in the yard. Tiger leapt through a window that was six feet from ground level, shattering the glass, and badly lacerating one paw, so frantic was he to get to the children; he could hear them playing, and obviously thought that he should be with them as usual. During school hours he would mope around just waiting for the kids to get home after which he would come to life and participate in all their activities.

There had been a number of complaints from the shop owner and landlord of the terrace, about Father driving his motorcycle and sidecar along the back of the houses and out to the main road; indeed it was the only way to reach it by vehicle and Father had no choice but to use it. At the time of building the terrace, there were no cars or motor vehicles, and the track was designed to cater only for horse drawn carts. With the invention of the internal combustion engine, and the development of the car and lorry, people were forced to use the same tracks that had been intended for horses, and transport became more mechanised as the horse-drawn vehicle gradually disappeared.

To solve the problem, and prevent further trouble with his neighbours, Father purchased the old stone wall and twelve inches of land from his neighbour on the other side of the house which was the end of the terrace. There had always been a fair size track there, but now with the addition of the extra twelve inches, and by building a single block wall at the new boundary edge, he had gained himself access to the road without having to pass by any of his neighbours', or the landlord's property ever again. It was now wide enough, just, for him also to drive his van through when he later updated his transport, it was a tight fit, but he became very proficient driving through the gap and was now quite independent, and there was no way the neighbours could complain again.

To finish the job, Father also built a high wall cutting them off completely from his property.

As the years passed Father acquired his first van; his ice cream business was doing well and called for some expansion. The back doors of the van could be removed and the fittings arranged to accommodate the barrels. Everything was painted up, and the signs still proclaiming to the world that Taylor's Pure Ices were still delicious, Father continued plying his trade in the new improved transportation.

When the family went out for a spin now, it was quite a different adventure to that with the motorcycle combination. Now the van was cleared out, and we either sat on the floor or on boxes. Mother was now able to sit in the passenger seat next to Father, still it seems with a child in each arm and one on the way. Our ride was supposed to be much better now but I was not so sure. The van was an early Austin seven, and soon lost power on the slightest incline, so we were all ordered out of the van, and had to push and shove it up the hill. Sometimes we failed to make it, and Father would reverse back down the hill to the bottom and make one more try, giving himself a longer run up to the hill. When we finally made it, we all got back into the van and continued on our way in high spirits. Of course, the manufacturer had never intended their product to stand the sort of punishment Father meted out, but nevertheless it was a willing workhorse and did its job quite well with a little help from its friends.

Chapter Six

By the time I was eight or nine years old, I had learnt that in order to purchase things one needed money and the only way to get that was to work. I did all the normal things that boys had always done in order to earn a few coppers, and quite a few things that they didn't. Quickly discovering that 'Penny for the Guy' time was very short lived, I tried carol singing with a friend, but the only problem was that we did it in August, and that did not prove to be very successful either.

I managed to get a job as a paper boy at the local newsagents. Twice a day, early morning and evenings, I pedalled round the town delivering papers on the only bike owned by the family, my sister's property really, but we all shared it. Father had made it up from odd parts salvaged from the scrap heap, and it only kept running with constant repairs and maintenance. I earned sixpence a week at this job which was not bad really for the times.

My brother Eric and I were also choir boys at our local church, St John's. We were paid one halfpenny a practice session twice a week, and I think it was tuppence for the Sunday. We were very keen to be asked to sing at weddings or funerals because the pay for those events was half a crown, high pay indeed. We looked like little angels dressed in our cassocks and surplices with a ruffle around our necks, and we could bring tears to the eyes of gentle old ladies as we sang 'Oh for the wings of a dove'. In fact though we were little monsters; we fired wads of wet paper using rubber bands at our friends sitting in the opposite choir stalls, we giggled and larked about during the sermon, and the choir master would frown and frantically try to quieten us, but he was helpless at such times and was not able to do anything to prevent our bad behaviour. We were too quick for him at the end of the service because as we proceeded slowly up the aisle to the vestry at the end of the service, we were busily undoing the buttons of our cassocks, under the cover of our surplices of course, so that by the time we had reached the vestry, our garments could be slipped off, hung in the cupboards, before you could say Jack Robinson, and we could make a quick getaway before the choirmaster could grab us. The same thing happened in reverse at the beginning of the next service because there was only just sufficient time to get dressed before the start of the procession to the choir stalls. We had the timing off to a fine art and were seldom caught out.

Choir practice nights were different of course, and we were soundly lectured by the choir master for our misdemeanours, and threatened with a deduction of pay which made us toe the line for a while. This was far too serious a matter to ignore because it was the main incentive for being a member of the choir in the first place, still we did have fun. One evening before practice, a group of my friends tied up one of the boys to a tree in the churchyard for a joke, and we all entered the church at practice time leaving him still tied to the tree. It took him some ten or fifteen minutes to free himself and he arrived red faced from his exertions, obviously late. The choir master, equally red faced with annoyance, shouted at the boy, 'You're late, you're late, and you have lost your halfpenny', thereby punishing him for his laxity, and maintaining strict discipline among the rest of us with the threat that we too might lose our night's pay if we did not behave. He never gave the poor lad a chance to explain the reason for his lateness, and we were too callous to feel concerned about it, though we did make it up to him later.

It was quite by accident that I got my next two jobs. Mother was in the habit of walking to Radstock market every Saturday morning, a distance of some two and a half miles each way, the reason being that she could obtain some of her groceries much cheaper there. She was obliged to take the two youngest children with her and they were pushed in a pram. All the various packages, provisions for the following week, were loaded into that pram for the return journey, and sometimes it was difficult to see the babies because of the great number of packages and parcels that had been included and distributed around them. In addition, one or sometimes two of the older children were allowed to accompany Mother on these trips as a special treat.

On one of these occasions I had been wandering around the various market stalls, when I was approached by a black man who asked me if I would like to work for him on Saturdays, I immediately said that I would, I certainly was not going to miss any opportunity to earn some money. In the thirties, in my home area, it was rare to see any coloured people, and they created a mild sensation when they were seen, especially by children. My job was to stand on a box, head and shoulders above and in full view of the crowd of shoppers and other people who flocked to the weekly market from the surrounding villages, and I was required to hold a towel to my face covering my mouth.

This act was purely for effect, and was sufficient to cause a crowd to gather, curious at the sight of a small boy standing in such a way high above them. When my employer considered that the crowd was large and interested enough to warrant a move, he would harangue them with plausible patter on the merits of the product he was selling. Tooth powder. Then in full view of everyone, he cleaned my teeth with a piece of cloth wrapped around his forefinger, dipped first in water and then in this wonderful stuff. When the job was finished, I had to turn full circle on the box, grinning like a Cheshire cat so that everyone could see the wonderful shine I had on my teeth. My boss then did a brisk trade selling his powder until everyone who wanted it had been served. We then had a break, but repeated the whole procedure every hour or so throughout the day.

Needless to say, my teeth had never been so clean before, nor indeed have they been so since. It was a good job and well worth it because I received sixpence for the day's work, a far better rate than the paper round which took a whole week's hard work to earn the same amount.

By pure coincidence, my Uncle Bill, who by this time had completed his army service and was married and lived in Frome, some six miles from Radstock, had obtained employment as a lorry driver and general assistant with that same Italian family that had given Father the idea to start his ice cream business. They also dealt in the fruit business and had a shop in Frome as well as a number of stalls in the various market towns round about, one of which was Radstock.

During the daytime, trade was quite steady and my uncle and his employer managed quite easily, but towards evening, crowds would gather waiting for the bargains they knew were coming. All the fruit had to be sold because it would not keep or remain fresh over the weekend; it would go rotten and any unsold would have to be thrown out.

At about seven p.m., having decided that it was time to start disposing of the remaining fruit, the paraffin lamps would be lit and hung around the stall. Uncle Bill would stand on a box and cry out for the crowd to gather round for the bargain of a lifetime. Everyone knew what was about to happen, and a large crowd would soon build waiting for the auction to begin.

'Here we are then,' Uncle Bill would cry, and into a large brown paper bag would go four or five oranges, half a dozen apples, a bunch of bananas, and perhaps a few peaches. 'Five bob's worth of fruit there, not five bob, not four bob, not three bob, not two bob, one and sixpence the lot.' Up would go a dozen hands indicating acceptance, and the bag of fruit was tossed to me or another lad who was the owner's son, and taken to one of the waiting customers who would pay us, and we returned the money to a box on the front of the stall which had been provided for that purpose beforehand.

This performance was repeated a hundredfold, and we were kept dashing back and forth for several hours. As the crowd gradually thinned out, and in an attempt to sell the remaining fruit, the bargains got even better. They really were genuine bargains, and much business was done by the time the market closed for the day. Again I received another sixpence for my work, and also a fish and chip supper, and with my shilling, and a bag of fruit, I walked home tired but well pleased with my day's wages.

Not far from our house was the blacksmith's forge. From early morning to late evening every day except Sundays, the ring of the hammer striking the anvil sounded loud and clear. I loved it and would stand by the forge fascinated as the smith, whose name was Lew Uphill, worked at his craft, shoeing horses, repairing parts of agricultural machinery and implements. I believe he could make anything in iron; he hammered the red hot metal into various shapes just as an artist creates a painting on canvas, poetry in motion it is called, and he was a joy to watch.

Because I was very interested and also big and very strong, he offered me a job after school hours. No wage had been discussed, but I liked the idea and accepted his offer anyway. I knew that the work was hard but I was not afraid of that. And so I became a blacksmith's striker, skilled at wielding the fourteen pound sledge hammer, striking exactly where indicated by the smith's hammer tap, tending the forge fire, heating the metal to the correct temperature and being careful not to burn the iron. I learned how to lift a horse's foot, how to shoe and a great deal more. It always amazed me to see how docile and gentle those great shire horses usually are, though I remember one occasion when one lashed out at the smith and kicked him a good half dozen feet when he touched the horse on a tender spot.

There was also a great deal of bonding to be done, that is the fitting of metal tyre rims around the cartwheels. There were more horses and carts, and ponies and traps around than there were cars, and these cartwheels were constantly in need of repair, as the metal bands became worn out and sometimes broke or became damaged, and there were broken spokes to be mended or replaced. The blacksmith was also a wheelwright, and there was a continuous non stop supply of work for him to do.

One day a week was usually reserved for bonding, and there was a special routine, quite a rigmarole it was too, when the wheels were placed flat on a large flat circular stone with a metal spigot fixed in its centre about eighteen inches high, to which the wheel could be pinned to prevent it from moving. Close to it, just a couple of yards away, a very large fire was built around the new metal tyre rim which had to be heated almost up to white heat evenly all round. It was quite a job and took a long time. Some of the wheels could be as much as six feet in diameter. When the smith judged the time to be right, using special tongs, he would lift one side of the glowing rim, and I would take the other and we would carry it to the prepared wheel, place it over so that it was dead central all around, and taking his sledge hammer, the smith would walk around the wheel tapping to position and get the rim correctly adjusted and in the right place, and then he would shout for water. I then had to quickly scoop up buckets of cold water and run around behind him pouring it over the red hot metal and cooling the rim evenly where he directed I should apply it. As it cooled it contracted and shrank and became tightly fixed to the wheel and needed no further fastening of any kind. The whole thing was not quite as simple as it sounds because when the white hot rim was placed over the wheel, there was a tremendous billowing of choking smoke as the wood caught fire, and following that, great clouds of steam rose up and together with the smoke, choked and blinded me as the water was poured in a slow continuous stream until the metal cooled down. I always got soaked to the skin at these times, and there were frequently three or four wheels to be bonded, but the feeling of pride in having done a good job was grand. A good bond would protect a wheel for quite a few years; the roads were often rutted and quite rough, and the wheels had to take a lot of punishment as they carried heavy loads over them. It was one of the miracles of simple engineering.

The blacksmith was also the local undertaker. He owned a very ornate Victorian hearse which was drawn by two large and splendidly matched black horses. Funerals then were very dignified occasions, and the horses were bedecked in magnificent black plumes of feathers, their harness was gleaming, and the coffin was visible through the glass sides, covered with a mass of flowers. The whole cortege proceeded to the church with the undertaker and the mourners following on foot, of course.

One winter's night, there was a catastrophic fire at the smithy and the hearse was destroyed. Father and other neighbours helped to fight the fire. The horses were saved, but everything else had been completely burned up, so it was the end of the undertaking side of the business. It was such a shock to him that he never recovered. Shortly thereafter he retired and I never saw him again. While I worked for him he paid me well, five shillings a week which was equal to my first wages after I left school and worked full time. But I did miss the smithy and the lovely sound of that anvil ringing out.

There was one other job I tried as a boy, I sometimes went to the local sawmills and watched the men cutting up the trees and lumber and turning them into useable lengths of timber, and I loved watching the two shire horses hauling the trees around the mill. Using special off-cuts designed for the job, and using a jig, one could produce fish boxes by nailing the various pieces together. I do not remember how much I was paid for the job, but it was very poor: one had to produce something like fifty boxes to earn about four pence. I never did find that job worth doing.

Chapter Seven

Father had brought his bugle home from the war, and it held pride of place over the mantelpiece for many years. When the mood took him occasionally on a Sunday morning, he would play reveille and wake up the whole neighbourhood. The quality of sound deteriorated after a few years, mainly due to lack of practice. Eventually the bugle was put away and became lost; I think Mother probably had something to do with that.

All through the years we still had work to do at home. Father delegated some of the garden work to me when I was quite young and would put two sticks into the soil to mark out where I should start digging, and finish on any particular day; if I did not comply I could expect a beating after he finished work that night. As I grew older I often rebelled against him. We did not see eye to eye, and once, after a particularly nasty argument, I left home and cycled to Bristol where I went to the docks and boarded a steamer.

I asked the Captain if I could sign on for work on the ship, and though I was still at school I was a big lad, and looked much older than my real age of thirteen. He was quite willing to take me on, but when he asked for my cards I could not produce any, telling him that I would return the next day with them, I left. I later discovered that the ship was torpedoed on that next voyage and all hands had been lost, so I had to count myself lucky that I was not able to sign on for that voyage.

Not having anywhere to go, I decided to return home, cycling back in the rain and cold. I arrived back in the early hours of the morning to find my mother waiting up and very worried about me. For some reason that I was unaware of, I did not get the usual beating I had expected from my father, and the problems we had been experiencing seemed to stop for a while. Nevertheless, I had made up my mind that I would leave home at the first real opportunity rather than go through the constant arguments with him.

Again looking back, I have to be fair about my rebellious nature. Times were hard, there was very little money and I must have been a thorn in my father's side and a trial to both my parents. The pressure of work on Father was made worse by the fact that he would not pay anyone to do things that needed to be done if he thought he could do it himself. In no way was he a car mechanic, for instance, but when things went wrong with the car engine, he would do the repair himself.

The kitchen table had to be cleared and it was then covered with newspaper; and Father would start stripping the engine down. Each part was placed on the table in a certain position, carefully numbered. And by the time Father had finished, there were scores if not hundreds of parts and bits and pieces on and under the table. Woe betide anyone that touched anything. Having identified the broken part, Father would buy a replacement and recommence assembling the engine in reverse order. It took many hours of patient work and much trial and error, having forgotten which way a particular piece had to be inserted or placed, but in the end, after much cursing and bad language and sweat, the job would be finished. One has to admire his courage and tenacity in tackling the job in the first place, and in his mind Father had saved a fair amount of money, as indeed he had, but only at the expense of time, trouble, and upheaval, and because of his other commitments, things had to be done in a hurry. This made him bad-tempered, and, not being his favourite person, the brunt of his anger was taken out on my hide. Poor Mother, who had lost the use of her only table for the duration of the repairs, and ever the peacemaker, had the unenviable job of placating Father, and cooking and cleaning at the same time.

When I was about seven or eight years old, I had found a sixpence in the road. We had been taught that anything picked up should be declared and returned to the owner. However I did not do that; it was very rare to find any money at all in the road, but sixpence seemed a fortune, and I kept it and bought fireworks and had a glorious half hour lighting and setting them off in the playing field outside my Grannie's house. Of course I had been spotted by her, and she assumed that as I had exploded a large number of fireworks, I must have stolen the money to buy them; how else could I have paid for them?

She took me in hand, and walked me home admonishing me and explaining the dire consequences of becoming a thief. It was generally believed that I had stolen the sixpence. Fear and intimidation, and the sure knowledge of punishment that I would get from Father, made me withdraw into myself, and I would neither plead guilty nor deny all the accusations and interrogation that I underwent at the time. I was beaten and sent early to bed. It was bonfire night and I bitterly resented the injustice of punishment for what I considered to be nothing. I never forgot it, I was a little boy, albeit a tough one, but a great deal of the love and respect that I had for my parents was lost forever. I could never bring myself to talk about it in later years, but I do know that it had an influence on my thinking.

Holidays were now a thing of the past. Aunt Rose, who was once able to visit us on her 500cc motorbike, was no longer able to do so, as petrol was in short supply, so instead of bringing her customary rabbit or two with her for our dinner, she started posting them. They were not wrapped in any way, and came just as they were, with a label around the neck. They were put in the post and always seemed to arrive safely. We missed staying with her and Uncle Fred who was in the habit of getting drunk regularly. We also missed his dog, also named Tiger, who amazed us with his cleverness. At a signal from Uncle Fred, Tiger would race away to the field where the cows were grazing half a mile away, open the gate, round up the cows, and bring them to the milking parlour, and after milking, he would return them to the field and close the gate. All without any supervision. It does seem amazing but it was true. He could also growl at Uncle Fred's command to 'cuss 'em Tiger'. He lived for many years, and was finally killed by a milk lorry. His loss was a blow to Uncle Fred who now had to replace him and train the new dog.

It was about this time that I received one of the very rare beatings from Mother. The local Red Cross and VAD were calling for volunteers to act as injured patients so that the trainee nurses could practise treatments and bandaging. There was an imaginary disaster of some kind with large numbers of casualties so I volunteered. It was early evening and I was told to lie down on the floor and was labelled up as suffering from a fractured femur, broken clavicle, and various head injuries. I was told to lie still, do nothing, and allow the students to carry out first aid on me.

I quite enjoyed it really, and by the time the repairs to my body had been inspected, and we had finished our tea and biscuits, it had become quite late. Mother who had been sitting at home and getting more worried by the minute, beat me on the backside with her slipper all the way up the stairs, never allowing me to make any explanation for my lateness until the next morning when I handed her the sweets I had been given for doing such sterling voluntary service. I think she was sorry, and more hurt than I was; she said she had no doubt that the punishment I had received, although undeserved on this occasion, would make up for other times when I should have been punished and wasn't.

The Second World War had started, and there were air raid warnings at night. We remained in bed, but Mother would draw curtains and put furniture up against the windows to prevent any glass from being blown into the room in the event of any bombs falling nearby. The nearest severe bombing was at Bristol fifteen miles away, and Father would walk around outside with a pipe in his mouth upside down for fear that the glow from it might be seen by enemy pilots as they passed overhead on their way to the docks. It was exciting for me, and I wished I could have been a Spitfire pilot to have a go at the enemy, but of course it was a boyish dream and I was much too young.

Still, I was rapidly losing my childish thoughts and ways, the adventures I remembered from earlier times such as falling into the river obeying mischievous orders from my elder brother Eric, being the willing underling when he played his games with his own pals; I was tied to trees, blindfolded, made to walk the plank and thousands of other indignities were heaped upon me. I was always the prisoner, the bad guy; all these times were forever gone. My brother was in the army, and I had started my first job at five shillings a week, times were changing fast.

Chapter Eight

Up to this time, the wounds that Father had received in the first war had not bothered him very much, or if they had he did not complain about them; he seemed impervious to pain, and would make everyone shudder when he practised do it yourself dentistry. Loose teeth he would pull out himself using pliers and a mirror, but what really caused astonishment was his treatment of cavities. Grasping a sewing needle with his pliers, he would get it red hot in the fire, and thrust it into the cavity in his tooth. After the initial pain shock the nerve in the tooth was destroyed, and he had no further pain, I saw him do this several times and never ceased to wonder at the practicality of some of the things he did.

It was not that he did not want to go to the dentist, it was just easier and quicker and far less trouble to do it at home; he had not wasted any time, and it did not cost anything. Most of us were horrified by some of the things he did, but he never gave such mundane matters a second thought. To him, it was just another nuisance to be cleared up as soon as possible, so that he could get on with the more important things in life.

The bullet wound that Father had in his knee was now beginning to bother him a great deal. The bones had been shattered by the bullet, and although the healing process had been quite good, time had taken its toll. The damaged bones and surrounding tissue were becoming very painful, and he was forced to seek medical advice.

The British Legion of which my parents were staunch members, took up my father's case and made application for a war pension, and were successful in getting one. In the meantime, various forms of treatment was being applied to his knee to try to alleviate the pain. None were successful, and he later underwent an operation followed by some months convalescing at a home in Cardiff. He greatly benefited from the enforced rest, but the doctors and specialists had to admit defeat in the end, and he was sent home, still suffering some pain, and having to wear a leather cast on his leg which prevented the leg from bending at the knee.

Having decided that he didn't intend to hobble around with a leather leg for the rest of his life, or be treated as an invalid, Father flung the leather cast up on the top of the wardrobe, from where it eventually disappeared, and ignoring the pain of his injury, carried on with life as if nothing had ever happened, I never heard him complain again, but he could always forecast rain by the amount of pain his knee was giving him.

Whilst he was in hospital, the family income suffered a severe blow and Mother had to manage on Father's club money and a small pension. Because Dad was a miner, we were entitled to free coal, but now that he was not working, that coal entitlement stopped. My Uncle Percy who was still a miner gave us a load of his when we ran short to help us out. Again I was the oldest boy at home, and I had the job of helping my uncle move the coal from his house to ours.

The truck that we used held a good ten hundredweight and it was extremely hard work pushing it. When we started out, Uncle took the shafts and I would be pushing behind. I am sure he thought that I was not pushing hard enough, and made me take over the shafts. When he did this, the weight of the coal would lift me clear of the ground, and I was not heavy or strong enough to hold them down, so we had to change back again and carry on as before. I think he realised then that I had been doing my best.

It would be impossible for me to leave these times without a mention of several characters who must have been known to almost everyone in our small town. One of these was a small farmer known as Charlie Fry.

A soldier from the First World War, Charlie had been discharged from the army suffering from trench feet, and my mother told me that he had lost several of his toes whilst serving in the trenches, and had been awarded a small disability pension.

The amount he was to receive seemed to Charlie so derisory that it was not worth having. Mother said that he refused to accept it, and never claimed it for the duration of his life. Charlie could be seen frequently driving his horse and cart around the town, doing whatever business he had to do, the horse always moving at a fast trot. Charlie spoke to everyone he saw. He must have been quite a bit deaf, because as is common among deaf people, he tended to shout. In fact his voice was so loud that he bellowed like a fog horn, and could be heard by everyone in the street. 'Mornin' Missus, mornin' Will, how be you getting on?' He was usually travelling so fast that he was gone before he got an answer. Charlie was never seen in anything other than his working clothes, which was not surprising as he was always working. Except for Norton Fair day every year on 23 April: on that day, Charlie did no work except feed his livestock. He could be seen around the town, resplendent and clean, dressed in britches, highly polished leather leggings and boots, and a tweed jacket and cap and looking very smart. A stranger would have taken him for a proper country gentleman, passing the time of day and chatting with his many friends and acquaintances. He was a very friendly, old time eccentric, and much respected.

Another character, and a regular visitor to our home was Gunner Nash. He was also an ex-First World War soldier who had received severe head wounds, been repatriated home and was unable to work again. Father thought he was swinging the lead a bit, but nevertheless had a soft spot for Gunner, and tolerated him because he was an old soldier pal, and had served in the same area and front. Their paths had crossed occasionally though Gunner had been in the Artillery whilst Father had been an infantry soldier.

Mother, who seemed to know the history of all our visitors, explained that Gunner's skull had been so badly smashed that the surgeons had to reinforce it with a silver plate. He was a frequent visitor, and always received a cup of tea and a cigarette. That had been the real reason for his visit. He had a small pension to live on, and though he did not beg, he used to supplement his income by running errands or doing small jobs for people.

He had a regular route and a large circle of friends and acquaintances that he would call on. He had a passion for whist, and regularly attended whist drives held all over the town. His other great love was horse racing, and he could be seen studying form in the paper, and trying to scrape up sufficient money to place a bet. He lost far more money than he ever won, but he was forever hopeful for that big win, and never lost his enthusiasm for betting.

One would have thought that such a massive injury to the head would have turned him into a simpleton, but the opposite held true for Gunner. He would come into the house and say, 'Now George, where were you at six o'clock, nineteen years ago today?' My father would have no idea. Gunner would then recount where they had been, the name of the battle, who had been killed or wounded, and most of the other details that happened on that day. His memory was phenomenal, and he could regularly bring to mind a great deal of the history of the war from first hand knowledge. He would make us all laugh, and claim that Father was lucky to have won and married Ethel my mother, because he had been after her himself. And Father had just beaten him to it. With just a bit more luck, he might have been our father.

Whether there was any truth in the story we never knew; certainly my parents treated his banter in a very light-hearted way, but I suppose as a young man, he may have taken a fancy to Mother, but I do not think she had been very interested in him at the time. Still, as long as Gunner was able to scrounge a Woodbine and a cup of tea he was content. And after half an hour chatting away, he would say goodbye and leave, heading no doubt for his next port of call, another friend or neighbour.

There was another twice weekly visitor to our street, who was known as Nutty. In the week he was a Rag and Bone man, and his special cry remains in my mind today. He had a unique way of rolling several words into one, 'Anyolraagsa, Anyolraagsa,' he shouted up and down the street, and out would come the women with their old unwanted woollens which Nutty would carefully weigh and pay over whatever the going rate was in return. He was a fair man, and did considerable trade.

His second visit was always on Fridays, and with a horse and cart as before, but this time he was selling fresh fish and vegetables. The cart had been changed, and the fish and vegetables laid out in boxes exposed to the elements. The women would gather round asking the prices, and choosing what their particular fancy was that day, Quite a bit of haggling went on, but everyone was satisfied in the end.

My mother often bought tomatoes from him, as they were fresh from the Channel Islands and cheap. They were packed in fourteen pound baskets, and that was how she purchased them. She would also buy herring, and cod roes, although when they were available, sprats were favoured. Mother would take along her large enamelled kitchen bowl, and get it almost filled with sprats; no one else seemed to want them, and that is why they were so cheap. She spent the afternoon cleaning and preparing them, and then spent ages frying them up for our tea, they were delicious. Of course they were not always available, but every now and then when they were, we had a treat.

When the war started, street trading gradually disappeared. There were no supplies available, and even the scissor grinder–knife sharpener, or the umbrella repair men no longer called. A familiar sight like old

Chapter Eight

Mr Durnford the lamplighter was no longer required because of the imposition of the blackout regulations, and the changing times affected almost everyone.

I was fourteen when I started work at the Standard works, supposedly as a printer's apprentice in the machine room where all the printing was done, having to work at all the dirty jobs as most beginners usually do. When a machine finished a print job, everything had to be cleaned up and the machine prepared for the next one. Or when a colour was changed, the old ink had to be removed from the storage ducts, and everything had to be perfectly clean so that not a trace of the old ink remained.

Printing ink is vile stuff, not at all like ordinary ink used for writing, but a thick glutinous treacle-like substance that sticks like glue to everything it touches. It required a lot of hard work to remove and clean up, even with the thinners provided.

All male newcomers to the trade had to be initiated. A gang of workmates would suddenly appear without warning on the young, unsuspecting youth. He would be pinned to the ground, his genitals exposed, and they would be liberally smeared with printers' ink. It must have been an awful problem removing it afterwards. I was extremely lucky, as try as they did on many occasions to initiate me, I always managed to outwit them or fight so hard that the attempt was always abandoned before the dastardly deed could be done.

I was not a timid little school leaver, weak, inexperienced, or unable to defend myself, neither were the majority of those who tried to overcome me particularly fit. I was a tough and very strong lad; my work with the blacksmith had hardened and built muscles on me like a man, and on the many occasions when I was not quick enough to outwit them, and was actually waylaid by the perpetrators of this horrible tradition, I would fight like a demon against five or six of them, until they wearied of trying to overcome me; but it was a close run thing at times.

The women were not as savage as the men with new girls, and it was considered sufficient just to smear ink on the faces of the uninitiated. Even then, it was quite difficult to remove.

At first I came under the eye and direction of an old time employee who was nearing the end of his working life and was soon to retire; he was called Jim. His main job was to keep all the big rotary presses and machines supplied with paper. They were not allowed to run out or stop production, so there was always a spare roll ready and waiting as the machine used the last of the previous roll. These rolls were of various sizes, and the largest ones might weigh several hundredweight. They were stacked on edge on top of each other in the stores up to fifteen or twenty feet high. They could be damaged very easily, and just to let them fall any old way was to invite disaster and the loss of a whole roll of expensive paper. If they landed on an edge, its weight could burst the roll and then it would not run on the machine because it would continually break with every turn of the roller.

If it landed on the length of the roll, it would become oval shaped and prevent the machine from keeping the correct tension, which caused further problems. I quickly learned that a certain measure of skill was needed to bring a roll of paper down to floor level, and then get it to the machine.

In order to accomplish this, the roll had to be manoeuvred by hand so that it lay with the edge overlapping the roll it was resting on to the point of balance. It was allowed to tip over, and as it fell, a push was made on the edge nearest the person carrying out the operation. In theory the roll fell perfectly straight, and landed flat on the edge. Jim of course with his years of experience could do it blindfold, but it was quite a while, and with a lot of practice on old unwanted rolls, before he allowed me to actually replace a roll with the proper paper. However with the enthusiasm of the young, I quickly learned, and found no difficulty in keeping the machines supplied.

Another part of training was working in the stores, where I learned the mysteries of many different kinds of paper. Cream laid, Azure blue, Conqueror, Bond: many and varied are the types and qualities of paper; terms such as quires and reams which referred to amounts were also new to me, and I used to watch fascinated as the storeman would find and count out the paper in amounts of five sheets at a time. This job also required considerable knowledge and skill.

Up to the time hostilities commenced with Germany, the firm had been a small but successful one, printing books of order forms, invoices and other business stationery; there was also a subsidiary making carrier bags. Now that a war had started, one part of the factory was put on war work. It had acetylene welding and cutting machines installed as well as drilling and milling machines, in fact all of the paraphernalia of light engineering. It busily went to work producing gun shields for merchant ships, and small parts required in the construction of Bailey bridges which were designed for the use of the Royal Engineers, who could build them in just a few hours to replace those that had been destroyed. They were only meant to be a temporary structure but were so good that they frequently remained in use for many years, even in peacetime Britain.

I was taught to cut and weld heavy sheets of plate metal, but more often than not used as a labourer, keeping the machines supplied with materials. I had a workmate called George, who was a handsome well built Yorkshire man. He was three years older than I, and had discovered the female sex. He spent most of his time chatting up the ladies for whom he had a fancy, and with an eye for a date, and with a great many sweethearts and husbands serving in the armed forces away from home. George's services were in great demand, and he had a very good time providing comfort to the lonely girls whilst their loved ones were away fighting for their country. All the details of his very successful sex life were related to me the following morning. I often thought in later years, that if I had entered the blackmailing profession when the men returned from the war, I could have made a very good living using the information I received from George. He was quite open about his conquests, and firmly believed that he was providing a need to the lonely females.

The large sheets of steel used in the factory were stacked in sizes on edge along both sides of the whole length of the roadway leading to the entrance of the new engineering section of the company. They varied in thickness from a quarter to one inch, and were some hundred or so feet square in area. They had to be manhandled all the way to the machines inside the factory. We had an old four-wheel truck which we would position alongside the steel plates and taking opposite top corners we pulled the sheet over onto the trucks. We then hauled it by hand, along the roadway to the factory lorry entrance, and used a chain block and tackle to lift the steel up to the floor level of the factory where we pushed it along the overhead girder and dropped the load on to another truck. From there we hauled it to the machine where it was required. It was quite hard work, and George was always asking the foreman for a wage increase because of the donkey work we were required to do.

The factory had been built with a number of skylights to allow more light in, but war-time regulations meant that all windows had to have blackout screens fitted. Any light showing at all would be met with a shout from one or more of the patrolling civil defence air raid wardens,

'Put that light out!' If the order was not promptly complied with, the person responsible could be reported and fined quite heavily.

These blackout screens in the roof were raised and lowered from ground level by means of a rope very much like a washing line; this ran over a pulley system which quite frequently got jammed or sometimes slipped off the pulley. At such times either George or I would be called upon to climb into the roof area, along the steel roof trusses some thirty or forty feet high, and rectify the fault so that the blinds would operate correctly. We rather enjoyed swinging around up in the roof like a couple of monkeys. I am sure that the foreman thought we had sabotaged the ropes by pulling them off somehow on purpose, so that we could get a break from our more tedious work.

Part Two

THE AIRBORNE FORCES PRAYER

MAY the Defence of the Most High be around us and within us, in our going out and our coming in, in our rising up and in our going down, all our days and all our nights until the Dawn when the Sun of Righteousness shall arise with Healing in His Wings for the Peoples of the World: through Jesus Christ our Lord. Amen.

Chapter Nine

For some time I had been thinking of joining the army. It was 1942 and I knew that if I did not hurry up there was a strong possibility that the war would be over before I could get in and see some action. I was fed up, and there were continuous arguments at home with my father. The only bright part of my life was doing military training with the Home Guard.

I had been in the army cadets for quite some time, but now I could for several nights a week attend the various military lectures and field training, and take part in the exercises that happened most weekends. One day I took the plunge. I took a day off work and caught a bus to Bath where I knew the nearest recruiting office was. I took a deep breath and entered without hesitation. In for a penny, in for a pound, I thought.

'I have been in a reserved occupation,' I said, 'but I am fed up with that and I want to join up!' 'How old are you?' the Sergeant asked. He was a tall guardsman, and looked very forbidding as he eyed me up and down. With the guilty feeling of one about to lie, and knowing that I had to act with confidence and without hesitation, I glibly answered with my older sister's date of birth. I had rehearsed my lines well beforehand, I knew that I looked old enough. It was just a matter of having sufficient aplomb to carry it off.

I was a big strong lad and certainly looked the seventeen and a half years that I needed to be. 'What regiment do you want to join?' he said. 'The Somerset Light Infantry,' I answered smartly. 'The same regiment my father was in during the last war.' 'I'm afraid there are no vacancies left in that regiment, but will the Devons suit you?' I did not mind what regiment it was as long as I could get in, and Devon was the next county to Somerset, so I agreed.

'Right then, just fill in the particulars on these forms, then go along to the doctor for your medical, then report back here to me, OK?' He waved me away with his hand. Trembling with excitement, I went along the passage to where there were three other lads waiting to see the doctor. I sat down on the bench to wait my turn. Each recruit entered the room and was there about seven or eight minutes. When my turn came along, I entered and was directed by an orderly to an elderly doctor seated at a desk who asked me questions about my health and that of my family. He examined me, tested a urine sample, and pronounced me A1.

We returned to the recruiting Sergeant who ushered us all into another room where there was another officer seated at a desk. Handing us all a Testament, we were promptly sworn in to serve His Majesty, and his heirs and successors. The officer shook hands with each one of us in turn, and congratulated us on becoming soldiers. We were handed travel documents and other papers, and he told us when and where we should report for duty. He then sent us on our way.

I was amazed and elated at how easy it had all been. The whole thing had been accomplished without any difficulties in just over an hour. I was very pleased with myself and whistled and sang all the way home. The thought of having to break the news to my parents sobered me up somewhat, but I was certain that they could not raise any serious objection; after all, I was sixteen and the same age as my father when he enlisted.

'I have joined the army, and I have to report to Gujarat Barracks in Colchester next Wednesday, so it is no good making a fuss because I am going.'

My father looked at me and said, 'If I tell them your correct age they will not let you join and you will have to come home again.'

'If you do that, I will leave home anyway.'

My mother looked on, concerned and worried. She felt that I was too young to go to war, and remembering the high casualty rate in the first war, had fears for my safety.

'I will be all right, Mum, and I will write to you and let you know how I am getting on.' I knew that the battle was won. Knowing that I would leave home if I were not allowed to enlist, she reluctantly agreed; at least this way she would know where I was. Father remained silent; he knew that I was as stubborn as he was, so he became reconciled to the situation and never referred to it again.

Having given in my notice at work, there remained nothing else to do but wait for the great day. I champed at the bit, eager to start out on a new episode in my life. When that day arrived, I said my goodbyes and caught the train to London where I would have to change stations to travel on to Colchester, where I arrived at about two o'clock that afternoon. Along the way, other young men had been joining the train bound for the same destination. Most of them had been conscripted and were very reluctant to join the army. There was much grumbling and bitterness at being forced to leave home and families to serve in the war. I thought that everyone would have been keen to do that, but my youth and inexperience of life was pointed out to me and it seemed that they thought I was stupid and a nutcase. Fancy volunteering to get your head blown off.

It soon became apparent that it did not matter what any of us thought, we were now in the army, and we had no time to think; we were all herded like cattle through the system. After having our names and addresses checked, we were escorted by an NCO, in groups of about a dozen, first to the barber's shop, where the speed of the haircut seemed to be paramount. The unfortunate recruit was seated in the chair, a cloth put around his neck, and using an automatic hair clipper, the barber started at the base of the neck and ran the clipper up over the head to the hairline on the forehead. After being repeated about six times, the hair cut was complete and the head was completely shorn, as close to the scalp as made no never mind.

I swear that each haircut took no longer than thirty seconds to complete: suddenly, and very quickly, one became a baldy. Many and varied had been the beautiful hairstyles, and obviously a matter of some pride to some of the recruits. There were quite a number who had to fight back the tears at the shock of losing their hair almost before they knew it. It did not bother me because I had been having similar style haircuts for years. All the boys were used to it. Father never wasted money at the barber's, he just put a pudding basin on our heads and removed every bit of hair that was visible. What hair had been left under the basin, and it was not much, was trimmed with the scissors, and we were all left with a very short fringe at the front. This army haircut was almost identical, but it did not leave a fringe, I never gave it a second thought. The army knew what it was doing though, and we all looked like a gang of convicts. Whatever feelings of class consciousness had all disappeared; that haircut was a great leveller of people.

From the barber shop, we were propelled to the stores where we walked along a huge counter and were loaded with kit bag, shirts, towels, underclothes, vests, and a housewife, which was not at all what I imagined it to be, just a small cloth bag filled with needles, cotton, and darning materials.

Berets and boots were thrown on the counter. The sizes were accurate because they were shouted out by us as we passed along. However the fitting of uniforms was a miracle of experienced judgement by a Colour Sergeant who passed his eye over each recruit in turn and called out the size to the storeman who then produced the uniform. He was more often than not very accurate with the fitting, and except for shortening legs of trousers or altering sleeves, in fact with the minimum of tailoring, there we were, kitted out and ready to start soldiering.

The rest of the day was spent in packing up our civvy clothes, and being instructed and shown how to behave, dress, and above all, do what we were told. It was not a requirement that we should have to think, that would be done for us, all we had to do was obey orders. We were now in the army, forget home and the comforts that went with it. Any misdemeanour would be severely dealt with, and instruction on every conceivable matter would follow in due course. We made our beds, and wondered what had hit us.

At six a.m. next morning, we were roused by the noise of shouting and sticks banging on our beds, by several NCOs. They got us washed, shaved and dressed, and on parade in double quick time, a phrase that we had not heard before, but would hear much more of during our training. It meant in fact, as quickly as was humanly possible, or in another term, like lightning. To enforce this, and to ensure that every man did move quickly and do whatever had to be done in the spirit of what the army meant, the last two men to comply with the order were always punished in some way, either by running around the parade ground in full kit holding their rifles above the head, or cookhouse fatigue, (peeling spuds). There was a never ending supply of punishment waiting for whoever the last two unfortunates were. It did also of course achieve what the army desired, namely to promote one hundred per cent effort, and also instill discipline. Each individual recruit did his best to avoid being one of the last two men.

After breakfast, we were paraded and sorted out into our sections and platoons. We met the officers and NCOs who were to be in charge of our training. The real power, we quickly learned, was in the hands of our platoon Sergeant. At the end of our basic training we felt a sense of pride and achievement. The platoons were judged and placed in order of merit in the passing-out parade. Each Sergeant was intent on producing the best platoon, and to that end praised our good points, and was merciless in meting out punishment to correct our bad points. The junior NCOs i.e. the corporals and lance corporals were like gods, and would also hand out extra punishment, but the platoon Sergeant who had over-all control, caused severe fear and trembling in everyone. He would stand no nonsense, and would make life a misery for those who would not toe the line.

There are those who complain about the methods of training in use by the army, but they have traditionally proved to be the best and quickest in producing good disciplined soldiers in the minimum of time. That standard, it might be argued, may not need to be as high in some of the Corps, or behind the battlefield troops. But it was and is required in front line troops, where immediate obedience to orders is crucial, and where one is usually under stress and the very real possibility of being wounded or killed. The outcome of the battle may depend entirely on the discipline and bravery of individual soldiers, and that is instilled by training, tough training, and it produces the pride and *esprit de corps* in the regiment. This comradeship will not allow a soldier to let down his unit, or do anything that might put the lives of his friends in jeopardy. But I digress.

I found the food to be very good. I suppose it depended on the style of life one had been accustomed to, but to me and most other working-class lads, quite satisfactory. In fact there was infinitely more variety than I got at home, and the rationing that had been so obvious there, was not at all evident in our cookhouse. There was also the chance that if you were particularly hungry, one or more of your pals was not, or did not like what was on the menu, and would hand over his portion or swap one dish for another. We usually finished up satisfied.

The army practice of dealing with complaints was quickly instilled into us, ensuring that we learned to be satisfied and happy with our lot. One day, whilst eating our dinner, one of the more dissatisfied recruits who had been tied far too long to his mother's apron strings, and who on occasions because of his failure to accept his new way of life, had caused our whole section to be punished, made a complaint.

The orderly officer accompanied by the Orderly Sergeant, walked along the mess tables briskly, enquiring if there were any complaints; this was the procedure every meal time, it was intended to show that the army was concerned that the quality and standard of food remained high. We all knew better than to complain, it would be inviting trouble to do that, but in any case, there was rarely any thing to complain about. However, such was the unhappiness of this particular recruit, that he mistakenly thought he could make life difficult for the army.

He did not want to be in the army, and everyone should know it. I expect his mum told the little darling not to put up with things if he was not happy, and to do something about it.

'Yes sir,' he said, 'I think that the windows in this cookhouse are filthy, and we should not have to eat our food in such conditions.'

The orderly officer was taken aback. Complaints were very rare, and this particular officer was young and inexperienced. Not so the orderly sergeant, who was an old soldier and knew exactly how to put this snotty nosed, jumped-up trouble maker in his place.

'The man is quite right, sir,' speaking to the orderly officer and taking the complainant's name and number. 'We need to get the Cook sergeant here. If you wish I will deal with the complaint.'

The officer, pleased to have such an experienced NCO who knew the procedure, continued on his way. In the meantime the Cook sergeant had arrived on the scene. He too was an old regular soldier, and he listened to the orderly sergeant as the nature of the complaint was explained.

There was a pause as he looked around his cookhouse, and then directly at the recruit. 'Yes, you are quite right, the windows are dirty, and you will report to me after your duties this evening to clean them.'

His mouth falling open, the recruit spluttered and protested, saying that he did not have the time because of his training etc. etc. But he was hooked and there was no way out. There were a lot of windows in that very large cookhouse, they took a long time to clean. The sergeant was not satisfied with the recruit's first or second attempts at cleaning them, and he lost his weekend pass and spent most of the weekend cleaning the windows again and again. Needless to say, never again did that man make any complaint about anything. We used to pull his leg and say it was about time he complained about the cookhouse windows again as they were getting dirty. He took it in good part, and eventually settled down and accepted the new way of life. The army has more than one way of persuading men to buckle under and accept the rules.

Chapter Ten

Basic training for the infantryman was of six weeks duration, and consisted of small arms handling, marching, drill instruction, and various field training with lectures. There was one series of these on Regimental history, which was given by our Company Sergeant Major who seemed to be an authority on it. He told us about the many battle honours won by the Regiment, also the names and histories of those men decorated for valour, who included three Victoria Crosses. He was very proud of the regiment, and it is easy to see how such pride and *esprit de corps* was passed on to the new members. At the end of those six weeks, we could march and look after ourselves and our kit, and we looked and felt like soldiers, very proud of our achievements.

Having now completed this first part of our training, we were put through a series of selection tests, the results of which would determine the actual posting to his place in the army for each individual. Some would become clerks, or engineers, or tank men, or one of the many other trades or professions in the armed forces, whatever our Lords and Masters had decided was in the best interests of the country. Anyway it meant losing some of our new found friends and we had a night out on the town to celebrate, and to say goodbye to those who were going separate ways. I do not remember much about it, but I was a bit nonplussed to wake up next morning in my bed, and to find a tattoo of a Red Indian on my forearm. I do count myself fortunate in this respect, because some of my pals had much bigger, and much uglier tattoos on them. The general consensus of opinion was that we had enjoyed a good night out.

Corps training, which consisted of a further ten weeks, took place at Bury St Edmunds; after that, we were considered to be fully trained soldiers and ready for active service.

Those ten weeks were the hardest of my life up to then, and very different to the type of physical work I had been used to in civvy life. Little did I know it at the time, but there were far harder times to come in the future. We learned to shoot, run, crawl and march in an endless succession of days and nights of concentrated effort, and we were inevitably turned from useless civilians into fit and proud soldiers. At least some of us felt that way, others were still bemoaning their lot and complaining about everything under the sun. Human nature being what it is, I suppose there will always be those who are unable to take to the rough and tumble of army life.

For myself, I was pleased and excited, and as the prospect of actually getting to the front line, and fighting approached nearer, I was looking forward with eagerness to getting to grips with the enemy.

The route marches which started off in a programme designed to harden the feet, were gradually increased in distance and regularity, from five miles and then nine, fourteen and up to twenty five. The tedium and pain were relieved at spasmodic intervals only by the order 'Sing you bastards.' And we did. The countryside around echoed to the sound of men's voices singing lewd and boisterous army songs, the words of which would bring a blush to the cheeks of any but the most hardened of ears. We would arrive back in camp at all hours of the day or night, weary and footsore yes, but as we sloped our arms, straightened our pain-racked bodies, and marched to attention through the gates, there came to us a great sense of pride and achievement. We had made it, we had not let the side down. We were pretty tough fellows, and we knew it.

We continued to train our way through the remaining weeks of that period, learning to read Ordnance Survey maps, and carrying out various exercises sometimes lasting several days. These would include marching to some distant objective, an attack on a hill or other feature against some mythical enemy, and end up invariably with the return march back to camp, both physically and mentally exhausted, having practised and used all the knowledge and skills we were so rapidly acquiring.

It was also at this time that we received our first experience of the army inoculation programme. These jabs, as they were known, were always administered on a Friday afternoon. They had more effect on some men than on others. At worst it could knock a man out completely to the extent that no activity of any kind could be engaged in, in others it produced symptoms of flu, or a very heavy cold. I suffered somewhere in between those two extremes. In general, it was a feeling of unhappy misery for some thirty six hours. The reason for the jabs being given on Friday of course, was that you had to suffer in your own time and not that of the army, not that one had much free time, but sometimes, after a particularly strenuous week, we were granted a Saturday afternoon and Sunday free, and this was one of those times.

The formation of a new airborne division was taking place at this time, and volunteers were being sought for inclusion. The First Airborne Division had been in existence for some time, and the powers that be obviously thought that a new division would be required when the time came to invade Europe, hence the call for volunteers.

It was just what I wanted; there will be plenty of excitement and adventure with them, I thought. There was an extra incentive, too: the pay was more, an extra two shillings a day flying money, almost doubling our pay, and if we completed parachute training, even more. The opportunity had come at the right time for me. I volunteered and was quickly posted to the 12th Battalion the Devonshire Regiment, in the new 6th Air Landing Brigade, 6th Airborne Division. Our regiment was glider borne. We were to be towed into action by Stirling bombers and released over the enemy targets wherever we were required, and after the landings hopefully intact, we were to go into action as specialised infantry.

Two other regiments made up the landing brigade, The Oxford and Buckingham Light Infantry and The Royal Ulster Rifles. The other nine battalions of the division were all from the Parachute Regiment, plus of course the additional specialist units which were the normal part of a fighting division. We were all living on Salisbury Plain in the Belford area. The division not only became a crack fighting unit, but it was also a lucky one in that it was successful wherever and whenever it went into action, the *esprit de corps* was magnificent, and morale could not have been higher anywhere in the rest of the British Army.

Morale is instilled by training and confidence. The physical fitness of the Division as a whole, was of the highest standard, the training was tough and continuous. First parade at 6 a.m., road run and walk for seven miles; this consisted of running more than walking. We only occasionally marched up hills, the rest of the time we went at the double. Then back to camp for a wash and shave followed by breakfast. Clean weapons and parade for training. Another seven mile road run and walk before lunch, after which there was football or some other field game followed by further training and you can guess, yet another road run and walk of just two or three miles.

The pattern of training was frequently changed; we sometimes had a route march, anything from five to twenty-five miles, again, sing you bastards, and we did. One can only imagine the extremely high level of fitness that was achieved. Quite ordinary people were changed into virtual athletes. With this extreme fitness, came a feeling of well being, of cockiness, of pride, of being the crack of the walk, the best. It also produced aggression which had to be controlled with firm discipline. Though sometimes there were fist fights among the many units that were crowded into the Salisbury area, it really was quite amazing that these extroverts were controlled with a minimum of trouble. One could sense the pride and verve emanating from these young men, who were waiting, like thoroughbred horses, champing at the bit, and eager to get into action against the enemy.

I previously mentioned that our division was a lucky one; it was successful in all the actions it undertook, also the casualties it suffered were fairly low. This was in contrast to our sister division which seemed to suffer bad luck and high casualties every time it went into action. At Salerno for instance, which was a combined Anglo American attack, the battle was very lacklustre, and not a success. Many of our airborne units finished up in the sea, the pilots having released the gliders too soon.

Again at Arnhem the 1st Airborne fought a gallant action for a far longer period than could have been expected. The operation failed, not because of inferior troops, they were every bit as good as those in the 6th, but by a combination of bad weather, which made re-supply impossible, a slightly over ambitious plan, which had it been successful would have definitely shortened the war, but mainly plain bad luck. There may be those who do not agree with that assessment, but that intangible thing which makes the dividing line between good and bad luck is undoubtedly a major factor in determining the outcome of innumerable situations. After experiencing many narrow escapes myself, some of which are recounted later, I will leave it with the reader to decide if there is such a thing. Certainly I am a believer in luck. Both varieties.

Anyway, there we were, fully trained and keen to get into action. It was pretty obvious that we were being prepared for the second front. We were visited by King George, and being a very young soldier, I was very impressed when I saw my first Field Marshal when he came to inspect the division on Salisbury Plain. We were all neatly drawn up in our regiments. Monty arrived, drove into the middle of the division, stood up in the jeep and called everyone to break ranks and gather round him, which of course we did.

Chapter Ten

It seemed to me that one could easily understand why he was a successful General, and that he planned the victorious battle of El Alamein, because in a very short speech of ten minutes or so, he instilled a wonderful feeling of confidence in us. Not only in me, but in discussion with my pals after the parade, I found that many of them also felt the same. He exuded confidence. He was not a large man, but his precise manner of speech, and his whole demeanour impressed everyone, and we realised that here was a General who knew what he wanted to do, and who would make the preparations and planning to do it, and mostly that he would not waste lives. Every individual soldier was important, and would know the overall plan, he would know his role and what would be expected of him in the battle. Somehow we knew that we could trust him.

Sometime after the war, on one of his rare TV appearances, I recall him saying that he was now going to retire, and one of the things he had to do, was to make his peace with God and with his soldiers who had died in battles that he had planned, and for whom he felt responsible. Not many of our Generals have publicly given thought and accepted the responsibility for the death of men killed in action in this way. Monty was one who did, and I have the greatest respect for his memory.

What a contrast to the Great War generals, most of whom were indifferent to the tremendous loss of life resulting from the outdated, set piece battles that took place in the trenches. Men were just cannon fodder, and were maimed and killed in their thousands. Battles were planned in the knowledge that casualties would be very high, and this was not a consideration in the plan: the objective was the important thing, it could be normal to expect 5000 dead, and 10,000 wounded in some battle or other, and it was not regarded as anything to be concerned about specifically, merely one of the hard facts of life.

I was sixteen years old and looked nineteen or twenty, and I had become proficient in the use of all the infantry soldier's weapons. Our training continued apace, and quite a number volunteered and completed parachute training, which produced an extra bonus of two shillings a day. We were the best paid British infantryman, receiving one pound fifteen shillings, much more than the ordinary soldier got.

My platoon commander decided that I should be the platoon 2-inch mortar man, and Ali, who came from London, my No.2. We practised the art of dropping smoke and high explosive bombs until we became efficient. One day we were called upon to take part in an exercise which involved a medical unit from our division, who had arrived in our area for a day's special training. A number of live bodies (ordinary soldiers) were placed all over an area equivalent to a ten acre field; they were dotted here and there, and they were required to act as casualties. It was the job of the medical unit to search for and carry out the appropriate medical treatment on these casualties, and then remove them from the battle area to safety.

The commanding officer of the unit was keen for things to be as realistic as possible, and had requested the use of mortar men of our unit to lay down smoke, thereby simulating battle conditions. Ali and I were given the job.

We positioned ourselves on a prominent hillock overlooking the whole scene, and with a large stock of smoke bombs beside us we started firing and laid about ten bombs at strategic points around the area in quick succession. Our orders were that we should keep the whole site covered in smoke for about two hours, and having started with this burst, it was only necessary to fire a further one or two a minute thereafter in order to keep a good thick blanket of smoke continuously billowing over the whole battle area.

Visibility was minimal, just about a metre or two, and it was very difficult for the medics to locate the casualties. They could not be seen, that was obvious, and so they had to methodically search in a way that would enable them to cover all the ground. More often than not, they found the casualties by tripping over them in the thick choking gloom, and I have doubts that such terrible conditions were ever encountered in real battle. From our place of safety on the hillock we enjoyed the operation very much. The commanding officer of the medics was delighted with the exercise, and as we were coming to the end of it, and the smoke was gradually thinning, he callously ordered us to actually fire a bomb directly at one of his jeeps. I questioned the order, thinking that someone might be injured or killed even, but he was adamant. I aimed and fired the mortar at low angle; it was only about one hundred and fifty yards range to the jeep, and the bomb struck it on one of the front wheels, the ricochet screaming away, bouncing with considerable velocity into the distance.

It was only then that I realised how terrifying the whole exercise must have been to those taking part. It was a lucky thing that no one was injured; what to us seemed a bit of fun, was to them very frightening, because they could hear the bombs screaming down to earth, but they could not see them, and undoubtedly some would have landed very close and been very scary. It was not long before their feelings were made known to us, because they had re-formed as a unit, and had to march by close to our position, back to their vehicles. Shouts of 'Bastards, wait till we catch you outside,' and many other choice phrases were directed at us as they went by, I would not have given much for our chances if we were ever recognised in town or anywhere else away from our unit. But we had steel helmets on which hid our hair and helped to disguise us, and it was unlikely that we should be recognised. Anyway, no one had been hurt, and the CO sent his congratulations on our skilful handling of our weapons, so we were not unduly worried.

Chapter Eleven

We had a very imaginative CO, who made sure the Battalion's training was as diversified and complete as he could possibly make it. He had the idea that every man should know what to do if they were taken prisoner. It was their duty to escape and make their way back through enemy territory to their own lines and rejoin the unit. And so he devised an exercise which would give us some experience in case it happened to us.

We were searched to ensure that we had no money, maps, or food, or anything that might help an escaped prisoner, and we were dressed only in army denim overalls, and army boots, but we had no hats. They did allow us our gas capes. These were a sticky, waterproof, oilskin type of knee-length jacket, designed for use in gas warfare. They were not lined, but they did offer some protection from the wind, and to a lesser degree from rain, and they could be rolled up into a small bundle so they were easy to carry. They provided a little comfort at night when sleeping in the rough, but not much.

As we clambered into the back of the trucks, we had no idea of our intended destination, or indeed what we were supposed to do. Tarpaulins were sheeted down all round so that we could not look out, and in complete darkness, we spread ourselves out on the floor of the truck, and tried to sleep. We had received orders to pair up with someone, and it was quite natural for Ali and me to do that as we were already a team on the Mortar. We had also been told to be ready to jump off the truck when ordered.

It was a very long boring time, and some fourteen hours later in pitch blackness, in the early hours of the morning we were ordered out of the vehicle, and we found ourselves somewhere in the countryside, all alone. The police, and the Home Guard had been notified of the exercise, and they were to act the part of the host country authorities and of course our enemy. If caught, we were to be held in custody for twenty four hours, our names recorded, and then we were to be released to continue the exercise.

We had no food or drink, no money and no timepiece, but we were given a bit of paper with instructions typed on it. But it was dark, and we had no light, and no means of producing it, so we decided that the best thing was to kip down and try to sleep until first light; we could then read our orders, find out where we were, and take it from there. Making ourselves as comfortable as possible, we curled up in a ditch, covered ourselves as best we could with our gas capes, and tried to sleep.

We awakened cold and stiff. It was misty and drizzling with rain, and visibility was only about twenty yards or so. We could not pinpoint our whereabouts; signposts had been removed for the duration, and it was only the fern and heather which gave us any clue. We were obviously on some kind of moorland. Having read our instructions, we made the decision to travel east. The first thing we were required to do was to proceed to Scarborough railway station, and get a platform ticket. To make sure that we entered into the spirit of things, the ticket had to carry that day's date which was quite a tall order.

Putting a brave face on it, we stepped out lively along the road, and after a few miles we came to a small cottage where our enquiries produced the information from an elderly lady, that we were on one of the North Yorkshire moors. We had decided to come clean and tell her the truth about the exercise. She was quite angry when she heard we had no food or money, I supposed we must have looked a woebegone pair, not having washed or shaved or cleaned ourselves up in any way. Fancy the army treating us poor boys in such a way; making suitable responses to our sympathetic listener, we were soon warming up by a blazing fire, and tucking in to a welcome breakfast. After a wash and brush up, we thanked our generous sponsor and went on our way.

Scarborough lay some 25 to 30 miles away, and my partner and I decided to try to appear as normal as possible. To be spotted acting in a furtive or suspicious way would have made it obvious that something was amiss, we would give the game away and we did not want to do that, so, making no attempt to hide, we marched along the road without a care. Traffic was very light and very few vehicles came our way, but five or six miles after leaving the moors, we managed to hitch a lift on a truck straight in to Scarborough arriving at 10.30 a.m. We made our way to the railway station, sat down on a bench, and wondered how we could get a platform ticket.

'Why not try begging?' Ali suggested, so we stood either side of the entrance to the station, selected likely looking candidates and spun various yarns to them hoping that we could scrounge sufficient money to enable us to buy the ticket, which if I remember correctly was only about two pence, I had never been in the situation of having to beg before, and never realised just how difficult it was; we were both complete failures, at a loss, and we were beginning to look very suspicious.

'Why not be truthful with the ticket collector?' I said. 'We were with the old lady, and she believed us, maybe he will too and give us a couple of tickets.'

'Suppose he reports us,' my partner argued, 'what do we do then?'

'Just make a run for it, they will never catch us. And if we get separated, we will meet up here again after an hour or so, what do you think?'

'I agree, let's give it a try.'

Much to our surprise, the truthful approach worked. We might have looked a little odd, but our answers to his questions certainly convinced him that we were genuine. He gave us the tickets and a half crown for something to eat, so we went in to a local café, ordered a cup of tea and discussed our next move.

Our orders were to get to Birmingham, and obtain a daily paper with that day's date on it. We discussed various plans, methods and ways in which we might get there. We had another cup of tea and it was some time before we arrived at the most obvious solution. The answer had been right there at the end of our noses. We would travel by train. We would find out the train times, wait for this ticket inspector to go off duty, use our platform tickets to get into the station, hop on the train and Bob's your uncle. Ali was enthusiastic about our chances and we were convinced it would work.

'We shall have to keep a sharp lookout for the ticket collector,' I said. 'We should stay somewhere in the middle of the carriage, then when he appears, we clear off down the other end and lock ourselves in the Khazi till he goes by.'

'No that's no good,' Ali had done this sort of thing before. 'He will just wait until we come out, better to wait until he enters the compartment before ours, then slip out, and go back the way he has come, that way he won't even see us.'

I agreed somewhat hesitantly, and thinking of the saying 'Nothing ventured nothing gained' I finished my tea, and left with Ali to return to the station to find out the train times.

There were three or four trains heading our way, and departing at different times. Most of them meant that we would have to change trains somewhere along the way, one however was a through train and went all the way and had fewer stops; it left at 6.10 p.m. that evening.

'That's the one for us,' Ali became excited. 'Takes us to Birmingham, and it gets dark on the way.' We planned our moves in great detail, and made our way to the park for a snooze. Having slept most of the afternoon away, we casually strolled back to the station. Our friend the ticket collector was nowhere in sight, and we walked into the station and on to the platform as if we did not have a care in the world.

Anyone who has travelled on a wartime train will know that they were always overcrowded with service personnel, and that the carriages were bursting at the seams; there was never a seat to be had anywhere. We squeezed into the corridor, elbowed ourselves a little more space and just sat down where we were on the floor. If a ticket collector had come along, there would have been nothing that we could have done. There was no way that we could have escaped him, because we could not move, the crush of bodies prevented it. The toilets were in use all the time, and in any case it would be impossible for any ticket collector to do his job in such conditions. It was a nightmare journey that started on time, but arrived in Birmingham two hours late. We consoled ourselves by celebrating the fact that we had arrived without getting caught.

Our spirits were high, but we were deadly tired; it was one thirty in the morning, passengers were streaming off the platform and out through the exits where two ticket collectors were taking tickets.

We quickly walked away from the exits into the darkness, and at the end of the platform jumped down on to the tracks and climbed over a fence, where we found ourselves on a road outside the station. We were elated with our achievement; we had made it, and it was a feather in our caps that we had got so far without discovery, and with relative ease. Tired and hungry, we legged it out of Birmingham toward Bristol, our next stop. Lady luck was still with us because we found a copy of a Birmingham daily paper in a litter bin, and we thought it wise to get away from the city as soon as possible; every minute in a large heavily populated place was dangerous and increased the chances of the police spotting us. As soon as we cleared the built-up areas we began looking for a farm where there was sure to be a barn and a dry place to sleep.

It was almost dawn before we came across a likely looking farm. We set a dog barking as we searched for somewhere to hide and sleep. We soon found the barn and were pleased to find it half full with sweet smelling hay. We climbed up into the back, covered ourselves with hay and fell sound asleep. The dog had stopped barking and we were a bit concerned that the house was very near to the barn, however the hay was lovely and warm, we were very comfortable and too weary to care.

It was not very long before we were awakened with the barking of the dog and someone shouting. It was the farmer who somehow knew we were there, 'Come on out of it, you can't stay there,' he said. And with no other choice left to us but to do as he demanded, we emerged tousle headed, but refreshed to face the music.

The policy of honesty having proved itself previously, we told the farmer the truth. He chuckled as we related the story of our escapades so far. 'How did you know we were in the barn?' I asked. 'Well, I often get travellers and tramps doing the same as you, looking for a bed, but my Ben never lies,' he patted the black and white Border collie, 'when he starts barking, there is always someone about, and I put two and two together, and there you have it. Anyway, you had better come in for some breakfast, would you like that?'

Would we like it! I'll say we would, and explaining the situation to his wife, we relaxed, and following her invitation, sat down at the kitchen table. It was lovely and warm, and we ate a large breakfast of bacon and eggs followed by toast and marmalade, and two mugs of hot sweet tea, just the job.

'I will be driving down to Bristol this afternoon if you want a lift.' The farmer's casual remark took us quite aback. 'Thanks very much,' I said, 'that will be a great help.' What luck, we could hardly believe our ears, Dame Fortune had certainly smiled on us up to now. Little did we realise that things would be changing for the worse after we got to Bristol; it would no longer be the easy ride that we had been experiencing so far.

The farmer dropped us off in the city centre, and we shuffled around disconsolately, discussing our next move. It was then that we spotted two of our pals who were on the same exercise as ourselves only their route was different. Their next stop was Taunton as indeed was ours, but after that they had to get to Exeter, we had to get to Bridport, roughly in the same direction.

On our briefing before the start of the exercise, we had been told that if we could obtain a bicycle that was not secured, and which had been left unattended, it was perfectly legitimate to confiscate it. The same applied to any vehicle, we were at war and no vehicle should be left unattended, and if it was, then it should be immobilized. It was in fact an offence, since an enemy spy or some other unauthorised person intent on sabotage could steal it and use it for some purpose not in the interests of the country. It would also be a lesson to the owner if through their own negligence they lost their vehicle.

There was a proviso that we should not damage any vehicle taken by us this way, also we were obliged to report its whereabouts after we had finished using it.

Of course, our orders had not stated exactly how we could or could not obtain a vehicle, and it was not very long before we hit upon the idea of waiting until dark, going to a likely residential area, and trying garage doors. If they were not secured, and there happened to be a non immobilized vehicle available, we would not be breaking the rules if we took it. Even if the vehicle was garaged, it had to be secured, and still needed to be immobilized otherwise it was fair game. We did not have long to wait for darkness to fall and the blackouts to be put in place when one of our number, Tom, found what he said was an unsecured garage door, and inside stood a nice little Austin 10.

The owner was to complain bitterly later that the garage door had been locked and the car immobilized; if that were true, how could we have removed and started it? Tom was very positive about it. It has to be said though that he was a mechanic and certainly knew what he was doing. Having checked there was petrol, we quietly pushed the car out of the garage, down the short drive and out into the road. 'We had better move it further away from the house, and someone should go back and close the garage door,' Tom said. And this we did, after all, we did not want the owner to discover his loss, and if everything looked normal, we might be clear away and at our destination before that happened.

Tom had very much taken over command of our little group; he was the oldest and seemed so full of confidence that it seemed quite natural for him to take over the leadership. He had been the instigator and prime mover in all that we did; he was also the driver. Piling into the car, Tom started it, and drove off through the city and up the hill on to the Taunton road. I had been terrified of being discovered during this escapade, but seeing just how nonchalantly my companions were treating it, I soon settled down and joined in with them singing our heads off as we journeyed on our way south keeping well away from the main road to avoid being caught.

Just as we came to the village of Ashcott in Somerset, we spotted yet another pair of our comrades also heading for Taunton. We made room for them in the car, and continued merrily on our way.

We were by now all very hungry. Ali and I had eaten a good breakfast, but none of the others had eaten since the day before. The thought of food and how it could be obtained had become an obsession.

'I know where there is a fish and chip shop in Taunton,' said Bill, one of our party, 'Why not let us all go in for a meal, we can draw lots to be the last one out, he can pretend that he is going to pay, then run like hell?' We were all quite enthusiastic about the idea, but it was not until I was unlucky enough to draw the short straw that I once again became worried. 'You will be OK, Ted,' said Ali, and knowing that I must not let my mates down, I resolved to do my part as well as I could.

I arranged a rendezvous so that we could meet up again afterwards, and rehearsed in my mind what I would say and the action I would take after the meal, I felt quite relaxed as we drove at last into Taunton and we left the car in the vicinity of the fish shop in a back alley. Making our way into the restaurant we found it quite full; we sat down at a couple of tables and waited impatiently for the young girl waitress to come over and take our orders. It was almost 10 p.m.

I had been watching and taking note of the system and how the meals were paid for. Having had the meal, one paid the bill at a counter almost at the entrance. It suited me very well because it would enable a quick getaway. We all thought that we might as well get hung for a sheep as a goat, so we ordered the works, fish, chips, peas, bread and butter with tea. We set to, enjoyed, and did justice to the meal as only hungry young men could, but as the time approached for the showdown, as it were, I once again became nervous. Why had I agreed to get involved in such a scheme, supposing I got caught?

My companions however were boisterous and lively, and now with full bellies did not have a care in the world. It was muggins that was in the hot seat. We got up and made our way to the door, laughing and joking amongst ourselves. My friends called out a cheery goodnight as they left indicating to the proprietor that the fellow at the back would be settling the bill. I felt quite sick as I neared the counter, and pretended to be reaching into my pocket for money to pay, allowing just a second or two for the last of my companions to leave, I looked up at the proprietor and said, 'I am very sorry but we don't have any money.' I did not hear what he said, but he gave an almighty shout as I opened the door and raced away into the night.

Chapter Twelve

I AM NOT AT ALL CERTAIN in which direction I was running, but the café owner had been quick to follow me, whether he had been a little suspicious and half prepared for what had happened I could not know but he was very determined to catch me. He did not really have any chance at all. I left him further and further behind still shouting after me and I turned into a side street hoping that he would pass by. Unfortunately for me, it was a cul-de-sac, and he, knowing the area, must have realised he had me cornered.

My mind raced, I was trapped, how could I get out of this? I had known all along it wouldn't work, it had been a stupid thing to do. Wait a second, though! Why not try to get through one of the houses? In desperation I tried one or two doors, they were locked. I could hear the steps of my pursuer getting ever closer, I was sweating with fear. I grabbed at another door, praise be, it was open; I quickly entered and found myself in a passage with two doors and a stairway obviously leading to the bedrooms. I chose the second door, opened it, and there sitting around a table were the family, eating supper.

There was a middle-aged couple, an adult lady, and a teenage lad. We looked open mouthed at each other. Making a very brief apology, I promised to return later and explain my intrusion, but I had no time now, I had to get away. There was a pounding at the door; the proprietor must have spotted me as I entered the house. The owner must have believed my brief explanation because he pushed me out of the door toward the kitchen and back garden, and I made my way quickly across it and out into another road. I had made my escape.

Having kept our previously arranged rendezvous, Ali and I returned to the house later. It was almost midnight but I felt I must explain to the owner what it was all about. The family treated it as a huge joke, and because of the time, we were offered the settee and floor for the night. We accepted their kind offer, were given blankets and saying our goodnights we settled down to sleep oblivious to the havoc we had caused. We had been lucky again. But now fully alarmed, the police and Home Guard had stepped up their activity; they were aware that a number of us were in the town and they would try to catch us if they could.

We had another good breakfast, and were sent on our way with a packet of sandwiches, and ten shillings each, a gift from our sympathetic host. I supposed we must have brightened up his humdrum life just a little. Having given us instructions how we should best avoid the authorities, he wished us good luck, made sure the coast was clear and sent us on our way. We thanked him and headed in the general direction of Bridport which was roughly south.

All our good luck now left us; we were to get the other sort from here on. It took us almost three days of hard foot slogging with occasional hitchhiking lifts before we made it. The last part of the exercise had taken us across country. We had to keep away from the main roads to avoid capture but that meant there was much less traffic. The money we had meant at least that we did not go hungry, and we spent our nights in farm buildings as before which were not too uncomfortable especially the hay barns. We tramped along the coast road to the village of Swyre and the end of the exercise at the village pub. It was 11 a.m. and we were the fourth pair home. The CO had arranged for our clothes to be in the Company vehicles at the pub. We changed out of our scruffy kit into our uniforms; we were also paid and given a leave pass for a long weekend as a reward for our efforts.

We had enjoyed it very much despite the unpleasant escapades; we learnt later that some pairs took over two weeks to complete the exercise. We had covered some 400 miles in five and a half days and had not been apprehended, quite a creditable performance really; we had a lot of luck to help us though, but many and varied were the tales that were told for a long time afterwards.

As our training progressed through the year we knew that something was up. Things were beginning to happen; we were gradually being involved in more live firing and more realistic exercises with other units. 1943 seemed to flash by and we were caught up in a huge machine heading inexorably like a runaway train headlong toward the second front and the real fighting that I had been waiting for.

The whole country was flooded with American and other foreign troops. We exchanged our men with those of other units just for short periods. I was privileged to serve for a while in the American Airborne, the idea being that everyone would get some experience of cooperating with our Allies. They were very tough boys too. I had previously thought that they were a bunch of undisciplined showoffs, but the easygoing manner they displayed masked a firm and determined resolve to get the job done and get back home. They were impatient to get the fighting started too. We were all waiting for the second front, and it could not happen too soon.

One had to admire also, their wonderful organisational abilities, and their efficient handling of supplies. Anything that was needed they could get, and whilst our units sometimes had to wait for replacement parts for engines or guns or other things, they had plenty of everything to hand immediately.

It did not go unnoticed by us that they had a much higher success rate with the British girls too, who seemed to like the easygoing American lifestyle. Americans had the benefit and advantage of far higher pay and a far nicer uniform. There were also plenty of clubs and other places of entertainment provided for them from which we were excluded. The girls had a far better time than the poor underpaid British squaddy could provide. It was asking rather a lot to expect any girl to turn away from free nylon stockings, the beautiful underwear, and the high lifestyle that was to be had with our American cousins who took full advantage of the situation, and who could blame them? There was much resentment by the British soldiers though, and many a fight started over which girl was with whom, but on the whole relationships between the different nationals was very good.

Life intensified in the early months of 1944; units were constantly on the move and began concentrating all along the south coast. I was getting excited, and looking forward to the action we all knew was about to take place.

The 6th Airborne Division had been given a number of special assignments. Quite apart from the marking and preparation of the dropping zones, units were to be landed behind the enemy before the seaborne invasion proper. This was to destroy various strongpoints such as gun batteries, and ensure that crossroads and other vital positions would be in Allied hands to help ensure the success of the operation. One infantry company was to capture a bridge over the River Orne, another was to do likewise with a canal bridge at the same location. The attack was made at night, just after midnight prior to the invasion. The gliders came in to land as planned; the troops with feet up and arms linked, the normal crash landing procedure, braced themselves for the landing. It was pitch black and after casting off completely silent except for the rushing noise of air. Horsa gliders were made of plywood, they creaked and groaned and made other frightening noises whilst being towed in flight; experienced men frequently blanched at some of the noises and erratic movements. We often wondered if the wings would stay on, but despite the nickname (flying coffin) I had never heard of any breaking up in flight. But as soon as they dropped the tow, they came into their own, they flew well and were very manoeuvrable.

Thank God for our well trained Glider Pilots, although the gliders were released in the vicinity of the targets. The pilots only had a short time to pinpoint the target, and find as safe a place as possible near to it to achieve the element of surprise, and avoid casualties; lives were in their hands. Our pilots were the best, and achieved a very high percentage of accurate landings.

Most of these gliders landed on a skid, but some retained their wheels. The floor usually collapsed as the weight of the glider increased the forces that were produced by the touch-down; it was really more of a crash landing since the landing areas were not runways, and were only selected because of their proximity to the target. They were usually dotted with hazards such as trees, hillocks, streams or rivers, and it was more often than not a matter of chance whether the landing would be a good one. The feet up landing procedure was designed to prevent injury to the lower limbs, and interlocked arms helped to take the shock of the abrupt crash and rapid deceleration. Sometimes the tail fell off, though it was more likely to be blown off by explosive after the landing. This was a means of providing for a quick exit, the large front door would also have been discarded.

A bad landing might not be the pilot's fault; without power he might not be able to avoid a previously unseen obstacle, the glider might have been damaged by enemy fire while it was still in flight or as it was coming in to land – there were many reasons that could spell destruction and cause casualties during the landing sequence, so it was a combination of skill and luck that often accompanied the brave and culminated in a successful landing.

The pilots on this particular night made perfect landings although it was dark, several of the gliders right on target, a superlative bit of skilful flying. The troops were quickly out of the aircraft and attacked the bridge, storming forward and firing from the hip. Suddenly the battle was over and the bridge captured intact. The canal bridge was also captured undamaged. Both were firmly defended and remained in Allied hands until handed over later the next day to the forces advancing inland from the invasion beaches.

These bridges had been earmarked for self destruction by the enemy, and preparatory work had been carried out on them for that purpose. Only the meticulous planning and courage of the airborne soldiers thwarted the enemy plans. They were saved and used as the Allies advanced, as munitions and supplies were ferried to the battle front over them.

The bridge was renamed 'Pegasus Bridge' in honour of the airborne forces that captured it. Pegasus was the immortal winged horse in Greek legend, ridden by Bellerephon who performed great deeds of battle. It was also the emblem of the airborne forces and was worn as a badge on the upper arm sleeves of British airborne divisions. The main bridge still exists some 50 years on, and the night of its liberation is still remembered and recorded in the café which stands on the bridge, and which holds a certificate issued by the War Office, stating that this was the first place to be liberated on D-Day. The canal bridge was dismantled in 1993 giving way to modern times and progress.

We now know that many of the units on the sea borne landings had met with considerable opposition when the Germans finally realised that this was indeed the long awaited invasion proper. Hitler and some of his Generals had mistakenly thought that these attacks were only a diversion to hide the real invasion which they had surmised would take place in the Calais area, and they held back from committing reserves for the defence thinking mistakenly that the main attack would come elsewhere, and the reserves would be needed at the point of that main attack. Casualties might have been much heavier otherwise; there were heavy casualties on some of the beaches as it was, the Americans especially suffered heavy losses. But despite the setbacks, it was a very successful operation, a bridgehead had been established by nightfall, and the Allies were pleased with the progress of their armies.

I feel some pride in having been one of those who fought against the tyranny of Hitler, and I do not regret the small part I played along with countless others in helping to defeat and destroy a regime that was intent on ruling the world and enslaving the people. I still believe it was an honour and a privilege to serve one's country and the words of that great Field Marshal, just like those of Nelson at Trafalgar, will I hope remain in the history books to remind and inspire future citizens that there were in these times ordinary men and women willing to lay down their lives fighting to keep the freedoms that had been their birthright, secure for posterity.

What a marvellous achievement! The meticulous planning and organisation of D-Day, the instantaneous co-ordination and movement of large numbers of troops and equipment, of units and vehicles, and the co-operation between so many different units, not only the three combined services, but also with Allied forces of different nationalities, marking the greatest military operation in the history of the world. I do not believe there was one man from the highest General to the lowest private soldier who did not know what his job or that of his unit was on that eventful day. Monty sent this message to his armies: 'To us is given the honour of striking a blow for freedom which will live in history, and in the better days that lie ahead, men will speak with pride of our doings.'

Chapter Thirteen

Most of Normandy where the early fighting took place was glorious countryside very much like my native Somerset. Small fields were enclosed with hedges and ditches and it was impossible to move through them quickly. Tanks were almost useless because they could be ambushed and destroyed in such bocage. It was heaven-made for snipers who caused many casualties, and who were almost impossible to locate. It was ideal country for defence and the advance perforce went slowly.

Everywhere we went we were met by excited farmers and other Frenchmen. Often as we were advancing and coming under fire they would be overjoyed to see us, running up with a bottle of Calvados in each hand, and insisting on shaking hands and pouring drinks. The Calvados is made from apples, and has a distinctive taste which warmed us up from head to toes, making us gasp for breath as the strong spirit took our breath away. Never before or since have I ever seen such joy, or received such a welcome as that given to us by the French people as we advanced through the countryside. But I run ahead; there had been a period prior to this when in the rest area, and we were being reinforced with new men to replace casualties, the battle had become static and as each new intake of men arrived, they were given their one and only lecture from our Sergeant Major.

'You are going into the front line,' he would shout, 'And there are only two kinds of people here, the quick and the dead.' He was very fond of this biblical quote, but of course he was quite right. Even though we were dug in, and spent most of our time in our slit trenches, the artillery and mortar fire which rained down at us came without warning and could kill or wound us if we were not quick enough to get our heads down.

It is extraordinary how quickly one learnt to distinguish between the sounds of our own and the enemy shell and small arms fire. It was essential to learn quickly before one became a casualty. The crack and whistle of an enemy 88 mm self propelled gun was quite different from our 18 and 25 pounders, and the German Nebelwurfers, a multi-barrelled mortar, set up such a screaming noise as they flew through the air that was truly terrifying; the noise was designed to instil fear, and they did have quite a bad effect on some men. Our rest areas were set up just behind the front and though they were hardly that because of the enemy fire, at least we got a bath and a clean up for a few days before being sent forward again, and I also remember the attempts to provide some entertainment when we were visited by George Formby, the ukelele playing comedian who brightened our day with several of his comic songs. But we had to return to the war and the Sergeant Major's advice to newcomers was quickly assimilated and appreciated.

It remains a mystery to me to this day, just how some men escaped death or injury at times of shelling and others got away scot free. I never did understand how on one occasion four of us had been sitting around our slit trenches when we simultaneously heard the cracks of 88 mm guns. It was normal practice to dive into the nearest trench at these times, and the devil take the hindmost. This time was no exception. My three companions beat me to it diving one on top of the other into the trench, I was last in but still managed to get my head down before the first shells arrived and began falling all around us. Some of them were very close indeed and the blast was severe.

After a few minutes the shelling ceased and I got out of the trench badly shaken but none the worse for wear, but the chap who had dived in before me was dead, though except for a trickle of blood from his ears and mouth he was unmarked. The friend who had got to the trench before him had been injured, his ear drums were punctured, and the chap at the bottom was like me, untouched.

How it had happened I do not know, but blast sometimes has a very strange effect. I can only say that my guardian angel was with me that day, and it was not to be the only occasion.

Because we were an airborne division and had to be prepared to move at two hours' notice, there seemed to be an unwritten law that when we were in England, we were entitled to a small amount of leave every three months. Anyway, we did get regular leave, and more than was usual among other units, I remember on one such occasion I met the mother of a pal of mine serving in the same regiment but in a different company. He was unfortunately killed in the rest area when we were being shelled one day, and up to the time I met her she had not been notified of his death.

'How is it that you are on leave and my Mark is not?' she asked, I did not have the guts to tell her the truth, and would explain that he was in another company and that I did not see him very often; this and other excuses I used on the several occasions that I met her before she was officially notified. She was naturally devastated; he was her only son.

As the Allies poured more men and materials into the bridgehead we were able to start advancing. My unit was on the extreme left of the Allied positions next to the sea. We got a message that the enemy were pulling out of Honfleur, a small fishing town about seven or eight miles further along the coast almost opposite the port of Le Havre at the mouth of the Seine. One of our platoons rode into the town on a commandeered fire engine, and the rest of us were ordered to follow up tout suite. Marching at top speed, we arrived at the town just as dusk fell, and as we made our way down the hill into the town centre, all the doors were opened and people crowded round shaking hands and obviously very pleased to see us. The enemy had not completely withdrawn but was at the point of doing so. By dawn the next day they had all left. We bedded down that night in a school hall, our first night under a roof since the invasion started. I remember that we were all very hungry not having been fed that day, but our quartermaster managed to get some food up to us; it was about 3 a.m. Each man got a packet of hard tack, and a hot tin of M & V which put us in fine fettle. Some other unfortunates went back on guard whilst the lucky ones were resting. I put my head down and slept the rest of the night away.

Quite early in the morning, we were abruptly wakened by the sound of women screaming, interspersed with rifle shots. I grabbed my weapon and dashed outside with the section commander and several others. Down by the harbour near the custom house we were met by an astonishing sight. A number of armed Marquis were holding a trial of known traitors and collaborators, who had assisted the enemy and some had been responsible for the death of local inhabitants. Now was the time of reckoning.

On being found guilty, the men were executed by shooting. The women found guilty were bound to a chair and had their hair shorn completely off and their heads shaved. It was from these that the screaming came. I was not used to seeing anything like this. I had imagined that there would have been proper hearings in a court room, but no such thing. It was explained to me by one of the Marquis that the evidence was well documented, and the traitors and collaborators had been discovered well beforehand and had in fact been tried by the people sometimes several years before. It had been decided that punishment would not take place until after liberation unless any action of the traitors was at the time likely to bring about the capture or death of other members of the Resistance. In such cases the traitor would be dealt with immediately. In all cases they had been warned.

Once the Allies had built up sufficient supplies and men, they began advancing and the enemy were forced to withdraw. Most of them had by now realised that the war was lost, morale was low and the enemy soldiers just wanted to go home. After the fall of Caen which had seen bitter fighting, most of the enemy troops had accepted that their defeat was inevitable; it was only among the SS units where personal allegiance to Hitler had created fanatical obedience to the regime that they were holding firm.

By this time the terrible loss of men in Russia had seriously weakened the German army. Hitler had to scrape the bottom of the barrel for manpower. All that were left were old pensioners and young boys most of whom had been indoctrinated into the Nazi system by means of the Hitler Youth.

They were fanatical and we frequently came across ten and eleven year old boys hardly bigger than the rifles they carried, quite fearless and determined to fight and die for their Führer. Some fifty odd years later, I still have recurring nightmares after having to shoot one of these youngsters. I know that had he been a little quicker he would have killed me, but despite that, I still harbour guilty feelings about it.

After the battle of the Falais gap, where the Allies encircled a very large number of enemy units and destroyed them, things began to go well; all the Allied armies were advancing into Europe and it looked as if the end was not too far away. My unit had several periods of leave at home and it was during one of these on a Sunday morning in September 1944 that the air was filled with the sound of hundreds of aircraft. I dashed out of the house to see what was happening and there was a never ending stream of aircraft in formation, and most of them towing Horsa gliders. They were obviously heading for Europe. I automatically realised that it was the 1st Airborne Division; it certainly was not the 6th because we were on leave and I was there to prove it.

Unfortunately, there was an explosion at the rear end of one of the gliders which blew the tail completely off. The tow-rope was released by the tug before it could be dragged down with the glider. It crashed in some wooded fields in the village of Paulton in Somerset just a couple of miles away from my home. Subsequent enquiries came to the conclusion that a soldier had been loading fuses in to hand grenades and had made a tragic mistake; somehow one grenade exploded and that was the end. I went up to the crash site and there were no survivors. I did recognise the shoulder badge of the regiment as the RAF recovered the bodies; they were The Kings Own Scottish Border Regiment.

The occasion was of course the assault on the bridge at Arnhem. It had been planned to capture this bridge and the one at Nijmegen together with several others in the same area. This would allow thirty Corps to race up the one road and connect up with the Airborne troops holding them, which would enable our armies to advance into Germany and its industrial workshop. It was hoped thereby to shorten the war. If the plan had succeeded it might well have been over by Christmas 1944.

Alas, it was doomed to failure. I have previously mentioned that 1st Airborne Division was unlucky. The failure to secure the Arnhem bridge was due to several factors, most of them in my opinion bad luck. It is true that the Divisional Commander had no communication with his Brigades because the wireless sets were not functioning. Apparently the wrong crystals had mistakenly been used. That was a grave error; the radios should have been checked and tested before the operation and it was sheer negligence that this was not done.

The bad luck was in the loss of important equipment which for one reason or another did not reach the drop zone, or if it did, had been taken by the enemy who had by this time recaptured the whole area. The weather too had prevented the RAF from flying and the re-supply of food and ammunition by air did not take place. Mainly however, it was the presence of an enemy Panzer division that was not expected to be there. It had been on hand as it were to immediately attack and overcome the much reduced strength of the British forces at the vital moment when they were landing and at their most vulnerable. They had only just moved in to the area to be rested and regrouped only to find themselves in the middle of an airborne attack and their Commander quickly took advantage of the situation.

There can be no criticism of the courage or fighting ability of the 1st Airborne. Just one company was available to capture the bridge itself and after a forced march of six or seven miles, they surprised the enemy and secured one end of it. The other units of the division had been scattered all over and were not a coherent fighting force at this time. There was no help for the men on the bridge, with heavy casualties, and short of food and ammunition. They held on to it for over a week without respite from shelling and counter attack and outnumbered by a much superior force. It was not the enemy that beat them, but a series of events that add up to just bad luck.

So impressed was one of our war correspondents, Richard Dimbleby, that in one of his broadcasts he stated that if at any time in the future you were in a pub back home and the man standing beside you said, 'I fought at Arnhem,' buy him a pint: you were standing next to a hero. The battle failed by a whisker, but that is war.

Chapter Fourteen

My unit returned yet again to the front. This time we headed into Holland and took up positions on the river Maas at Blerwick. We were opposed by the enemy who faced us at Venlo on the opposite bank. Because there was no direct fighting, we were able to take refuge in deserted houses, and during rest periods have some home comforts like a roof and cover from the weather. The front line was the river with us this side and them the other. The river was quite wide at this point and both the enemy and we were in full view of each other. Shelling was a regular occurrence, and we took up positions in houses where we were out of sight of the enemy by day. We did our cooking at night so that there would be no smoke to give our positions away to the enemy and bring shelling down on us.

On watch at night we could see the launch of the enemy V weapons just over the horizon at Peenamunde. It was difficult to imagine that London was being bombed. One could see the trail of the rockets as they climbed high into the night sky and the luminous tail of fire fading away until it gradually disappeared into the distance.

One night I spotted two men cross in front of the house where we were. There were no reported patrols of our own out that night, so anyone we saw must be the enemy. I signalled the inside of the house and was quickly joined by the Platoon commander. I explained what I had seen and he decided to get the whole platoon on a stand to; everyone had to take up their firing positions.

As the night wearily wore on, many were the jibes I had to endure from my mates, 'Get a new pair of glasses,' one would say, 'Blind as a bat,' quibbled another. They were annoyed at losing their sleep time and our commander would not stand us down until daylight. We heard later that a couple of our own men from another company had been out hunting for chickens for dinner. They were very lucky that no one had opened fire and shot them.

Occasionally we carried out patrols across the river in the dead of night with the intention of capturing a prisoner. The river was a serious obstacle at these times because an enemy flare would light up everything and bring fire down on the unlucky patrol if they were spotted. Of course, it also gave us the benefit of a natural defence barrier in the event that the enemy chose to attack us.

Shortly after this we were withdrawn back to England where we were reinforced up to full strength and sent on leave again.

Christmas time was fast approaching and there was a competition to see who would produce the best decorated dining hall.

There were three large domed huts built of corrugated steel, each of which catered for two companies. At meal times, food was collected from the kitchens, enough for each section of eight men. This was apportioned out by the section corporal, and after the meal we washed our mess tins and utensils outside in large prepared tubs of hot water.

The dining halls were looking very gay and quite attractive, the decorations were made with coloured crepe paper and the hall was full of holly and mistletoe and almost ready for judging and the Christmas festivities. There were only two or three days still to go when it happened.

Without prior warning as usual, we were ordered to pack and prepare to move. Well within the two hours notice we normally had, we were on parade in FSMO, loaded with weapons and ammunition. Our kitbags had been stored and we were ready to go into action. We had no idea what was happening or where we were going. Were we just returning to the front line, or were we going to be dropped somewhere to carry out a special mission? We had been looking forward to having Christmas at home, and were a little disgruntled at not having our turkey and pudding in relative comfort instead of facing action somewhere. Never mind, our extra two bob a day was paid to make up for these little inconveniences, and we did get more than our fair share of home leave.

I was not in the habit of following the news particularly, but I learnt that enemy troops and armour had made a serious attack in the Ardennes which was on the American front. They had penetrated some miles into the Allied lines and had in fact broken through and were heading for Antwerp, the nearest port.

We were rushed on to trucks and transported to Southampton, loaded on to a small cross Channel steamer and landed in France the following morning. We were again loaded on to trucks and transported in the general direction of the fighting. We spent another night in a slaughter-house in Belgium before arriving the following day in the Ardennes. The enemy had not been halted and were still heading for Antwerp and causing havoc amongst our American Allies. As if the attack itself was not enough, the enemy had let loose a large number of men, dressed in American uniforms. They all spoke fluent English, and purported to be American military police. They took up positions at important road junctions, and then directed scores of units in the wrong direction.

There we were in the snow. Just a couple of days ago we had been at home looking forward to Christmas, and now we were having to spend it in action, digging our slit trenches in the snow covered hills in the forest to defend ourselves. I do remember that the cooks did a wonderful job in getting a Christmas dinner up to us despite the difficulties of feeding soldiers in battle.

For the moment we remained dug in at the top of a hill overlooking the village of Tellin. They were defensive positions at which we remained awaiting orders to advance. They were not fully occupied except at times of 'stand to' after which a proportion of men remained on guard. The others were allowed back to the village where we had taken up quarters in a house and were allowed to sleep and rest before returning to our trenches at the top of the hill.

We were still obliged to take part in the 'stand to' whether we were resting or not, so for about an hour at dawn and the same at dusk, every man jack of the unit took up firing positions. It seemed that these were the times when the enemy was likely to attack, it was a normal practice. And whilst I 'stood to' some countless times, I never experienced an enemy attack. I think it must have been a continuation of what had been the practice in the First World War and had been written into the instruction manuals for battle. It was uncanny though how the enemy seemed to know about the habits of the British, because as if timed by a watch, as soon as we started to move to our positions, as sure as eggs are eggs, we would come under enemy shell fire, mostly 88 mm. self propelled guns. Naturally we all dived for cover, but it was frightening to be caught out in the open at these times. When we had to collect meals was another such time. The enemy seemed to time it perfectly.

I was just as frightened as the next man, but if one was in a slit trench with one's head down, at least one felt safe from everything except a direct hit of course, but out in the open was a different game; fear made one a gibbering idiot, trying to scratch and rake a hole with one's fingernails, sweating and pressing the body as flat to the ground as possible, praying that the next one would miss, shells falling all around, all of them aimed at you. There is not much that could be more frightening. This shelling could last half an hour though about 15 minutes was about usual.

I am reminded of a time back in peacetime barracks, when our Sergeant Major was lining up agnostics and non Christians who wanted to be excused church parade. He was berating them about their non Christian attitude and he said, 'If you ever get into action and come under shell fire, I bet you would start praying then.' No words had more truth in them than these. The big strong men and the small weaker ones all prayed when undergoing constant shell fire. I saw many acts of bravery at such times but I never knew one person that was unafraid.

It was at the dawn 'stand to' one morning, we were on our way up the hill to our positions. I had reached a small hamlet of three or four houses about halfway up when the shelling started. Almost dirtying my trousers in panic, I dived into what seemed a pile of straw as the first salvo of shells screamed over, it was the only semblance of cover to be seen, and I did not care what it was as long as it gave me some protection. For about fifteen minutes we were pinned down, unable to move under the constant barrage. As I raised my head slightly, I could see shells striking the eaves of the house just across the road from me, and others bursting all around me, the noise was horrific, would it never end? Blast from the explosions continually hit and buffeted me and after one particularly loud and obviously close one, I was struck on the back of my thigh with shrapnel.

My leg went completely numb, there was no feeling at all. I recall thinking that is it then! You have lost your leg, if you get out of this alive you will be going back home. The shells continued to rain down seemingly for ever. Blind panic engulfed me, I was petrified, sweat poured down my face: if the shelling does not stop and I don't get medical help soon, I will bleed to death anyway.

It did finally stop, praise be. Extricating myself from the straw pile, I got up and ran back down the hill to the platoon HQ shouting as I ran, 'My leg's off, my leg's off!' It was not until someone said, 'You bloody fool, how could you have run down the hill with one leg?' that I came to my senses and realised that I was OK. I had been hit with a small piece of shrapnel just hard enough to deaden the nerves, but it had not penetrated the skin. What a fool I felt. It was a lesson in the control of fear and what blind panic can do to the mind at such times.

It was a funny episode but could easily not have been so. Later, the platoon commander measured the distance from where my head had been, to the edge of the shell crater that had been the closest, the one that had hit me, and nearly put paid to my life. 'You are the luckiest man alive today,' he said; the distance was just nineteen inches and could not have been closer. I had not come up covered with roses though because the pile of straw that I had hurled myself into, and into which I had vigorously tried to bury my head in my panic, was the animal manure heap. It was only now that the smell hit me and I swear that there had been no awareness of it by me beforehand.

It took a long time to live down that episode, and my friends did not allow me to forget it for quite a while. I know that many had felt the same as I did and were just as shy of shelling as I had been and they recognised that it could have happened to any of them. I was able to laugh at myself afterwards and still do today. But I never forgot how close I had been to death, and I had learned how to control fear. I never again allowed it to take control of my mind.

Field Marshal Montgomery had been ordered to take over command of the area and had taken charge of both the US and the British forces on this front. One of our Battalions was ordered to attack the enemy holding Bure that night of the 7/8 January and my Battalion was to pass through them after they had consolidated. As we marched toward the battle front, we came across numerous Americans in small groups and some individuals. Most of them were confused and bewildered, not knowing where they were, or who were friends; they were heading away from the front to escape the murderous attack, and looking for the front line which had yet to be re-established and stabilised. The enemy attack had been a complete surprise and totally unexpected. The Allies had got used to an ever weakening enemy who were short on manpower and equipment, most of whom knew that the fight was over; these had lost the will to be really aggressive. It was only a personal order by Hitler to his beloved SS that enabled an attack of such ferocity to take place at this stage of the war.

As we passed through Bure after the Para attack, we were sickened at the sight of pigs eating the bodies of dead soldiers. There had not been time to recover the bodies after the battle but we could not stop; we had been ordered to attack the small town of Grupont on the night of 9 January. We had information that the enemy were withdrawing and that our objective was only lightly defended.

Snow lay quite deep but it was frozen hard like ice. We were brought to a halt by the River Homme which was flowing quite fast. We were fortunate to find that it was only just above knee depth.

Mines of all descriptions had been laid everywhere by the enemy, but because of the weather conditions they had been made safe by the soil and snow freezing hard over the top of them, they did not explode when stepped on. The following day one did when a jeep drove over it. We had been guided to the river, but from there on we were on our own; it had been decided that one platoon would ford the river and advance into the town. The job fell to my own platoon and we moved forward across the river and took up defensive positions in the town. The enemy had gone but one could never be sure if they would counter attack. God, it was cold; our lower legs and feet froze and became enclosed in a case of ice. Some men collapsed and were taken into their houses by the local inhabitants for the night. I was called to Platoon HQ.

'Will you volunteer to go back over the river, there is hot tea and rum for the platoon back at HQ if we can get it across.' My platoon commander looked anxiously at me, half expecting a refusal, but I was glad to go because anything was better than waiting in defensive positions, not being able to move in the freezing cold, and I thought that the movement might possibly warm me up a little.

I went back over, but to my horror I found that the water had risen since we crossed earlier, and it was now over waist height. I got the tea and rum OK. And although it had risen, the water felt warmer because its temperature was just that bit higher than the air outside so I did derive some momentary comfort. But how I suffered later as my clothes froze and became encased in ice yet again, only now, I was frozen not just from the knees down, but from the lower part of my chest to my feet. We were not relieved for a further eight hours or so, and only then were we able to find a house with a large open fireplace, get a huge fire burning to warm ourselves, and dry our clothing.

I had been regarded as a bit of a hero for fetching the hot tea and rum and I cannot recall any other time in my life when I have been so cold; every one of us tinkled like musical chimes as we walked around encased in ice. Lucky that no one suffered any frostbite, it was nothing short of miraculous really. Perhaps those that collapsed and were taken in by kind residents might have, but were saved by the generosity of their hosts. They all finished up in warm comfortable beds, lucky people!

I do recall being extremely cold when I was serving in Korea, but there was no wading about in water on those occasions, and running on the spot vigorously and beating the arms for ten minutes was usually sufficient to produce some warmth. However I was not very happy at Grupont and will never forget it. But like many other incidents, we put it all behind us as we continued with the war.

The following morning, my pal and I walked round the village trying to buy eggs. We were invited into a house and much to our surprise saw a body of a middle-aged man lying on a bed surrounded by grieving relatives. It was the Mayor. When he realised that the enemy troops were withdrawing, he had followed hoping to discover what he could about the enemy dispositions, intending of course to pass any information on to the Allies. Unfortunately he was discovered and shot by the retreating German troops. We expressed sympathy to the grieving family and left the house. It seemed to be bad luck that he had survived the war for so long, only to be killed when it was almost over.

Continuing our walk round the village we came upon the local church which had been almost completely destroyed. Two nuns were trying to salvage what they could from the ruins, but there was hardly anything left to save. One of them gave me a Flemish Bible and a rosary which I gave to my sister Jean when I returned home on leave.

Many years later I learned that she got rid of them, believing that I had looted them from the church. I was a little hurt about that.

I have never thought that I was an angel, but if I had intended to go looting, I would certainly have chosen somewhere that had not been destroyed, and where there was something of greater value than an old Bible and a very cheap rosary. I think we just looked like a couple of villains and they thought we needed saving.

Eight of us under command of a Sergeant were selected to go out on a reconnaissance patrol one night. We intended to take a circular route so that we did not cover the same ground twice; our intention was to try to discover the location of enemy positions. The enemy were still withdrawing but would leave a heavy machine-gun and its crew, together with a few infantry soldiers at the occasional strong-point to harass and hold up the following troops. These machine-guns would open fire spasmodically just to let everyone know that the front was defended. However they were very thin on the ground and could not have held these positions for very long against a determined attack, nevertheless they were good soldiers and usually gave a good account of themselves. Their purpose in life was to cause problems to the enemy and hold them up, and then slip away quietly hoping they had deceived the enemy into thinking that the position was still being held.

There had not been any significant movement in the disposition of troops of either side for a little while, and patrol activity was the normal thing, so dressed in our whites for snow camouflage, we set out at 3 a.m. and passed through our lines into no man's land.

Moving slowly, we made our way along a rough track in the general direction of the enemy. It was a fairly dark moonless night but the snow lightened the darkness and we could see quite well up to a distance of 40 yards. We would stop and listen every 50 yards or so and then creep forward again. We had gone about two miles and reached the extent of our patrol and would soon be turning for home when we came to a small hamlet with the houses scattered and far apart. The first one was boarded up and seemed to be empty. We slowly moved on. I had a terrible feeling of tension and foreboding; it was another time in my life when I was in real danger and I could feel it. All my senses became razor sharp, my nerves were as taut as a bow string. Even in the bitter cold I was sweating, and I was terrified.

Still moving with extreme caution, I had reached a point on the left of the track immediately opposite another house. I was number five in the patrol and there were just three men behind me.

The house was of the normal farmhouse type that accommodated the family on the ground floor, and it had a large double cellar door opening out into a large yard where it seemed that the animals were kept in the winter, although there were none present at this time. The upper storey consisted of a large open barn type room where the harvest and the winter fodder was stored.

It could obviously be reached from within the house, but it had two large doors at the front which would allow easy loading or unloading directly into the room. It was these doors that were suddenly flung open, revealing an MG 42 and two or three men manning the machine-gun who opened fire on our patrol with steady bursts.

Having had plenty of practice, I hit the ground and flattened myself against it as quick as a flash. I knew that the man in front and the one behind me had definitely been hit. I heard their shouts, and later, what was to be their dying groans. The enemy continued to rake up and down the length of the patrol for what seemed to be several minutes, but actually was probably only half a minute, the intensity of the fire magnifying everything in my mind; I could feel the bullets tearing up the earth close alongside of me, and I do not know to this day how or why I survived, except to say that I do not believe the gun could be depressed sufficiently for me to be hit, and the bullets passed over me and were hitting the ground beside me. It was too dark for them to see if I had been hit, but I could only assume that they thought I was dead.

Those readers who have heard an MG 42 fired at them in anger and survived to tell the tale, will undoubtedly remember the unmistakable noise they make when fired; it sounds more like a terrific rushing wind than a series of bullets. The rate of fire of the British Bren gun was about 500/600 rounds a minute and seems quite fast, but one can recognise the individual reports of each bullet as it is fired; the Spandau (MG 42), however, fires twice that number in the same minute and is so fast that it is not possible to recognise the report of individual rounds. It was an unfortunate fact that if one was unlucky enough to have been hit by a burst of fire from an MG 42, one would suffer from as many as a dozen wounds from that very short burst, and not too many could survive such punishment.

I could not be sure, but I believed that the whole of the patrol was dead. The enemy must have observed us coming for some time, and we did not think there were any enemy units left in the area, how wrong we were. We had been cautious, but evidently not cautious enough.

The thought flashed through my mind: play dead! And so I did, I froze my body, forcing myself not to move. I tried to breathe as slow and shallow as I could so not the slightest movement could be spotted. I had fallen into a rest position with my right leg bent at the knee and my foot up slightly, my head was resting on my arms as if I was asleep, and my head was facing the enemy position across the street. I could clearly see and hear them congratulating themselves on their successful action. I assumed that there must have been an observation post in the house we had passed, the one we thought was abandoned, and they had alerted the MG post of our approach. At times, although the upper doors remained open, soldiers seemed to disappear from the opening back into the house and though I could not see anyone, they probably did have a lookout on duty all the time; maybe he positioned himself back from the opening for warmth as well as for camouflage. We too had been trained to keep back from a window: it was far more difficult to spot anyone there in the darker interior of the building. Anyway I was not going to lift my head or change my position to find out. I was still very afraid and at a loss what to do. I remember that Hitler had ordered his armies not to take prisoners of enemy soldiers wearing Green Berets (Commandoes) or Red ones (Airborne). They were to be shot, treated as spies. If I moved, or if the enemy soldiers came over to inspect the bodies closely, they would discover me still alive and I would be as good as dead anyway. For some reason they did not, and I could only think of a couple of reasons why that was so.

German patrols were carried out in a very similar way to our own. We had to leave behind at base, all letters and documents and personal effects that might identify us, or anything that might inadvertently make a noise whilst we were on patrol, so we carried nothing on us that might be worth searching our bodies for, and the enemy knew that. The other reason and maybe the most likely one, was the cold. The temperature was well below freezing point, at least that is how it seemed to me, and never knowing when new orders might force a change in circumstances, all soldiers of whatever army, try to make the most of a nice warm billet when they can. They would be very reluctant to leave the comfort and warmth of a house just to inspect a few dead bodies which they knew very well had no valuables on them, or anything else worth having.

It was by now quite light, and I estimated that the time was about 8 a.m. The man ahead of me in the patrol had died of his wounds, but the one behind was moaning occasionally, and was obviously in a bad way. I just wanted him to shut up, the noise he was making, though not particularly loud might induce someone to come out if he was heard. After several hours his moaning ceased, he had died.

The hours passed so slowly and the cold was intense, but the panic I had felt at first now subsided and I began to think quite rationally as if I was quite detached from the incident and as if I had a problem to solve in the classroom. Instead of remaining in a state of panic and fear, I was thinking of how I could get away. If I waited until nightfall and the cover of darkness, I could slip away off to the left away from the track and into the woods which would help to conceal me. There was a good chance I could escape and get back to my unit. I knew that panic would be my downfall if I allowed it to take over my mind, and it would be far better to concentrate on working out a plan and then carry it through. At least I would have tried. From that moment on, I resolved to keep cool and not allow fear and blind terror to take over my mind again. I felt a great deal better after this, and never again did I get in such a state as to be so helpless.

Occasionally I could see the soldiers moving around the area of the open doors of the upper floor, and there was a long period when the MG was stripped and cleaned. My heart seemed to stop as the enemy soldiers looked out through the doors, and it seemed as if their eyes were looking straight at me. I felt so exposed, I was the nearest body, and of some interest. I prayed they would remain indoors in the warm, and not want to come out.

I needed very badly to urinate, and had been suffering for some hours. However if I relieved myself, would the steam rise up and give me away, what could I do? Eventually nature took its course, I could hold it no more; what a blessed relief as I let go. The beautiful warmth spread over my upper legs and abdomen, and the steam did rise up in a cloud but thankfully was not spotted. I suffered greatly later on though as the water froze and chilled me to the marrow.

At some time during the afternoon there was some commotion as the enemy changed their personnel. A relief guard had taken over and they were no more inclined to inspect the dead bodies and even less inclined to come out in the cold than their predecessors. What did give me hope was that the two upper doors that overlooked me had been shut, I supposed to get the house warmed up for the night. I felt elated, and much less exposed. Of course I could still be seen from the ground floor windows and I was forced to remain still, but there was no one overlooking me now, and that machine-gun was not sticking its ugly barrel out ready to pepper me in a hail of bullets.

I must stick it out until dark whatever the cost. I was bitterly cold, my body ached from being held in one position for so long, my legs felt numb and I wondered if I could move when the time came, or whether I would be too frozen and give myself away when I made the attempt. The long hours dragged on, the dusk gradually changed to darkness. I must not move too soon they would be watching. I urinated again and started very slowly and quietly to exercise my body into life. I could not move anything at all at first, but gradually felt some life come back into my limbs as I eased myself up and down just a few millimetres, then sideways, then flexing my arms and legs a tiny bit. I then relaxed for a couple of minutes and repeated the same exercise. I will wait just one hour longer then go, I thought, that would be the safest thing and I settled down to wait … Having worked myself up into a state of readiness, I still found that I could not go, my mind was unwilling,

I will wait just another ten minutes and then definitely move, I argued with myself. This same thought occurred again and again but at the critical moment I would fail to act, I found myself reducing the waiting time before I moved down to five and then two minutes then one, coward that I was.

This is no good, you must make a move, you just cannot lie here forever. I was just about to make a definite effort when two soldiers came out of the house and set off back along the track in the direction from which we had come. I had been right, there was a listening post in the first house and these men were about to relieve whoever was on guard there. Some minutes later I heard the relieved sentries return to the house. The incident frightened me after the long inactivity. I had built up sufficient courage to make my move, only to have it demolished by the latest enemy move albeit a routine one. I will wait a little longer then go.

Once again I went through the agony of flexing my body to get life into my limbs and preparing my mind for action. Forcing my whole being into movement after a mental countdown of twenty, I got up and crept away into the woods opposite the enemy post. Elation! I kept moving for twenty minutes before I stopped. I was gaining confidence and bodily strength by the minute but where the hell was I? Which direction should I take? I worked out roughly where our friendly positions were and headed in that direction. It was beginning to get light again and I realised that I must have lain where I had fallen, far longer than I had thought, too scared to move, and almost for twenty four hours. I must still move very cautiously, there must still be enemy positions between my unit and where I found myself now and I certainly did not want to jump out of the frying pan into the fire.

I moved steadily, and got back to my unit having been gone for thirty two hours. One other member of the patrol had also returned the night before; he had been one of the first men in the patrol and had survived; like me, he thought that all the other patrol members were dead. And so it proved to be.

I never went on another patrol whilst we were in this sector; obviously I would have gone if ordered but I was not required again. The experience had affected me quite seriously in that I felt sick when we had to 'stand to' or when we took up front line positions. I seemed to have lost the natural zeal which I had hitherto displayed to my comrades and the world.

Later, when thinking about it, I realised just how lucky I had been, although being afraid in times of crisis and danger must be a natural thing I had not treated it formerly with any respect at all. It had been something that the majority of soldiers would experience at some time or other, but I had treated it in a flippant way, almost frivolously in fact, something that had to happen, but which would pass again without any after effect when the danger was over. In fact it could paralyse some men, and turn others into gibbering idiots (shell shock). I went through a period of agonising fear, dreading those times when I had to be in any dangerous situations at all. However time does heal and with youth on my side, knowing also that I had so far in this war been very lucky, I quickly recovered and soon reverted to my normal confident self. I also learned that if you got on with the job in hand fear would disappear, but I never treated it with disrespect again.

I would also mention premonition; it is related to fear, and is a phenomenon which frequently raised its ugly head. What is it that could make a man know he is going to die? When one mate says to another, 'See that my mum gets this letter, I won't get through this next lot.' Or 'Don't let me suffer if I get a bad hit, I will do the same for you.' It was no good trying to jolt someone out of it, because once expressed, I never heard of a survivor. It is one of the genuine unexplained mysteries and in my opinion remains unsolved. It happened too many times to be classed as coincidence; the genuine and sincere feelings of the unfortunate victim was accepted by them as a fact and the more one tried to pooh-pooh the idea, the more certain they were that they would not survive.

The Ardennes was not good tank country but the enemy hoped that they could break through into open country and capture Antwerp, and with it, all the petrol and supplies they needed to prolong the advance. They almost succeeded, but the determined resistance of the Americans and the Para attack broke them. It was evident that the battle had been a savage one to judge from the heavy casualties. Enemy vehicles were out of fuel and the will to fight diminished as the Allies hastened to plug the gap. The battle quietened down as the enemy withdrew back to their previous positions, forced by the unrelenting pressure from advancing troops. It was the last attack of any significance by the Germans in the Second World War.

Chapter Fifteen

Except for the shelling, we were experiencing a quiet period in the Ardennes and we were taken out of the line for a while and billeted with Belgian families in the village of Heers sur Meuse near the French/Belgian border. The people were very friendly and kind to us. Jean Devaux with whom I stayed, and his neighbour M. Lambert opened countless bottles of different spirits and wines that had been hidden away from the Germans, and became intent on celebrating the fact that they were no longer under enemy occupation. Jean took four of us into his house, and we spent hours trying to make conversation as neither we nor him spoke each other's language.

In the short time that we were there, the battalion produced a variety show for the troops and the locals, the artists coming from our own unit of course, and despite our mutual ignorance of each other's language, the locals thought that some of the acts were hilarious. We were glad they enjoyed the show, and we were very appreciative of the way they were looking after us despite the shortage of food and fuel and the deep snow.

The local young men and women used to sledge down the hill through the village on the main road now covered with snow; they would hurtle down the hill and take off as they hit the crossroads halfway through the village, land some distance ahead and continue the trip at breakneck speed to the bottom of the hill. I took many such rides and found them exhilarating and estimated that with six adults on the sledge (a normal load) we were probably travelling at some 60 mph through the faster sections. Alas, our stay was only a short one. Several months later my parents received a letter from Jean written and translated with a dictionary; it hardly made sense, but they understood from it that he wanted them to know that we had met and got on well together. He was a fine fellow and treated us with kindness.

Yet again we returned to England and were granted more leave. It was the custom for service men who had been employed at the Standard works prior to enlistment, to make visits back to the factory when they were home on leave to renew old acquaintances and friendships with their former workmates.

Chapter Fifteen

It was on one such occasion that I had met and fallen for my first love.

There had been a succession of girlfriends and casual dates beforehand, but nothing serious.

I had been walking through the various departments and chatting with people and I arrived at the boiler room; this was a small area which housed the boiler which provided constant hot water for various uses, one of which was to make paste used in the manufacture of carrier bags. The girls would come in to renew their supply of paste and they had to mix and make it themselves.

I spotted a new girl. I knew most of the girls of course and was on speaking terms with the majority but I had not seen this one before. She was tall and slim with beautiful dark chestnut hair and I was immediately attracted to her. I took the plunge and spoke to her. 'Hello, I've not seen you before have I?' 'No,' she replied, 'I have only worked here a short while.' I recognised from her accent that she was from London. 'What part of London are you from?' I asked, and went on to explain that I had previously been on a course there and had spent some time looking around and visiting some of the places of interest.

Ivy, for that was her name, lived with her mother and sisters in Holcombe, a small local village. They had moved to Somerset because they were weary of the nightly Blitz, carrying bedding down to the underground shelters where the city tube trains ran in the hope of getting more sleep there than they could at home. They did war work during the day, and had to undergo the bombing raids of Hitler's Luftwaffe night after night. Eventually the family could take no more; the lack of proper sleep and rest forced them to move away from the besieged capital. Somerset was the home of a distant relative who was able to provide temporary accommodation, and the whole family thought they had moved straight to heaven; the peace and tranquillity of the quiet village was something they had never experienced before.

'Would you like to come to the pictures with me tonight?' I asked. 'Why don't you come over to Stratton this evening?' she replied, 'We have a cinema show in the village hall there.' Stratton was a neighbouring village and I quickly agreed to meet her at 7 p.m. outside the hall. Ivy was there but she had brought her sister along too. We looked in vain for a seat; there was one at the front and another at the back. I was persuaded to take the front one and we were separated the whole evening. After the show I walked both sisters home, said goodnight and left.

Ivy was painfully shy, I later discovered, but we agreed to correspond and it was from her that I would receive parcels of goodies containing fruit, cigarettes and cake which my less fortunate mates were also very pleased about since they were keen to participate in the carve-up. We rarely saw any home baked cakes, and they were consumed straight away after they had been divided. I always seemed to have plenty of friends when a parcel arrived.

A lot of scoffing and fun took place at the mail delivery. The post corporal handing out the letters would smell and roll his eyes at some of them, frequently reading out the abbreviations that were commonplace on the letters between wives and sweethearts during the war: SWALK (sealed with a loving kiss) or BOLTOP (better on lips than on paper) would always bring a ribald cheer when read out suggestively. The list was never ending, and when a Dear John arrived (letters breaking off engagements, or informing the recipient that his sweetheart had found another love and he was no longer wanted) we all helped to jolly the poor fellow out of his misery. We had to make him feel that he was better off without her, and she was not really worth knowing if she could throw him over so easily. But these letters often were the cause of much misery and unhappiness and took a long time to get over.

We continued with our training. There was still one great natural obstacle to overcome, the river Rhine still had to be crossed before the Allies could get into Germany proper and finish the war. The Russians now had the upper hand on the eastern front and were steadily advancing, forcing the German armies back.

We had been dispersed to departure airfields a week or so before the battle. I think we were somewhere in Essex and the name of Mushroom Farm sticks in my memory, anyway we were living in huts there and eating RAF rations out of our mess tins. We knew that we were going into action again, but we had no idea exactly where. We were soon to find out though, because everyone was called to the briefing the day before. It was the 23 March 1945. I remember it so well because it was my 18th birthday and I was thinking, what a birthday present, I won't forget this one!

The briefing was very thorough and every man jack of us knew exactly what we had to do. There was a superb model of the small country town, Hamminkeln near Wesel which was to be the Battalion Battle-ground. Our company objective was the main crossroads in the town centre. From this model we could see quite clearly the houses and the roads, and one landmark which I was later to recall. The church.

Chapter Fifteen

Later that day the whole Battalion was called on parade: the Brigadier was to speak to us. I recall much of what he said, 'I know you have a reputation for killing the enemy, so tomorrow, get stuck in and do your job.' He then went on to specifically ask commanders not to use smoke after we landed, as it might confuse following waves of gliders who might not recognise their landing areas if there was too much of it. He wished us luck and moved off presumably to other units in the brigade.

Reveille was at 3 a.m. next morning. We were up and quickly washed and shaved and our kit packed. It was cold and bleak as my pal and I returned from breakfast at 4.15 a.m. and I recall the clanking of mess tins as the men walked to and from the cookhouse. Shortly after, we were assembled and taken to the airfield and dropped alongside our glider. In the half light of dawn we could see it and the tow rope looped in waves on the ground in front, and just ahead, our tug aircraft, a Stirling bomber. Tugs and gliders were lined up each side of the runway. This system allows for a very quick take-off, one from the left and the next from the right until the whole group in that particular flight was airborne. They were then able to take up their flying formation with the minimum delay.

We were flying in familiar gliders, the Horsa; it would carry just one platoon fully armed and ready for action. The British used it for troop carrying, and a larger glider, the Hamilcar, for small tanks and guns and other vehicles. It was made of plywood mostly, and flying in it would put the wind up the most experienced traveller, fondly known as the flying coffin. They would creak and groan and make the most horrifying noises as the stresses of flying tested the structure and joints; these sounds were alarming to first time flyers in the otherwise silent flight of the glider.

At times the glider pilot would decide to alter position. One normally flew above or below the slipstream of the tug aircraft which avoided the worst of the movement; any change however meant flying through this slipstream and although this normally was not too bad, frequently the glider was tossed about like a leaf in the wind. Also, just like towing a car, the glider would sometimes move up on the tug aircraft allowing the tow rope to slacken off, and when the tug took up the tow again the subsequent jerk seemed enough to pull the wings off. The sequence would be repeated for half a dozen times until normal towing was resumed and the terrified passengers could relax again. Sudden air pockets could also cause a drop of twenty feet or more without warning, and one's stomach would be left up in the air somewhat like a roller coaster at the fairground. Of course we did get used to it but the issued vomit bags were in frequent use.

It was time to load up and we took our places. I was the two inch mortar man, and with my No.2 we were near the front of the aircraft with platoon HQ and the platoon commander almost opposite the front door. I could look into the cockpit and when we were flying, see the tow rope and when I leaned forward the tug too. Just before take-off the tug pilot poked his head in the door and wished us good luck, cheerfully adding that he was glad he was not landing with us. The door was fastened and shortly we felt the jerk as we were towed out onto the runway, and ever faster as the tug increased power. The glider became airborne first being lighter, and we swung from side to side as the glider pilot settled down to his work holding the heavily laden glider in the correct position.

I have forgotten most of the names of my companions except for the first names of those to whom I had been close, but there was my friend Tom Gittings, Allibone my No.2, and I recall Bert and Frank, Con Primrose and Stevenson who during the flight continually kept our spirits up by pretending to be airsick and making conspicuous use of the vomit bag. He was older by just a few years, and a nice chap. I think most of us were a little apprehensive, I always was before going into action, but I had learned that as soon as we had actually started to move, all fear and dismal thoughts of getting wounded or killed disappeared as we threw ourselves into the job. It is the waiting that is hard.

The flight was a good one with very little disturbance, and before we knew it the pilot had turned and shouted back, 'We are over the coast,' then it seemed to be no time at all before the call came, six minutes to the Rhine. We re-fastened our belts which we had previously been allowed to undo, and arranged our equipment comfortably. 'We are over the Rhine, prepare for cast off.'

Feet up, link arms, we took up landing positions which was followed just a few seconds later by the shock of deceleration as the pilot dropped the tow. Then at first there seemed to be a silence as we lost the sound of the tug's engines; the noise of the wind roaring past decreased to a whisper as the speed dropped back, and the glider felt as if we had suddenly stopped moving. For a while, probably just fifteen seconds or so, we flew normally, then there was the loud crack of a bullet as it came through the fuselage. We looked at one another with surprise, and the sudden realisation that this was it. Several more bullets came through the glider then all hell seemed to be let loose.

Our pilot almost turned our glider into a fighter. We banked very steeply to the right and dived at a sickening angle corkscrewing first one way and then the other as he picked out his landing spot. We could now hear the automatic fire and explosions as the enemy did their best to destroy the aircraft as we came in to land. As we straightened out from the final spiral we heard the shout 'stand by' and we braced ourselves for the landing. There was a loud hard thud as we hit the field, the floor collapsed and came up and we scraped along the ground to a bumpy stop.

We quickly opened the door and found the glider more or less still intact and lying across a hedge. We had made a good landing and so far had no casualties. We scrambled clear and took up the normal all round defensive position and tried to work out where we were exactly. It was made difficult by the tremendous noise of battle, yet more tugs and gliders were coming in low overhead and despite the Brigadier's orders quite a lot of smoke was covering the area.

The next half hour was murderous; small arms and automatic fire from our own weapons added to the noise. I saw one of our gliders shot down with the loss of all on board, a four engine bomber flew across on fire, engines screaming, and obviously heading for a crash, and a heavy glider, one of our Hamilcars, came in low overhead and crashed straight into a railway signal box. It would seem impossible that anyone was left alive but although both of the pilots must have been killed, out of the wreckage came a small tank, intact and firing its machine-guns. The boys inside must have landed already in their positions inside the tank and ready to fight. Other gliders were landing all around us and adding to the general confusion as they in turn opened fire. We had landed about half a mile from the town, but managed to locate it through the smoke and haze. The platoon commander ordered us to move off in that direction.

Some three hundred yards or so from the town we became pinned down by heavy small arms fire and began taking quite a number of casualties. In one section near to me Bert and Frank had been wounded and Stevenson killed, and I believe there were more casualties in other sections. The platoon commander called for smoke, and I reminded him of the Brigadier's request, but before he could reply we were joined by the Colonel who quickly took command of the situation. He obviously knew where we were and what our objective was. His fearless attitude and personal bravery instilled courage into all of those present, and we were so inspired by him that when he shouted 'follow me' and dashed away, all of us were up and behind him to a man. I was the first man next to him, and we ran, then crawled, then ran again toward the town.

My friend Tom Gittings was hit and doubled up lying over a barbed wire fence. I thought he had been killed but I had no time to stop; it was not until some months later that I found he was still alive. There was a gap between a house and a wall which was a death trap to those who were not quick enough to cross it. It was the last twenty yards of a long exhausting run under fire. It was only natural that one would slow down at the end of that run just when safety was in sight, but enemy snipers overlooked the spot, and caused a lot of casualties. Each man that got across safely stayed there in turn to warn and urge speed from the next man across. The snipers were hidden in the church spire which I had seen in the model at the time of our briefing. Our return small arms fire did not seem to have any effect, and they continued to cause havoc and heavy casualties for quite a while.

We rushed the enemy still ensconced in a few houses and captured our objective, the crossroads. About one hundred enemy soldiers surrendered to us there, a mixture of young and old, Home Guard and regular soldiers; we disarmed them and shoved them in to a hall of sorts, I think it was the school. We would not have made it but for the CO. He had disappeared, and we found out soon after that he had gone to find the 6-pounder anti-tank platoon, and having done so, used them to blow those enemy snipers in the church steeple to kingdom come.

Suddenly the noise of battle ceased; it seemed just as if someone had waved a baton like an orchestra conductor at the end of a concert. One moment it was very loud and noisy, and the next moment, silence. The battle was over. I looked at my watch. It had taken only one hour and twenty minutes from landing to finish, but it seemed as if we had been fighting for hours, such a lot of action had taken place in that short period of time. We were cock-a-hoop now that it was over, and feeling on top of the world at the success of the operation.

Although we had suffered quite heavy casualties, I could not help but compare our good fortune as opposed to the bad luck that always seemed to be the lot of the 1st Airborne Division at Arnhem; almost every operation they took part in was a disaster, whereas we in the 6th were successful in all of our battles. Early the next morning, the appearance of the advance troops of the 51st Highland Division completed the link up with the airborne units and so confirmed the complete success of the battle for the Rhine. They marched through our positions and probed forward to maintain contact with the retreating enemy, leaving us to clear up our kit, and wait for further orders. I had survived another battle, luck really was with me. I was going to get through this war unscathed.

We were so impressed with the bravery of our CO that day, I remember it vividly over fifty years later. He continued to serve in the army after the war, and his obvious ability was rewarded with promotion and high command. Soldiers would follow and die for him.

He was possessed with a phenomenal memory, and some years later, twelve to be exact, I too was still serving in the army in Cyprus. He had occasion to visit my unit, a different one now since the wartime one had been disbanded, and the Sergeants' Mess was earmarked as one of the places he was scheduled to visit. Now a high ranking General, he had lost none of his charm, or memory in the intervening years. Glancing round the mess as he entered, and ignoring everyone and everything else, he spotted me some distance away. He came straight up to me and asked if I remembered the visit George Formby made to our unit in Normandy shortly after D-Day. He had recognised me instantly. How he could do so after so many years was amazing, I have no idea. I had just been a very young Private soldier at the time and had obviously altered a great deal in appearance since then, yet he recognised me as one of his men. It was said that he knew the name, and could recognise every man jack under his command in the 12th Devons and I believe it.

Much to the chagrin of his entourage we chatted at some length about old times and he told me that reunions of the 12th were now annual events and that perhaps I would like to contact our ex-orderly room sergeant who organised the event. He gave me the address and then left to carry on with his busy schedule. The Sergeants' Mess visit was over, and he had spent most of it talking to me. But what a man! And what a memory! To remember one man of a thousand after so many years. He was a fine soldier and a great CO.

We were now really convinced that things were going our way, and the war was finally going to end soon. We felt on top of the world and pleased with ourselves. We had come through the fighting and so far had been successful in every battle. We were showered with congratulations and praise and we gloried in it. With our heads held high, and feeling as proud as peacocks, my pals and I would stroll down the middle of the street just like fighting cocks, fearing nothing and no one, that is until we were pushed up into the line again.

Nothing dispelled the euphoria we were experiencing more quickly than the knowledge that we were going back into action again. One or two successful battles does not win a war. Although very weakened now, the splendid discipline of our opponents in the German army still held many surprises for the attacking Allied forces as they pushed ever onward deeper into Germany.

The general direction of our advance was north east and we were soon confronted with the river Weser. It was nothing like as formidable as the Rhine, not very wide, perhaps 60 or 70 yards, but it was quite deep and very fast flowing. We knew that there would be no air drop over this little obstacle, and my Company was ordered to cross it. How? Using army issue 'Assault boats, Infantry, for the use of.' These boats had a plywood floor with sides that telescoped down flat in the collapsed position. They could be loaded and transported in this position, about seven or eight in a three-ton lorry. When delivered by the RASC drivers to the destination where they were to be used, they could be unloaded, and the sides, which were canvas, would be pulled upward from the floor to their fullest extent which was about 18 or 20 inches and held in place by wooden struts. Plywood paddles were handed out, and there was your water transportation for one infantry section of eight men and all their weapons, ammunition and kit.

In ideal conditions, it was military policy that the users of these rather primitive craft would have time to get practice in using them. The NCO, the section leader, would be in charge and become the helmsman and call out the timing of the paddle strokes, synchronising the efforts of everyone and so controlling the boat as it made its passage.

In fact this seldom happened, and it did not happen on this occasion either.

It was the first time that most of these big hairy tough airborne soldiers had seen these boats let alone handled them. We turned pale and cringed at the thought that eight heavily laden men with weapons, ammunition and equipment could possibly be loaded and moved in such frail little boats, why, they were just a bit of plywood and canvas! We would have faced anything rather than the escapade we were about to embark on. Even the very good swimmers among us were terrified at the thought of capsizing. If one went overboard, the weight of one's equipment would carry the unfortunate down like a rock, straight to the bottom, and the not so good swimmers were petrified, goggle eyed and frightened, many believed their end was near. We were called together behind the raised banks of the river and given advice on how to use our boats. Most of us were landlubbers and would have preferred some practical tuition, but our hard hearted masters were intent on getting across the river regardless of the potential casualties we might sustain.

We had not been meeting a great deal of resistance from the enemy since the Rhine operation, but we knew that they were over the other side of that river. We also knew that the only anti-tank weapon that we could carry with us was the PIAT, a small weapon that might offer some protection, but which was useless against the thick armour of the Tiger and Panther class tanks held by the enemy. There were no bridges and it would be some 36 hours before the engineers could put a bridge across capable of carrying anti-tank guns and reinforcements to relieve us. So we were setting out across a deep fast flowing river, never having handled these boats before, and we had no idea what enemy force would be waiting for us, but we might easily be destroyed during the crossing. If by some miracle we did get across, we had no weapons capable of destroying enemy heavy tanks, so if there were any in the vicinity, we would be unlikely to survive. Charming.

Finally to put the icing on the cake, it was almost twilight; our crossing was to be made in total darkness.

Talk about a recipe for disaster! To this day I can hardly believe our luck. We crouched behind the river bank preparing our boats, and discussing how we should actually make the crossing. We learned that it was to be a silent attack without the support of artillery or machine-guns from our side, the element of surprise supposedly giving us a better chance of success. If a boat was lost, or ended up somewhere it should not be, we knew where we had to make for to find our unit. We were wished good luck and we settled down behind our cover to wait.

At the appointed hour, 7.30 p.m. on the 5 April 1945, near the small town of Petershagen we carried our boats over the bank to the river side where we were supposed to load our boats, and await the order to cast off. As we arrived at the water's edge we were horrified to see that there was no gentle slope, but a sheer drop of between 4 and 5 feet to the river. There, the water was racing past just as fast as it did midstream.

This meant that the boats had to be dropped over the edge of the river bank and held by one man lying flat on the ground with one arm hanging down over the bank, holding a small painter in one hand, and holding on for dear life to the grass tufts on the bank to keep himself from falling in with the other. This inadequate painter being very short even at full stretch, held the front of the boat out of the water, and the back end almost under.

Pandemonium, chaos and sheer panic took over as men tried to lower themselves into the boats. Thankfully quite a number of sections were successful in getting loaded, only to turn even paler if that were possible, when they realised just how little freeboard there was, just six or seven inches. They were convinced that the river would slop over the gunwales and sink the boat, but their confidence increased with time, and they accepted the situation albeit with a faint heart.

I never heard the order to go. Some boats were already out of control, some with only one or two men on board had broken away prematurely and were hurtling away downstream into the black night with white faced panic-stricken men, helpless and frightened, calling for help which was unavailable. Suddenly we were on our way, heading supposedly to the far bank. In reality it was more like into the unknown; the men cursing and swearing as only soldiers can, gradually made their way, fearfully at first, but with more confidence as they became more proficient. Skill was either acquired quickly, or control was soon lost.

Just over half the force managed to get across without serious mishap. Even and regular paddle strokes by three men either side of the boat, time being called by the section leader, enabled reasonable control to be maintained, in-out in-out, desperate voices calling in the dark, in-out in-out. Many and varied were the courses of some of the craft. I saw one turning in a continuous circle speeding away, carried by the fierce current down the centre of the river making no headway toward either bank. Lord knows where they finished up. One or two boats were actually heading back for the starting bank; try as they might, they just could not control their craft.

An estimation of the time factor involved and the speed of the current enabled a rough estimate of where the landing area should be, and also the assembly point on the opposite bank had been decided upon. However, no allowances had been made for the lack of handling experience and other numerous errors that occurred and contributed to the general cock-up which, when one thinks about it, was only to be expected. The eventual landing area was well spread out along the opposite river bank for several miles, and it was well into the next morning before the stragglers found their way back up to the unit. A few men never did make it back and had disappeared forever it seemed.

Probably into enemy hands somewhere downstream. It would not have surprised me if one or two boats had actually reached the sea and were still sailing on like the 'Flying Dutchman', forever doomed to wander the ocean.

Because the enemy had been retreating, and I presume the surprise of the action, we reached the far bank without a shot being fired. We were very lucky again that night: had there been just one enemy machine-gun post on the far bank, and with the scene brightly lit with flares, there would have been such a slaughter, and we would undoubtedly have been destroyed. Still, there it was, we had made it across, but I would not want another experience like it. Those safely across could now crack jokes and treat it as if it had been a piece of cake, full of bravado now; it was in sharp contrast with the fearful terrified men of a few hours before. Still, the war had to go on. The planned landing area having been very badly misjudged, we moved back upstream, finally reaching our original intended area, still without discovery by the enemy, but several hours late we took up positions around a group of farm buildings.

Stragglers had been rejoining us all night, but at dawn, the unit still not 100% complete, and saw us moving forward with the intention of making contact with the enemy. Listen! Was that the sound of engines? Indeed it was, engines that we did not want to hear, tank engines, heavy tank engines, Tiger tank engines, even worse, Panther tank engines, the enemy's latest and best tank – not just one, but a troop of four slowly advancing toward us. We had not yet been seen, and our only inadequate anti-tank PIATs were ordered forward to attempt to stop them.

If we had been armed with pea-shooters we would have created just as much the same effect on those tanks. The PIAT rockets just bounced off the armour plate. Even direct hits on the tracks had no effect, most exploded leaving a white blast mark on the tank but they had no other effect than to alert the crews that we were there, and that we were without effective anti-tank weapons. In other words, sitting ducks.

We went to ground, scattering in all directions; some headed for the cellars of the farmhouses and about six or seven of us stayed on the ground where we had dropped, in the hope that we had not been spotted, but it was not to be. Opening up with their machine-guns they began firing at us as we flattened our bodies forcing them down, and digging with broken fingernails into the earth hoping that we were not going to die.

It was another of those occasions when I should have been killed. I have to believe in luck, or fate, or call it what you will. Why is it that comrades either side of me were killed, some terribly wounded, yet I was left untouched? I saw the ugly bullets raking the ground just inches in front of my eyes. One of my mates, the lower part of his face missing and pouring with blood, looked up at me for comfort and help, and then his head fell forward. I thought he was dead, but later he was picked up by the enemy, still alive, and with what must have been considerable skill, his face was rebuilt in a German hospital. I have mentioned this earlier in the book. I met him at one of the large railway stations in London after the war; he had come home and taken up his previous job as a porter. I had been so surprised because I had thought him dead, his face had been so disfigured that one would not have thought it possible to perform the miracle they did. The surgeon must have been very skilled indeed.

Those of us still unhurt scattered. I rolled away from danger, and quickly moved behind the wall of a farmhouse which gave cover from the murderous machine-gun fire. The damn tanks were still advancing, but now of course they knew where we were. We were helpless against such superior force and could not defend ourselves, we had no weapons that could stop those tanks; armed only with rifles and light machine-guns, our bullets struck that enemy armour with about the same effect as a fly landing on a bare arm.

There was an awful feeling of helplessness and fear as we realised that this was finally it. We could run away, but the tanks would catch up with us at the river. We could surrender and hope to escape later, or we could continue to put up a pointless resistance until we were all dead.

Common sense pointed to the surrender option and about sixty of us put up our hands and were rounded up. We were herded back to enemy territory and imprisonment. Unknown to the enemy and us their prisoners, over half the unit remained free; they had hidden in cellars which were not searched and they remained undiscovered. Later that day they were able to link up with relieving forces who had crossed the river over a bridge that had been built in record time by the Royal Engineers during the previous night.

Chapter Fifteen

Those of us that were prisoners were ordered to give up our weapons, which we did, however none of the tank crew searched us and most of us carried hand grenades in our smock pockets which gave some of us the idea of dropping one down the tank hatch if we got the opportunity. We were told to get on the tanks, and we were driven several miles back into Germany. We saw no enemy troops, but we passed through two or three small villages and the people came out of their houses to take a look at what for most of them was their first sight of the enemy.

Strangely, they were mostly silent, but gazed at us with sullen eyes as we drove by, I must admit to having thought that we might have got some rough treatment from them, but not so. Perhaps the realisation that the war was lost had knocked the stuffing out of them. Anyway they showed no sign of hostility toward us.

The one thing that the enemy armour feared were our aircraft, and the most feared of these were the deadly Typhoon attack fighter/bomber, and rightly so. They had an awesome reputation for destroying targets with their amazingly accurate rocket attacks. Repeatedly in the past, infantry units had called for their assistance when confronted by enemy armoured vehicles and tanks that were proving stubborn to destroy and causing serious problems by pinning down the advancing infantry with superior fire power. Within very few minutes after the call for help was sent, one or two Typhoons would flash across the sky overhead, and be directed by radio on to the enemy tank positions. Banking round at high speed, their engines screaming, the aircraft would line up on their targets in a long low dive, a flicker of flame from under the aircraft wings would indicate that the rockets had been fired, and seconds later, the tank or target would explode in a mass of flame and smoke.

The kill rate must have been nigh on 100%. I had witnessed many such attacks and never saw a miss. By some miracle of chance, two flashed by over our little convoy at that very moment someone shouted out, 'Typhoons!' and everyone jumped off the tanks and ran as far away as we could get, the tank crews were just as lively as their prisoners. They also knew that to be caught anywhere near the tanks if they were spotted, meant curtains, certain death awaited the slow.

Glory be! We were not spotted. Yet again luck was with us; had we been seen, the tanks would have most certainly been destroyed and probably most of us killed or wounded. We were behind enemy lines and could not have been identified as anything other than enemy troops to an attacking aircraft; we would have been an easy legitimate target for them but it was not to be.

After the scare, the tank crews began rounding us up again so that we could continue our march into captivity. A companion and I had rolled into a ditch which had the cover of some small bushes; we were also the furthest away from the tank which had been carrying us. We indicated to our colleagues that we would try to remain out of sight and thus escape. The crew had not counted us and had no idea how many of us there were. We relied on that fact: surely they would not notice a couple of missing prisoners. The men that were near to us and also visible to the guards stood up, and talking amongst themselves made it obvious that they were re-assembling for the move back, and the guards began shouting at everyone to hurry up and climb back on the tanks again, and the column proceeded on its way. We were left in the ditch, still behind enemy lines, but free and happy in the knowledge that we had escaped, and were not far ahead of our own advancing troops.

It was late afternoon and we decided to wait where we were until dark; it was sensible not to risk recapture by moving too soon. We had no food other than a small bar of chocolate which my companion shared with me. We had not eaten since early morning so we were getting hungry, but there was nothing we could do about that at the moment, so we settled down in the warm afternoon sun and slept.

It was dark when I awoke, and rousing my partner we moved off heading back the way we had come earlier that day. We arrived at the last village we had passed through earlier and decided to make a detour around it to avoid the chance of being spotted. A dog in one of the houses started barking as we passed but quietened down afterwards. About two miles further on as we approached another village, we could hear the sound of voices. Several people seemed to be having an argument, but neither of us understood German so we had no idea what was going on. Again we avoided the village, creeping past the few houses on the outskirts and into the countryside beyond. We thought that our own lines could not be too far away even though we had been very cautious and slow, being anxious not to be caught again.

It was just after 2 a.m. and we were hungry and tired. The strain of moving around enemy territory with all our senses stretched to the utmost had taken its toll on our nerves. We decided to look in one or two chicken houses to search for eggs, and then make our way to some woods that we could see about half a mile away and hide up for another night. We crept around the village looking for hen houses and collected five eggs then left.

Making our way to the woods we found that there was sufficient undergrowth to hide us from anything but a very thorough search. We also took heart from the knowledge that no one was looking for escaped prisoners because no one knew that we were missing in the first place. We made ourselves comfortable and settled down to sleep the remaining part of the night. Dawn broke and a fine day seemed to be ahead of us. The weather was dry and the temperature rose and warmed us up as the time passed. We spent the day drowsing with one eye open and hidden from the world in our temporary shelter.

We were not far from the front, we could hear gunfire and the sound of small arms occasionally, and we knew we could make contact with our own forces some time during the coming night. The time passed slowly but eventually dusk and the coming darkness enabled us to move again. Stealthily we made our way toward the sound of firing and we saw no enemy troops or positions; they must have been quite thin on the ground. As we drew closer to our own lines we became nervous, we had no idea what the password was, and it would not take much for a sentry who might be of a nervous disposition to open fire on us before we could properly identify ourselves.

We had previously decided that we would get as close as possible to our positions and call out that we were two escaped prisoners coming in, and then comply with any instructions given. It turned out to be the correct thing to do because that is exactly how it happened. We were identified and returned to our own unit which was close by. We had not been POWs long enough to qualify for special leave, so it was a very brief interlude into our normal lives. Of those other prisoners captured at the same time, I did not hear or see anything of them until after the war.

They had suffered some hardship as prisoners, but were immediately released when the war ended. On reflection, I was glad that I chose to escape. Battle was over, we all took advantage of the fires, and small groups of three or four soldiers began to brew up tea and cook food whilst we had the opportunity.

It seems rather callous now, but an old man in his late seventies, and the obvious owner of the farm, wandered around with tears streaming down his face, heartbroken at the loss of his home and the senseless destruction of war, shaking his head and sadly trying to recover odd bits of chattels and belongings from the burning wreckage, his dejected face showing utter despair.

Suddenly he shouted a warning that startled everyone! He had seen the still standing but burning wall of the house begin to fall. Directly underneath at its foot there were several groups of our men, oblivious to everything else but concentrating on the cooking of their meals. Miraculously they were able to scramble clear before the wall collapsed. Without that shouted warning, at least a dozen men would have been killed.

I have often thought about that old man, who despite the destruction of his home, saved a number of his enemies from certain death, including the very person that had fired the shells that destroyed it. I wonder how many men would have shown any compassion at all for those who had just destroyed their lives?

Before we left, we plied the old man with cigarettes and food. It was not much compensation but he did not show any animosity, and we left him still raking through the remains of the smouldering ruin that had once been his home.

We continued our advance across north Germany meeting little resistance and taking ever more prisoners. The enemy soldiers were completely demoralised and beaten, almost six years of war had taken its toll. During the early years when they had been victorious and advanced rapidly over most of Europe; naturally, success, and good living on the spoils of war elated them, but as the tide turned against them, defeat became more inevitable, the terrible fighting, the starvation and the extreme weather on the Russian front, destroyed their resistance, the will to fight gradually disappeared. Millions of men had died in Russia and the army had seen enough, they wanted an end to the war.

It was now easy for the Allied armies to advance rapidly and deeper into the Reich. My section was in the van on one occasion when we came upon a column of enemy motorised infantry. Resplendent in an immaculate uniform was a high ranking General seated on a beautiful black horse. He was attended by several other officers, also immaculately dressed, and behind them stretched the entire regiment mostly on transport, but with some on foot. The contrast in appearance between the officers and the other ranks was remarkable. I had noticed on other occasions when we had taken prisoners that the German officers were always clean and immaculate. They only gave orders, quite unlike our own officers who gave orders too of course, but who were also prepared to fight and get dirty in the process (as in the battle at Hamminkeln). They were hardly distinguishable from the other ranks in battle. The weary, unshaven, dirty and ragged regiment that were halted in front of my section of seven men, looked as if they were a separate entity from those proud and arrogant officers that led them. It was obvious to me that these men had been in constant action for a long time without proper rest and were at the end of their tether.

The thought crossed my mind that they could have killed us and no one would have been any the wiser, but with the confidence of youth, and realising that the enemy were not in any sort of battle formation, I guessed that they wanted to surrender. Pointing my Sten gun at the General I ordered him to dismount.

Speaking in perfect English, the General said that he wanted to surrender his entire regiment intact, but honour required that this should be done to an officer of equal or higher rank. He could not surrender to me. I sent a runner back to the platoon HQ, and within a few minutes my platoon commander and sergeant arrived on the scene in a jeep. What followed was quite amusing as the proud general continued to insist that he could not possibly surrender to a mere lieutenant.

The platoon commander roared off in his jeep and returned a little while later with the company commander, a Major. The scene was re-enacted with same result, an impasse, there was no way that the general could surrender to such a low ranking officer. Away drove the major and returned eventually with the Colonel, our battalion commander. He spoke at some length with the General, who was still holding to his original position. It must be, he insisted, at least an equivalent ranking officer that must take the surrender. I watched the crimson flush of blood creep up the Colonel's neck and face, and with a very cool and controlled voice told the general that there was no other higher ranking officer available, and if he did not surrender immediately, he could take his regiment back where he came from, and be prepared to fight when we caught up with him.

The General struggled with his thoughts for a few moments, but realising that he was in a hopeless position handed his sword to the colonel and drove off with him in the jeep. We directed the column into a large open area after disarming them. They were required to throw their weapons on to one huge pile, and we impounded the vehicles. For two days thereafter we did nothing but direct long straggling processions of surrendering soldiers into the compound, taking control of thousands upon thousands of prisoners. It was impossible to organise anything at such short notice; we had not been expecting this sudden change of role. All we could do was to mount four Vickers machine-guns, one at each corner of a vast imaginary square, order the prisoners not to cross the imaginary line between them, tell them to dig their own latrines, and to be responsible for their own control and administration within the compound.

They were obliged to make their own sleeping arrangements, obey all orders, and we would undertake to supply food and register them as soon as possible. It was a job we were not trained for and we hated it. It was with smiles on our faces and much relief that we welcomed the arrival of the Royal Pioneers who were to take charge of the prisoners a couple of days later.

As we continued our advance, we came across a place called Belsen about which much has been written. Needless to say we were horrified at the condition of the survivors there. All the guards and officers who had been in control of the camp had been dealt with or had disappeared. Many of the poor starving inmates were close to death and did not survive their liberation. In the meantime a staff of doctors, orderlies and administrators took over the camp, caring for and feeding the inmates until they could be removed to hospitals and other places away from that indescribable hell. It became a correspondent's nightmare and a photographer's hell. I will never forget the sights I saw at Belsen, they will be with me till I die; I know that many people were affected in the same way. What depraved minds could do such a thing to their own species?

It was very soon after, that the battalion put in its very last attack of the war. It was a small village called Roche near Uelzen, where it had been reported that there was some resistance being met from remnants of several fighting units. Intelligence had suggested that there were a number of SS troops with them to stiffen morale and to prevent desertion.

We had been given our orders, and as we assembled on the start line before dawn that early April morning, the dry throats, and the knotted stomachs, in fact all the usual signs of nervousness and fear, gripped us. The evening before had been taken up with briefing and instructions, and as I cleaned my Sten gun, I had the usual thoughts, would I get hit

Chapter Fifteen

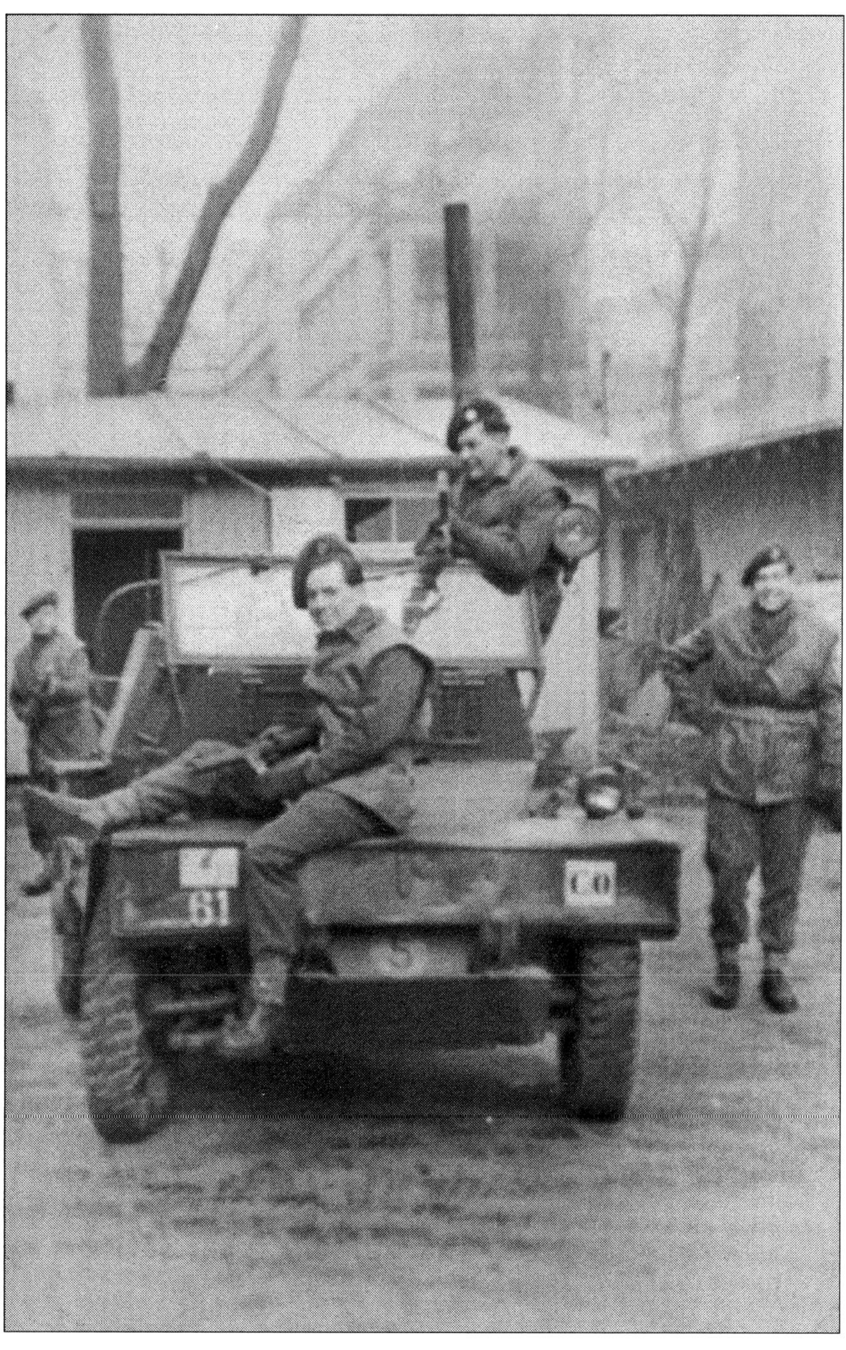

tomorrow, was it my turn at last? I had been incredibly fortunate so far, the odds must be against me now.

I thought matters through, and came to the inevitable conclusion that what was to be, would be, and there was nothing that anyone could do about it; if my time was up, well that was it, why worry? So I put all the bad thoughts out of my head, wrote a quick letter home, and got my head down for a sleep before the next morning's battle.

Just as the attack was about to start we came under heavy machine-gun fire from the village. The attack had been planned as a two company assault, one company each side of the main road which ran down to and through the village. Enemy troops were dug in either side of the road at the entrance to the village and had the support of a light tank which is what was firing at us as we assembled for the attack several hundred yards away. The attack was stopped before it had begun and we were pinned down by the heavy fire.

I had recently been promoted to section commander, and my section was the leading one of the attacking company left of the road. There were seven men in the section but our numbers were made up from the last reinforcements to arrive. The problem was that they had been posted from the RAF and had no training as infantry. What is more, they had never been in action and were very apprehensive about the attack that was about to take place. The bullets that were cracking around our heads terrified them, and no amount of reassurance could pacify them; with heads pressed into the earth and bodies pressed flat, they became frantic with fear. Only four out of my seven men were battle hardened, the other three were virtually useless.

My platoon commander, also new to me but at least he was from an infantry background, ordered me to perform a left flanking attack into the village with the purpose of capturing the first house on the left hand side of the road thereby getting a foothold and a means of driving out the defenders. In front of it were enemy trenches, and beside that first house was the tank.

Try as I might, I could not get my new men on their feet, such was their fear; in the end I ran along behind them actually kicking their backsides and firing my Sten gun into the ground close behind their legs. I threatened to shoot the bloody lot of them on the spot for cowardice if they did not get on their feet and follow me. I must have frightened them more than the enemy because it seemed to have the desired effect. Off we ran toward the left side of the village with the intention of attacking from there. Some fifty yards from the house we halted and I gathered my men around to give them my plan of action.

We would advance in extended order toward the house, open fire with everything on my order and take cover along the outside wall. Two men would then clear the house, and I would decide our next move after we cleared it. Off we went.

As we neared the house we opened fire and ran in the last few yards screaming loud enough to frighten the devil. The enemy, realising we were now behind the house, sent the tank round the back to get us out. As it appeared, we opened up with every weapon we had. I told the men to aim at the slits, and threw a couple of grenades hoping to fool the commander that we were there in greater strength than we were. The tank withdrew back round to its original position.

We did not have a hope in hell of knocking out the tank with our small arms fire, but I believe that the crew must have been an ad hoc one, unused to working together. No tank commander worth his salt would have been driven off by small arms fire, and we should have been wiped out. I can only think that this crew must have been inexperienced, the fact that it was dark may have helped us too. Anyway, the sound of our intense fire power as our bullets hit the tank may have frightened the crew enough to make them withdraw.

The house was quickly cleared, and we took up a position next to the road, separated from the enemy only by a six foot high wooden fence and the width of the road. The tank was now just the other side of the fence in its original position. Of course the enemy did not know how many of us there were, or exactly where we were. I signalled the men to reload and change magazines, we would take a brief rest. I was hoping that the attack would be coming in behind us, and wondered what to do in the meantime. I was concerned that the tank would hold up the attack and decided to try a couple more grenades. I threw two over the fence on to the tank in quick succession, hoping that the impact of the grenades would fool the commander into thinking someone was using an anti-tank weapon against him. One of the grenades entered the hatch and killed the crew outright. The tank was out of action.

I shouted to my men to take up firing positions again. We spotted one man moving across our front between us and our by now attacking troops. He was probably a runner taking a message somewhere. My shout of 'get him' was followed by a fuselage of shots from my men and down he went.

Unfortunately his groaning and shouting was so loud and un-nerving in the semi darkness, that one of the men went over and put him out of his misery.

Shortly after, the main attack came through, and the opposition withdrew through the village and disappeared. One man carrying the PIAT anti-tank weapon fired a rocket into the already destroyed tank, and was later awarded the Military Medal for his gallant action, much to the annoyance of my men who tried to rectify the mistake. The true story of the action was loudly proclaimed, but one could hardly take away the fact that the award had been made, and the decision stood.

We worked our way through the village clearing each house as we went. Most of them held frightened civilians hiding in the cellars; they were terrified of us and had been told that the British and the American troops tortured and did unspeakable things to all their prisoners including women and children, and they believed all these lies. Of course these things were said to make people more determined to resist the enemy and they were most surprised at the unwarlike attitude of their captors who after a brief cross examination allowed them their freedom.

This battle was the last one before the end of the war. It had been a success because we achieved our objective, and there were no casualties on our side. Those same new ex-RAF replacements that had been so reluctant to go into action just a few hours before, were now cock-a-hoop, full of bravado and courage now that the battle was over. Of course this was a natural reaction: everyone is fearful and apprehensive before the action really starts, but as soon as it does, and one becomes involved with the job in hand, fear vanishes as adrenalin pumps round the body moving, firing and protecting one's pals; there is no time to feel afraid, then suddenly the fight is over and tension is released. Things look rosy again and everyone talks about the action and the part they played in it.

Just a few days later we got word of the end of the war in Europe. I remember that we had found an abandoned wine cellar and two men had filled a small tin bath of some 10 gallons or thereabouts, and were carrying it up to platoon headquarters. There was much cheering and drinking and a lot of jollification taking place helped, of course, by the endless supply of wine. That night, rifles and other weapons were fired up into the air, and the sky was lit up like a Guy Fawkes night celebration.

At one of those famous meetings of the heads of state earlier in the war, Churchill, Roosevelt and Stalin had come to an agreement that at

the end of hostilities Germany would be divided up into areas of responsibility. The demarcation lines had been decided at the time, each of the four powers, the USA, British, Russian and French would occupy and administrate its own previously arranged area.

Churchill however did not trust Stalin whose armies were even now in Berlin. He thought that Uncle Joe would keep moving into Germany as far as he could and then stay, conveniently ignoring the agreement. Stalin already had taken much of eastern Europe into his sphere of influence, and Churchill, wily old statesman that he was, decided that the agreement should be enforced.

Our division was dispatched post haste to the Schwerin lakes area up near the Baltic Sea. All available transport was used to get us there and we arrived at the same time as our Russian Allies. We were on one side of the lake, they the other. Next day we found an old rowing boat and my section headed for the opposite shore. There was only one oar, but we used our rifle butts as paddles and slowly made our way across the lake. We were met by friendly Russian soldiers who plied us with cigarettes (hand rolled in newspaper) which tasted vile. We reciprocated with ours and rather a large quantity of vodka was consumed.

Eventually we had to leave, but not before our new found friends, who wanted to compare our weapons with theirs, were allowed to look them over and handle them. Reluctantly we agreed and they tried them all out, firing up into the air and shouting with enthusiasm and happiness. We spent a noisy half hour doing the same with theirs and were eventually allowed to leave after promising to return for a party to celebrate the end of the fighting. We finally got away and made our way slowly back over the lake to our own positions.

We did get together again some days later and what a party we had. We were plied with food and drink, mostly vodka, and treated to some wonderful Russian music and dancing. We returned to our own base about 4 o'clock in the morning and somewhat the worse for wear. Their generous hospitality and zest for fun and love of life made it a unique experience; it was the stuff that golden memories are made of, and I would not have missed it for anything. It was however in complete contrast to a later experience I had with them, and about which I shall pen later.

We were now being moved rapidly about from one place to another as the authorities set about dividing and controlling the beaten enemy. It was a chaotic time. Thousands of prisoners of war had to be vetted

Chapter Fifteen

and sent home, millions of displaced persons, refugees from all over Europe had to be sorted out and redirected to their former or new areas where they could be found homes and start new lives again. Starving and bewildered civilians had to be fed and cared for, destroyed services in the cities and towns had to be restored. It was an immense task for the Control Commission that had been set up to govern, but it had been well planned, and on the whole, the job was well done.

There followed an idyllic period; we swam in the lake and sunbathed, and we allowed the tensions and worries of wartime to slip away as we relaxed and waited to be sent on leave again. Some of the older men were chafing at the bit, they wanted to be released from the army now that the war was over, but of course it was not over, there was still the enemy in Japan that had to be defeated, and no one was going home yet.

We served for some time controlling the border between east and west not too far from the town of Uelzen. Regiments were being disbanded, battalions too were being amalgamated with others in the same regiments, and that is what happened to the 12th Devons men that were considered to have important occupations in civilian life: were demobilised and sent home. There was a great number of individual movements of men and units. Those of us that were left were posted to the 2nd Battalion, The Devonshire Regiment, and we were sent to Berlin.

Chapter Seventeen

Like most of the other important cities in Germany at the end of the Second World War, Berlin had been almost completely destroyed. Entire streets had been razed to the ground, large areas of desolation covered those parts of the city where bombs had blasted apartments, shops and theatres into huge piles of masonry and partly demolished buildings. In some places an effort had been made to clear away the rubble and mess to allow those vital services that still existed to reach at least some parts of the city despite the great damage.

To fly over Berlin at the end of the war, was to travel over destruction of nightmare proportions. It was a ghastly scene that was etched forever in the mind, the horror and terrible consequences of war. I was not able to see any part that had not suffered some destruction to a considerable degree and I would imagine it was difficult and a rarity to find even one house that was not damaged at all in some way. The walls of apartments that remained standing stood out in sharp contrast to the rubble beneath them, and one could but wonder how life survived the

The Brandenburg Gate.

nightly pounding that the city received at the hands of the RAF. Add to that the ground fighting as the Russian army fought its way in to the heart of the city during the last days of the Third Reich, and the picture of devastation is complete.

There was no water, gas or electricity when the fighting finally ceased, but the occupying authorities restored the more important services very quickly. The war weary and bewildered citizens were grateful for the food and medicine provided even though there was very little available, and it was some months before sufficient food and other commodities were delivered on a regular basis. At the time however, there was near starvation amongst the population made far worse by the many thousands of displaced persons and refugees that had fled their homes to avoid the fighting.

This was the situation when the 2nd Battalion The Devonshire Regiment were ordered to take over control of the British sector of Berlin. Division of the city had been pre-arranged by the four Allied powers some time before and they quickly took control of their own sectors. We maintained a constant guard on some key areas, the Flour Mill was one, Westhafen Docks another; it was from six identical and very large warehouses situated in the docks that food supplies for the whole of the western sectors of the city were stored and distributed.

The transition from a fighting infantry to a police type unit was made quickly. Ordinary soldiers had to learn to deal with the hundreds of workmen and women that passed through the guard posts daily. It would be very much against human nature for near starving people not to attempt to steal food and other necessities that seemed to be in abundance at the warehouses, and it was rare indeed to find anyone that could avoid the temptation.

Food was secreted in many weird and wonderful places, about the body, in underclothes, jacket linings, strapped to the body, in the hair, and often quite brazenly in a handbag or rucksack. Naturally some got away with it, but the guards quickly adapted and became quite skilled, many acquiring a natural instinct in stopping and searching guilty suspects. I recall one of our men, Mervyn Loughinan, doggedly searching a suspect and being more than ordinarily persistent despite protestations of innocence. Mervyn eventually found the goods, hidden in the handlebar frame; he just had a gut feeling about this particular man and he was right.

We were not harsh in the treatment of those that were only minor offenders; in desperation they might have taken a bar or two of chocolate for their sick child, and we knew they were starving, so a severe reprimand, and the threat that they would lose their job if they repeated the offence was sufficient to keep them on the straight and narrow path. For the big time crooks it was a different matter, these were handed over to the special police and we never learned what punishment they received.

The Battalion was stationed in Spandau barracks, but one company, 'B' was billeted in a very large block of apartments in Thomasius Strasse, Tiergarten. We were in a building that did not have the best of accommodation, but in which we made ourselves as comfortable as possible in the cramped circumstances. It was from this detached company that most of the patrols and guard duties were taken.

We had a good relationship with all our Allies, but the Russians gave us the most problems. One factor was that the British, French or Americans had not actually fought in Berlin, their main armies had been elsewhere employed. The Russians had fought for and captured Berlin by arrangement with the other heads of state though Churchill had been opposed to it, but it was now part of their military territory. The legal Military Command acted very proper in its relations with the other Allies, and seemed friendly and cooperated perfectly well in all our dealings with them.

The system of attack during the war most frequently employed by the Russian command was to use only partially trained Mongol peasants and other illiterate uneducated men, usually on horseback and armed only with rifles and sub machine-guns. The vast majority were of a very low mentality, undisciplined and brutal savages. These in their thousands interspersed with Commissars to goad them on and to shoot deserters, were sent into battle against intelligent, disciplined and well prepared troops, frequently the best, and often the cream of the German army. It did not matter, explained a Russian officer with whom I had been discussing the war, that many thousands of these peasants were killed in these attacks. They had died doing their duty for mother Russia, and had made the enemy use up large amounts of ammunition and other supplies which might have been used against the regular troops that followed up the first attack. Manpower was the one thing Russia had plenty of and it was used to full advantage.

These savage and brutal regiments were allowed to loot and destroy. They were promised all the women and drink they wanted, and all the goods they could carry. They left behind them, misery on an unprecedented scale; no young girl, woman, or grandmother from 5 to 90 years old was left unmolested, they were all raped and beaten many times. Berlin was full of women whose skirts had been cut apart, slit from waist to hem after the manner of the Russian rape. '*Komm, Frau,*' was the only German most of these monsters knew. Children, especially girls, were hidden, but few were saved. Those that went undiscovered were lucky, those that were found suffered the fate of all the others, and the Russians thought nothing of shooting the parents who tried to save their daughters.

Following behind these first troops came the normal fighting regiments, the bulk of casualties having been sustained by those in the initial attack. They had to advance against a much weakened enemy whose strength had been sapped by the first onslaught. Where troops had to be left in permanent occupation the Russians always used their best regiments, the Russian Guard. These were mainly European, well educated and perfectly rational, and the moral equivalent of most of the other Allied troops. They were all firm Communists without exception.

The explanation I give above is necessary so that the reader can understand that at the end of the war, with no more battles to fight, many hundreds of these savages deserted the Russian army, and went on a permanent binge of raping, drinking, shooting and looting, not only in their own sector of the city, but in the western ones also. I need to mention also that the penalty for desertion in the Russian army at that time was death. But more of that later.

Such was the mentality of the majority of these deserters that one could hardly credit their ignorance. I am convinced that many of them had never seen a modern house or apartment in their lives until the war brought them into contact with the towns and cities of eastern Europe. We were so surprised to see them drawing water to drink from the toilet bowls, they would play for hours just flushing them, and they would laugh and chuckle as the water gushed in to the bowls. Yet they would defecate on the floor of the bathroom not able to comprehend what these weird and wonderful wells were designed for.

I once saw a Russian soldier, mystified by the electrical power that worked the radio. He examined the wall plug closely and was able to tune the set up and down through the various stations. He was delighted with the music and wanted to take it with him so he physically pulled the shelf and radio from the wall, pulling out the plug as he did so.

Furiously twiddling the controls, and getting increasingly agitated and annoyed because the music had stopped and he could not get it back, that eventually he got so mad, threw it on the floor and gave it a burst of fire from his sub machine-gun.

It became common knowledge that these same Russians were interested in alarm clocks, the big old fashioned wind up type with the large bells on top. They would eagerly swap a gold jewelled Hunter worth a great deal for the alarm clock. The reason for this was because the alarm clock had the alarm. They would spend hours winding the clock up and setting off the alarm, laughing and thoroughly enjoying this new plaything just like children.

The North Patrol was devised and implemented. Commanded by an officer, it consisted of a sergeant or corporal, and five men plus an interpreter who spoke both Russian and German. Our transport was a small Daimler armoured scout car and a driver. We were armed with our normal weapons, pistols, rifles and Sten sub machine-guns and our tour of duty was for twenty four hours. Several times a day we would drive around the northern perimeter and through the north of the British sector. During the day, life appeared to be fairly normal most of the time, but I remember once when we were trying to clear away a large number of black marketeers near the Brandenburg Gate, we were almost attacked by a mob of Russian soldiers for interfering with what they saw as perfectly legal business. Lacking the strength to enforce our policing efforts we discreetly withdrew from what was becoming a very nasty situation.

At night it was a different matter, our officer remained in an office all night and was in constant contact with the local civilian police. He would receive reports that there was shooting and screaming or some other incident in a particular area and he would decide whether or not the patrol would investigate. More often than not it would be a genuine incident and the patrol would swing into action.

Racing to the area, we frequently found that the problem was being caused by one or two Russian deserters, completely drunk and trying to rob and rape women in their homes. They would think nothing of shooting and terrorizing to get their way. Sometimes it would be a small gang attempting to carry out a robbery. Russian deserters would frequently join forces with displaced persons and these armed gangs would roam the area looking for opportunities to steal. They saw no wrong in what they were doing and treated these occurrences as the spoils of war.

One should also remember that the German army carried out many atrocities in Russia and hatred of the Germans was intense. To these simple minded but brutal savages it was pay back time and the retribution they extracted was to them perfectly normal and just.

Many were the fire fights we had, and we shot to kill when our lives were endangered. I recall a battle with a group of terrorists in a railway goods yard with automatic fire from both sides, with bullets whistling round our ears and lasting for a good two hours before the gang beat a retreat without us apprehending anyone. They had been intent on robbing a goods train before we arrived to spoil their plans.

On one occasion I recall automatic fire coming from the top floor of an apartment in a building that we were searching. We normally cleared a building from the top down. Terry Herbert and one other man had been ordered to the top floor to start this particular operation and came under fire as soon as they got there. Terry saved his life by diving to one side but unfortunately crashed into a damaged banister which collapsed under his weight and he fell some fifteen feet or so to the next floor and severely damaged his ankle. He still suffers considerable pain today from the effects of that injury, but he was lucky to be alive. We did manage to capture the criminals on that occasion but we were not always successful.

If we captured an offender he was taken to our HQ, then searched and interrogated. DPs were handed over to the civilian police. Russian deserters were locked up in cells for the night, papers relating to the incident were completed in three languages and the next morning the offender was escorted back to his own Kommandantura in the Russian sector.

It was on our first visit to the Russian HQ that I had the shock of my life. Terry Herbert and I escorted this Russian deserter back to his HQ. We were marched into a room, the prisoner between us. Sat at a desk was a Russian officer who was about the same age as us, at any rate he only looked about eighteen or nineteen years old and he spoke broken English. I handed him the papers relating to the incident. He studied these for a few moments then standing up he walked around the desk behind the prisoner, pulled out his pistol and shot him in the head.

In terrified amazement Terry and I looked at one another, horrified by the summary justice meted out to the deserter. The officer shouted out and two men came in and dragged the body away. The officer went to some pains to explain to us that desertion was punishable by death. No trial or other explanation was necessary, and if we had any more deserters we should shoot them ourselves rather than go to the trouble of bringing them here.

It happened many times, and the officer would shake his head and look at us in a strange way. He could not understand why we bothered to bring the prisoners back to him, and would repeat that we should shoot them ourselves, they had been caught red-handed, why go through all this trouble when we could have sorted the matter out quite easily ourselves. I tried to explain that our methods were different and we could not do as he wished but he obviously could not comprehend our system.

There was a South Patrol too, which was far more agreeable than the North Patrol for two main reasons. Firstly there were far fewer incidents and we got more sleep. But the main and more important reason was that the South patrol skirted the American sector and our generous Allies allowed us access to their PX, which we had to pass by on our patrol. Leaving our weapons under guard at the entrance, we entered the club and were plied with free coffee and doughnuts, and as many free repeat helpings as we liked, all served by friendly and attractive American lady volunteers. On reading our company orders, there were moans if one drew the North Patrol, and cheers for the popular South. Top American theatre and film stars appeared regularly at this club to entertain the troops. One evening we had the pleasure of seeing and hearing the famous Andrew Sisters perform and our patrol was a little delayed.

As time passed control became more normal; there were fewer deserters and the DPs were shipped home or settled in with the indigenous population. German armed forces were being released and returned home on a regular basis and gradually the Control Commission took over the administration, employing these returnees and other local people to take care of the many peacetime jobs now available.

Our stay in Berlin became more enjoyable. We had more time off and we travelled around the western sectors, and unofficially the eastern one too using the U-Bahn, sight-seeing or visiting the night clubs that had opened up in the ruins of this once famous city. Christmas 1945 was unforgettable. The company saved some food for a party for the kids in the area. There were always a number of them hanging around the entrance to our billets in Thomasius Strasse; whenever a cigarette end

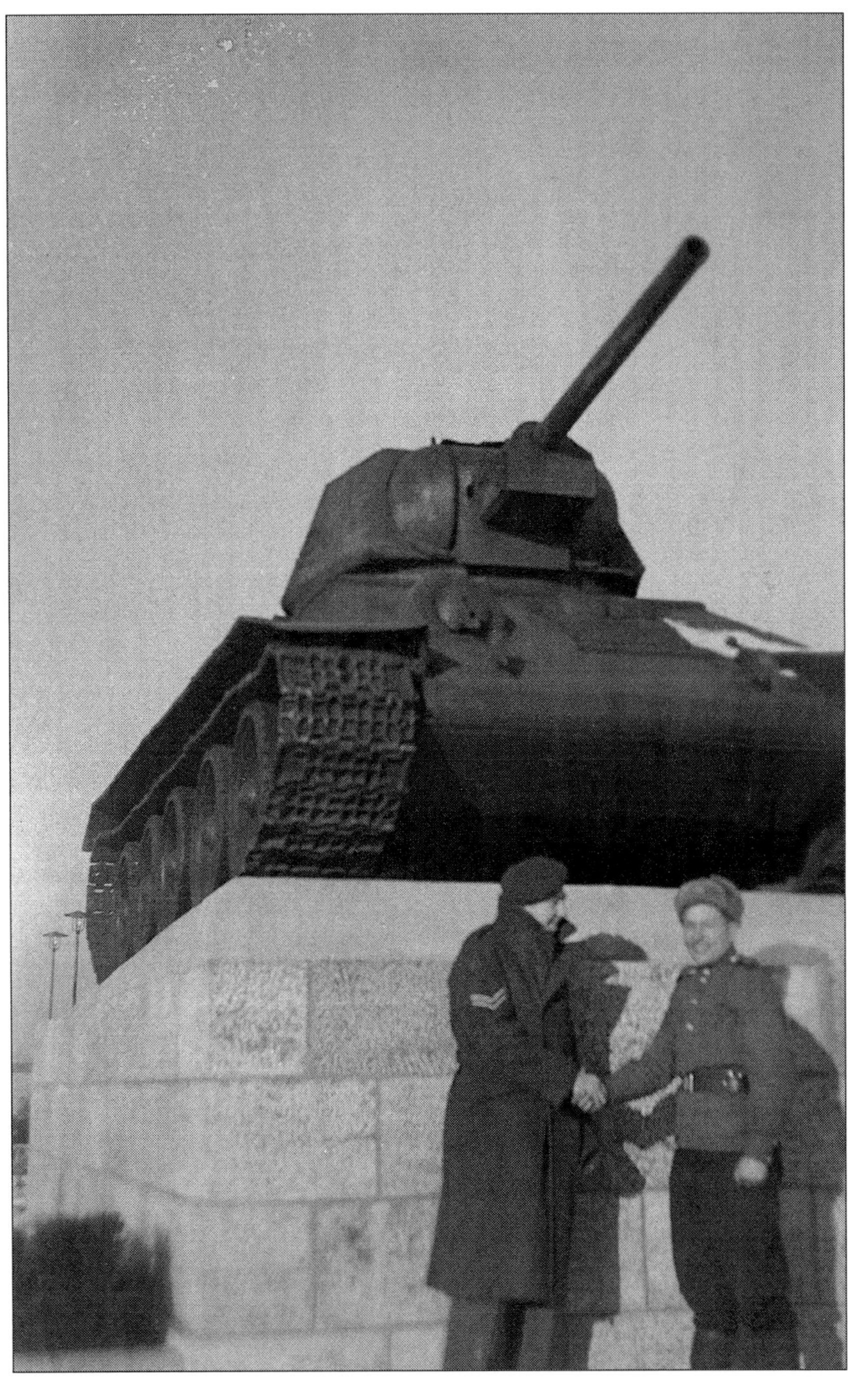

Author and Russian soldier at the Russian War Memorial in Berlin.

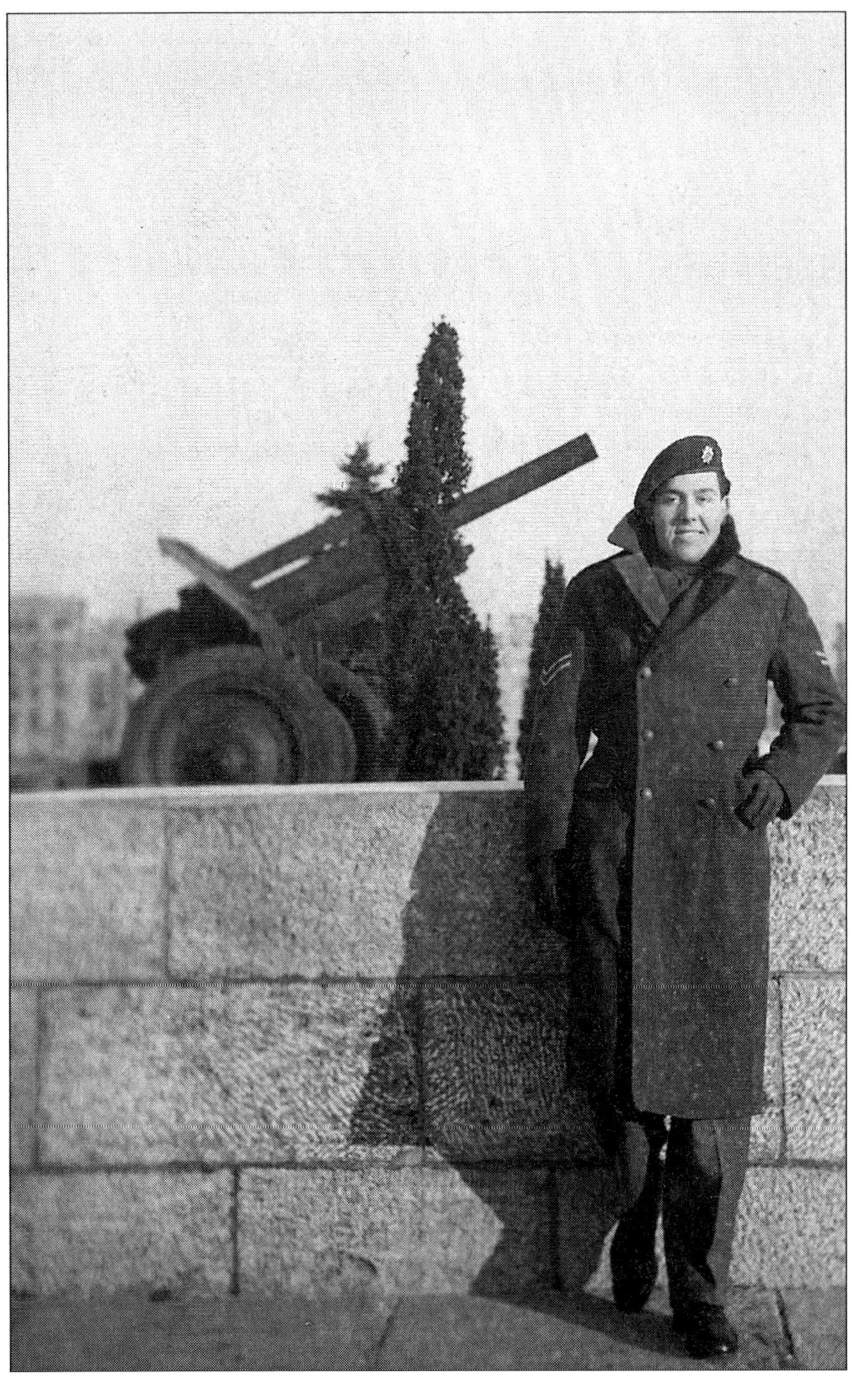

Author at the Russian War Memorial in Berlin.

was thrown away into the gutter, at least a dozen children would make a dive toward it and there would be a fight for possession. These dog ends would be meticulously taken apart, the tobacco saved and eventually bartered for necessities on the black market.

Most of them had never been to a party, they had never seen such a display of food. It was a joy to watch their faces when they received their oranges and bananas, never having seen any in their lives before, they were at a loss as to what to do with them. I think our men enjoyed the party more than the children. These foreign soldiers were nice and not at all like the monsters that these children had been brought up to believe the British and the Americans were.

No longer needed in Berlin, it was with reluctance and sadness in our hearts that we moved to Wolfenbuttel. We left behind many new friends and a lot of sweethearts, some destined to become the first British brides. Those that were there will never forget the North Patrol, and the difficult problems that we had to deal with in the transition from war to peace in those early days.

Chapter Eighteen

All the time we had been stationed in Berlin there had been a thriving black market economy. German currency had little real value and cigarettes which cost just a few shillings for a pack of 200 in our Naafi were worth 300 German marks to the dealers on the streets; that was roughly the equivalent of fifteen English pounds, a large profit indeed. Everyone was at it, and items like coffee could command many thousand per cent profit on the normal price at home. A pound of coffee beans could easily be sold for 2000 marks or about £100.

Consequently, British troops were coming back to Germany from leave carrying suitcases filled with luxury items including coffee for which they bartered for all kinds of goods on the black market. Much jewellery and objets d'art passed hands and there was many a fortune made by the entrepreneur. It took quite a long time before the authorities became aware and were able to clamp down on this illegal trade.

One could hardly blame the people though, they had been a long time without even basic commodities, and even longer for luxury items.

I had an orange in my pocket one time, intending to eat it later. Whilst I was waiting for a train I saw a mother and her little boy standing nearby. I gave the orange to the child who stood looking very perplexed, he had obviously never seen one in his life. His mother had also not seen one for a long time and was dumbstruck at the sight of it. I got on my train leaving them both on the platform looking a bit like lost sheep.

Immediately after the end of the war there had been a non-fraternization order issued. No Allied soldier was to speak to or attempt to befriend our former enemies, only contact on an official basis was allowed. Can you imagine it? Thousands of young hot-blooded sex-starved men in close contact with thousands of just as young, sex-starved women, and they must not even speak to each other. Of course it was ludicrous, and it just did not work. Human nature being what it is forced them to mix and do what they have done all over the world since time began. They fraternized all right, and very soon there were hundreds of applications from service personnel, wishing to marry German girls.

There must have been hundreds of girls expecting babies, hundreds of expecting dads wanting to marry them, and there were thousands of other men suffering from one form of VD or another.

Special clinics were set up for the mass treatment of VD. Thank God for the new wonder drug penicillin. The treatment for the more serious disease of syphilis was sixty injections over a five-day period, but for gonorrhoea and the less serious infections, which were far more numerous, only five injections were required. After the manner of common soldiers since time immemorial there was a song called 'Sixty needles for you', sung to the tune of Happy Birthday, when it was discovered that yet another poor unfortunate had contracted one of the diseases. The whole barrack room would break out into song. Camaraderie and sympathy for the sufferer was instantaneous, a lot of soldiers were affected, and there were very few barrack rooms that did not have at least half a dozen or more cases at any one time.

The fraternization ban had to go and it did. I have never understood its purpose and it never had a snowball's chance in hell of ever working anyway: I suppose some high ranking person deciding what was best for everyone else. Anyway, the ban was lifted, it had been a non starter in the first place.

The men had a chocolate ration and were able to obtain other goodies so naturally their girlfriends and her family benefited from the association. The troops got their socks and other smalls washed, and many other benefits too.

The authorities did everything possible to deter marriages between servicemen and German girls and every kind of obstacle was used. There were lectures to the troops advising against such unions. Individuals were interviewed and all kinds of possible reasons were advanced as to why the marriage would not work. Problems might arise and cause difficulties in the future, and what about the folks back home, might they object and cause trouble?

If after all this, the man had stood firm and was determined to marry, the girl was put through the mill; she had to be interviewed, have a medical examination and fill in a questionnaire of some fifty-six pages, it was called a Fragebogen if I remember correctly and it was a work of art on the part of the authorities. All this having been done, there followed a long period of waiting, up to a year or more before permission came through. Sometimes it didn't, and many marriages were abandoned because of the delay, indecision and hopelessness of the situation.

Chapter Eighteen

Sometimes of course the soldier was discharged, demobbed and sent home long before permission came through. In spite of everything, there were a large number of mixed marriages in those early years just after the war. My own was one of them.

My girlfriend back home was painfully shy and did not respond to me in the way that I thought she should, thinking that I could improve the situation, I told her that I had another girlfriend. Her response had the opposite effect to what I wanted and in no uncertain terms she sent me packing. The silly pride of youth! We often cause more hurt to ourselves because of it, so I stuck my nose in the air and left, with regrets, but that is another story.

Men were going home quite quickly now, units and regiments were being disbanded and I was posted to different locations, from Berlin to Wolfenbuttel, Celle, Bielefeld and Lüneburg all in quick succession; everything was in a state of flux. Now that the war was over men were anxious to be demobbed and there was a lot of resentment when they were forced to wait their turn to be shipped back home. Ex-policemen, builders and men who had previously held what were considered to be the more important occupations before the war and essential now, all these were released early, those others had to wait, and how they groaned, complained, and chafed away at those in authority until their turn came.

Among the millions of displaced persons wandering around all over Europe at this time were a large number of Yugoslav royalists. They were enemies of Fascism and also of Communism. The emergence of Tito, that great Yugoslav leader, had united the various national groups into a communist state and forced the downfall of the royal family there. Large numbers of people loyal to the throne fled the country.

Having bonded the people into one nation, Tito moved his army into the mountains from where he waged a bitter and successful partisan action against the Germans. He received a lot of aid from Britain, who were happy to help anyone that was fighting against their common enemy, supplies and arms were parachuted into Yugoslavia on a regular basis and these partisans became a large thorn in the flesh of the German army. By frequent attacks, destroying German supply routes, and causing alarm and despondency among their troops, a small group of partisans could tie up large numbers of the enemy way out of proportion to their size. By the time the Germans had got organised and went out searching for their tormentors, they had faded away back to the mountains where they were almost impossible to catch. They made an important contribution in tying up large enemy forces that were needed elsewhere.

Referring back to those royalists who fled Yugoslavia, it was discovered that many of them had been soldiers in the imperial army; they were trained, disciplined, and had always been keen to fight the Boche. Someone had the idea that we could use these soldiers, who even though the war was over, were quite happy to be of service to the Allies.

They were not to be used in the strict military sense, but if they were organised into units, retrained and armed, could they not be used to guard supply stores, petrol dumps and in fact anywhere that needed to have a military type guard?

There went out a call for voluntary military instructors who were to be formed into a training unit solely for the purpose of turning this collection of displaced persons into efficient useful guard units.

The officer commanding the training establishment happened to be from my own regiment, and I volunteered my services as a Sergeant instructor. We were based in a barracks in the country town of Holzminden in Westphalia and there were about a dozen instructors all from different regiments. There were also thirty to forty other junior NCOs to run and administer the unit. We became a close-knit and friendly outfit, and regularly produced efficient and trained units every six weeks.

For our social life we arranged dances every Saturday night. We laid on beer and hired a band to play for us and we invited our officers and a small number of our Yugoslav trainees to join in; everyone enjoyed these dances immensely. They became widely known as the place where a good time could be had. We were inundated with requests from the local girls for tickets to attend, and as they greatly outnumbered the men, we were able to pick and choose, and vary the allocation of tickets so that we always had a fresh selection of girls to invite. A very satisfactory state of affairs indeed, for the men at least.

These Yugoslavs were registered as they arrived. They came in batches of four hundred or so and were divided into platoons of thirty men, all dressed in their many and varied uniforms; there hardly seemed two alike. Their ages ranged from 30 to 50 years, some were bearded and they came in all sizes. They spoke very little English which caused some problems in training. They were expected to learn sufficient of the language for the purpose of the training course. Most of them spoke German which was a fortunate thing for me because I did as well and it was a great help at times for those in my squad. One had to feel sorry for the other instructors who became exasperated when having to teach something difficult. All communication had to be by way of a mixture of English, German, Yugoslav and sign language, mostly the last. It was hilarious at times, and our Sergeant Major could frequently be heard haranguing and gesticulating at one or other of the platoons with a mixture of languages when there had been some misunderstanding.

'Listen what the sergeant *alles sprechen*,' he shouted at the non comprehending Yugoslavs, adding 'silly buggers' in a quieter aside. This would be repeated with him trying to mime what he wanted to get across. He did not have much knowledge of German but used to the full what he did know even if it was wrong. He took our comic impressions of his performances with a good heart though.

I had been allotted the officers to train, not for any particular reason, but I had been the first instructor called out when the intake was divided up. Thereafter with every new intake, I trained the officers. There was no difference from that done by the other squads, but I did feel good about it. With the confidence of youth, and sure in the knowledge of

Complete staff, all from different regiments, at Holzminden Barracks, Holzminden, 1945–46. Selected to train Yugoslav loyalist refugees to guard British installations.
Author is on far right.

my ability as an instructor, I considered myself to be the best in the unit. I felt that as officers, my squad should be the best and seen to excel over the others. Praise from my CO confirmed what I had already known.

Most of the trainees were approaching middle age and I could not expect the same fitness that was normal in younger men, but with a gradual build-up, and sensible planning, they progressed in fitness and ability to a very high standard indeed. They were very proud of themselves, and although they thought that I was a very hard taskmaster and that the training course had been very hard for them, without exception I was personally thanked by every member of the platoon before they left the course at the end of their training. They could now do the work for which we had trained them, and they were sent off to take up their duties all over West Germany.

Every six weeks with only a short break in between we had a new intake and it continued for almost a year. Several thousand men had completed training and they took over important duties from our men waiting to go home. It was one of the happiest periods of my life, coming as it did just after the war.

More and more regiments were being disbanded, and I was posted hither and thither becoming occasionally attached to a different regiment which in its turn would also disappear as the men were sent home. I remember having to suffer the wailing of the bagpipes playing reveille as we came under the influence of one famous Scottish regiment, and the few unwanted Englishmen temporarily awaiting discharge with them, complained bitterly at the invasion of our early morning slumbers. We could not do anything about it, though.

Mind you, I love the sound of the bagpipes when played in a Scottish regimental band, and who is not stirred when they see such a sight as it marches along with their kilts swinging and their drums tapping; it is something special. But to be awoken from one's slumbers by the sound like that of a dozen cats being tortured is something else.

Chapter Nineteen

There came into being at about this time, Operation Woodpecker. War reparations had to be made by Germany to the British, and the powers that be had decided that some of the troops still serving there should be used to cut down the forest and ship the timber back to the UK.

Volunteers were needed and as I was once again quite eager to have a go at this new venture, I was one of those that took up new employment as a lumberjack.

We were based at Lüneburg at first, weapons were exchanged for saws and axes and we were transported at an unearthly early hour by truck to the forest. There, under the supervision of German forestry workers, we quickly learned the lumberjack's trade. There were a number of different jobs and I in time did them all. First of all there were the cutting teams, which consisted of three men, two sawyers and one axe man. Of course they could interchange their jobs in the team whenever they felt like it and frequently did so. The trees for felling were marked out by a forester and the cutting team would fell it and remove the head and branches leaving the bare tree trunk.

Then there were the men driving the large tractors, who worked with another team who hitched wire cables around the bare trunks of the now felled trees and they were dragged from where they had fallen to the track side where large ramps had been set up. Here the timber was sorted by size and quality, marked by the foresters, and loaded by crane onto special timber carrying trucks and driven away. The life was quite pleasant and different from soldiering, though of course we were under military authority and discipline was supposed to be the same; in fact it was very relaxed, and as long as the quota of wood was cut and removed, no one seem to worry.

There were various incentives for those teams actually cutting the timber down; it was the hardest job, but to someone used to physical labour it was not particularly difficult and I used to enjoy it. The incentive that my own team participated in was one that allowed us to finish work once a fixed amount of timber had been felled and trimmed ready for haulage. We would return to barracks early and could then do as we liked for the remainder of the day, and for Mac, Paddy and me that meant dashing off to see our girlfriends.

Once the tree had been felled and trimmed, the stump was measured across its smallest width. The trees came in various sizes so one might measure twenty-two inches across and another only fifteen, and yet another thirty. We discovered that it was possible to get more production by cutting smaller trees. We could not always choose them however because they had been marked for cutting by the forester and not by us but we found that we worked twice as fast if we had smaller trees to fell. The big trees took longer to cut down, that was obvious, but they were also harder to fell and when we came to have them measured up we could almost double our output by felling the smaller trees.

There was a minimum quota too: we were expected to fell and trim fourteen feet. This could take a full day when working at a normal speed and under normal conditions; it was not always achieved but was about the average. The goal we had to achieve in order to finish early was twenty four feet and could only be achieved by a good fit team cooperating, planning our course of action, and working very hard non stop.

Mac, Paddy and I having the same aims, in that we had all made applications to marry German girls, we had also all signed on to serve in the army an extra six months because we were all waiting for our marriage applications to be approved, and because we all wanted to spend as much time as possible with our respective fiancées, decided to make a sustained effort to finish early as often as we could. To this end we chose the best crosscut saws and axes, and sharpened them to as high a pitch as possible, and did our best to choose the trees that would help us reach our goal. We could all do each other's job efficiently, and could thereby interchange whenever we wanted to break the monotony, and to relieve the strain and stress on our aching muscles as we worked. It helped to change over and do a different job with a different posture.

The system that we used was to make a saw cut at the base of the tree we intended to fell; it was made as near to the ground as possible and was cut into the tree about one fifth of its diameter and made on the side in which direction the tree was intended to fall. The axe man chopped a large wedge out of the base above the saw cut and the two sawyers working the opposite side of the original cut and slightly above it would saw through the trunk and as they gradually reached the original cut gravity would pull the tree down. It was customary to shout TIMBER to warn anyone nearby that a tree was falling. Sometimes a tree might be leaning at an awkward angle, and one would have to use iron wedges to get it to fall in the desired direction, but that was time consuming and we avoided any trees that might give us problems or delay our progress. We became experts and could drop most trees within a foot of where we wanted. We often had a little bet to brighten up the dreary toil.

Off we went on the day of our first attempt. We were the first team off the truck and into the woods and the cutting area. Mac and I made our first cut and Paddy cleaned it out, working like beavers and keeping up a steady rhythm we soon felled our first tree even before any other team had started work and we kept it up all morning without a break. By two-thirty we had made it and were happy to be taken back to barracks early.

It was the beginning of many such days. We continually broke our own record, and we were the only team that regularly finished early often by lunch time. We built ourselves quite a reputation, and everyone, including our superiors, stood in some awe of these workaholics who became expert lumberjacks. Some of the other teams would come and watch us, and the forest would ring to the sound of the axe and saw, and the regular cry of 'timber' as we felled the trees.

We remained as a team for a long time and were then posted away from Lüneburg to a village called Gorleben. It was situated near to the river Elbe and we were living under canvas. The forest we had previously worked near Lüneburg was now depleted of mature timber, and we were required to work in this new area.

It was great for a while. After work was finished for the day we would go down to the Elbe and swim for miles. The current was quite strong and one had to be careful not to stay too long in the water because one could be carried many miles downstream, which meant of course, a long trek back to one's clothes. I used to ask a non swimming pal to take my clothes to the beach near the camp, and whilst he was sunbathing and guarding my clothes I would make my way upstream. Sometimes I was able to cadge a lift for five or six miles then swim down to where my friend was waiting, it was very enjoyable. Some time later, Paddy got his marriage papers through and left, Mac too left, then Operation Woodpecker closed down and I was posted back to Lüneburg.

It was the autumn of 1947 before I received authorisation to marry;

it had taken a year to get to this stage. We had intended to have a small quiet wedding but my intended's family wanted otherwise, so to please them we agreed to fall in with their wishes and we were married on the 19 December 1947 in the town of Hameln of Pied Piper fame. My new in-laws had managed to obtain a lorry which took us the 40 odd miles to the church. It was uncomfortable, cold and snowing. The three days of celebration that followed were memorable ones; there was no honeymoon.

The duration of the emergency was now over as far as I was concerned. We returned to England and I was discharged from the army in April 1948.

I started back to work as a civilian again with the same firm I had left when I enlisted. The problem was that the engineering side of the works was now closed down. There was no further requirement for the war components that had been in such demand just a few years earlier, now it was important to get back to the peacetime production of printing.

'I am fully aware of your brave actions in the army and I want to assure you that we want you back working for the firm, the problem is the only vacancy we have at the moment is in the packing department.'

These were the kindly words my employer greeted me with during my interview on returning to work. We knew that employers were obliged to take back into employment, those personnel that had been conscripted or who had volunteered for military service during the war, but doing what was the important question.

Many employers offered returning heroes dead-end jobs with no possibility of decent pay or the chance of advancement. They were complying with the ministry order as laid down but were not acting in the spirit of the thing. Not all employers were bad, but I was being shoved into a non skilled job from which there could be no advancement. I could remain a low paid packer for the rest of my life. I was prepared to accept this situation for a little while, but not forever.

And so I started back to work. It was a dreadfully dull and uninteresting job, humdrum and very poorly paid. I quickly decided that I was not prepared to accept this situation and one day I approached one of the directors, the brother of the MD. He was frequently seen walking round the factory. I waylaid him and voiced my concerns regarding my future career and asked him to increase my pay as my present wages were a pittance and insufficient to live on. I could see that he was very annoyed and implied that I was not entitled to more pay, I should keep my place and think myself lucky that I had a job at all.

Chapter Nineteen

I just saw red and lost my temper, I gave back every bit as good as he had given me, I told him that whilst he had remained back home on the gravy train making a handsome profit from the war, people like me had been risking our necks in the front line, fighting and doing the dirty work and keeping people like him in the lap of luxury, it was OK for him to make money, but the peasants could go to hell! That was the end of that job.

There followed a period of my life that was not happy. I tried a number of jobs one after another but could not settle down to the routine of civilian life. Men returning from the forces had been promised a wonderful new world just as they had after the first war: there would be full employment and good housing for all the boys coming back. It was all right for them to risk their lives and indeed lose them as many did in war time but their sacrifice was in vain really and in most instances it was all forgotten, a typical case of Kipling's 'Tommy this and Tommy that' when the need for them was over.

I had made application to the council for a house. We had temporarily lived with my mother after I was demobbed, and later, my brother had found us a cottage which was a little primitive but nevertheless most welcome, and into which we quickly moved, but we really wanted a proper modern home and my name remained on the housing list. On one of my visits to the council offices to enquire about my prospects, I was informed that it was no use my expecting to get a house because priority was being given to coal miners, not ex-servicemen, so although I did not really want to follow my grandfather and father down the pit, I thought that if it would get me a home it was worth a try.

The work was hard, I became a carting chap. Two breakers got the coal at the face and shovelled it out to the topple, and I would load the tub, take down the topple incline, mark our identification number on it, then in this particular place have to run the tub of coal some half a mile out to the main area where the coal tubs were concentrated and sent on out to the shaft bottom. An empty tub was then pushed back to the coal face to replace the full one sent out. On a good day I could make that run 23 or 24 times, so I would be running at some speed with the full tubs out and pushing the empty ones back and covering up to 23 or 24 miles each day five days a week. I was young and fit and did not mind the work but I hated the conditions. We went down the shaft at 6 a.m. each morning and did not see daylight for eight hours. It was wonderful to see and smell the light and air at the end of each shift. I suddenly realised that I could not take a lifetime of this; surely there must be other work I could do.

Leave before it is too late, I told myself, so when on a subsequent visit to the council offices I was informed that not only did one have to be a miner in order to qualify for a house but one had to have at least two children as well, in my usual hot-headed way, I told the council where to stick their houses, and the pit manager where to stick the pit and I left.

I rather fancied the idea of emigrating to Canada: there were one or two special schemes being offered to potential emigrants at the time. One was to purchase land from money loaned by the Canadian government. It was very cheap land but it was virgin with no amenities whatever. It was also very isolated somewhere in the more northern parts of Canada, it had to be cleared and a dwelling erected on it, there were a few other conditions too but the land title did become the émigré's if these conditions were fulfilled. It was a good offer and I wrote off to Canada House, filled in the application forms and returned them.

Patience is not one of my virtues, and I champed at the bit, what was taking so long? Surely it only took a few minutes to look at an application form and make a decision and inform the applicant. I expected an answer in days as opposed to the two months or so that such decisions normally took. Annoyed by the delay, I made another application, this time to the Australian authorities. They also had a scheme whereby one could contract to work on building the railways across the outback, and after the contract period, one would be accepted as a bona fide emigrant, all expenses were paid. This was also acceptable to me so I applied for that too. Whichever was the first to accept me, that is where I would go.

But it was not meant to be. I just did not have the patience to wait, and one day, no longer able to stand the delay, I made my way to the army recruiting office and joined the army as a regular soldier for twelve years. Within a month of my posting to Exeter, I received notice from both Canada and Australia house that my applications were successful and I could expect to be on my way very shortly.

Naturally I was very annoyed, I really had wanted to go to Canada especially; still it was too late and there was nothing to be done. Reluctantly I informed the respective parties that I was now a serving soldier, and that was the end of it.

Because I had been out of the army for two years I did not get my old rank back and I was obliged to go through training again. I was then posted to Plymouth as an instructor, and spent some time training conscripts. They had to serve eighteen months in the forces, later this was increased to two years. These conscripts did not like service life one bit, but the training and discipline did turn them from boys into men.

My superiors had decided that I should become part of the permanent staff at the depot in Exeter and I found myself running the Quartermaster's stores. I was not particularly enamoured of the job, but it was considered to be a good one. I wanted something more active and adventurous but I thought if I stuck this out for a while, perhaps later I might obtain a better posting.

Running a store is really very simple and from the Quartermaster's point of view it was important to ensure that the stock of uniforms and other military items remained in balance, preferably a small surplus one. During the hustle and bustle of organising a new intake of 400 men and the issue of their new equipment, it was normal for small errors to occur. They had to be issued with two uniforms, two sets of denim uniforms for work, boots and berets, underclothes, towels, socks and all kinds of other equipment. With such large receipts and issues of kit the stock constantly varied and small mistakes would come to light; it happened in all stores. It was common knowledge that if the inspecting officers found everything exactly correct, he would suspect that there was some sort of fiddle going on, and he would usually be correct in his assumption.

Hence the stock of items at any given time in the stores would read a surplus of a few of one thing, another might be correct, and yet another could be deficient. In other words as an example, there could be a surplus of 21 blankets, greatcoats might be correct, and tunics 19 deficient. Most military storeman would agree with my assessment.

The method of rectifying and normalising the stock figures was as practised by army storemen everywhere: if there was a deficiency in boots, for instance, one waited until it was time to replenish the stores and replace all worn out equipment and other items. Some of the old worn boots were broken apart and mixed in with other less worn ones, tied in pairs, and what was 300 pairs of worn boots became 350 pairs. The Indent was a request for 350 pairs of new boots to replace 350 pairs of worn out boots, quite a natural request. The issuing store quickly counted the 350 pairs of old worn boots. Naturally very little attention was paid to these old boots that were destroyed almost immediately, and the new boots were issued. The store making the request for replacements now had 50 pairs of boots surplus.

This could be done and was indeed regularly done with all kinds of items. From the foregoing one might surmise that there was one huge fraud going on all over the country at every army depot, and that hundreds of criminals were getting rich on the proceeds, but in fact I only knew of one CQMS who was doing this and he was caught. Most storemen practised it in a very small way purely to keep their stores in a reasonable acceptable balance.

There was another way of normalising the balance of items in stores, and that was for the storeman to keep in contact with other storemen in other units; he might be deficient in items that were surplus in yours, a trade was done and both were satisfied. This was a method I preferred.

To my cost and regret, some unknown enemy of mine discovered that I was about to carry out an exchange. I had fourteen pairs of trousers in my possession which I was to exchange for half a dozen tunics and a few other items. We had arranged to meet in the town but before we did I was approached by a policeman who had obviously known that I was carrying goods that were not mine. He challenged me and of course I was caught with what appeared to be stolen items in my possession.

A hue and cry took place back at the stores, and a check was made to see what items were missing. There were none and so no charge of stealing could be brought against me. But of course, everyone knew what I was doing and the only charge against me that would stick was one of unlawful possession. I was subsequently charged and found guilty, and reduced to the ranks and given a suspended sentence. I was also posted to a different regiment.

What I did was not with criminal intent to feather my own nest; if I had wanted to do that, there were other and much easier methods. I would not get very rich on money obtained by selling a few pairs of trousers, no, someone was after my blood, and it was a very simple matter to take advantage of what was common practice all over the army. There was a lot of jealousy amongst some of the other ranks, I had made a rapid advance up the ladder and someone resented it. Still, I was never one to cry over spilt milk and once again I started at the bottom rung of the ladder. I knew I was a good soldier and that I would regain my rank again. The old saying that you could not keep a good man down rang true, and when I returned to the UK some three years later, I had been promoted and was back in a higher rank than I previously had.

My next posting was to Vienna, a wonderful city, and whilst I was there I took every opportunity to see the sights. Wine was cheap, and it was an easy matter to travel around: Schonbrunn palace, the opera house, Vienna woods, St Stephens, the park, I saw them all and delighted in their beauty. Unfortunately my stay was not a long one; the four powers that had been occupying Vienna since the end of the war were now leaving, she was getting her freedom back. It had been decided that since Austria had been annexed and forcibly occupied by Germany, she should not be punished even though she had been a willing partner in the event and the Allies were now about to leave. There was a large military parade in which all the powers participated, and the Dorset Regiment carried out a 'Fire of Joy', an impressive display of controlled rifle fire in celebration. It commenced at one end of two ranks of soldiers, and each soldier fired his weapon one after the other in rapid succession along the front rank of the parade and back along the rear rank to the end. It was a very impressive display with the sound rippling along, and the smoke leaving a haze over the parade. There were many congratulations from the spectators. With that, administration of the city reverted back to the Austrians.

Word came through that the Battalion was going to the far east, I was delighted, I wanted to go and volunteered for the advance party. We were posted back to the UK, issued with our tropical greens, and our small party of about 60 embarked on HMS Troopship *Empire Pride* sailing from Liverpool to Hong Kong.

The ship was the smallest trooper in service and also one of the oldest. Its accommodation was a number of cabins for the use of officers, wives and a few other special passengers. For the other ranks, mess decks in the traditional naval system. These were a number of long fixed tables which seated about twenty men on fixed benches. Three men from each table were detailed to report to the galley at meal times, and they collected the food for their own particular table; the food was served out at the end and passed along the table until everyone was served. Unequal serving portions meant that sometimes those who were the last to receive their meal might get short rations, so that there was great interest and minute observation frequently followed by intense argument if the distribution had not seemed to be fair.

After the meals the tables were cleaned up, and if there were no other parades or duties, the men used those same tables to write letters, play games, clean kit, read or just yarn to one another. It was only after the last parade, or 8.30 p.m., that hammocks were allowed to be slung. That rule had to be strictly observed otherwise it would not be possible to move around the mess deck. The height of the deck was about seven feet, and once slung the hammock hung down from the fixtures below the deck head about three to four feet so there was only about one foot of room between the hammock and the table top, and if it was badly slung sometimes there were only a few inches between hammock and table.

Imagine if you can the pandemonium at hammock slinging time! Everyone struggling, pushing and fighting to be the first to claim the best places. These were near to the gangways and ventilation points which were the coolest places to sleep. It was also a comparatively easy matter to move, to get out of the hammock to visit the heads. It was quite another matter if one was placed against the side of the deck away from the exits, or even worse, somewhere in the middle of that seething mass, because to visit the toilets one would have to turn the hammock over whilst still in it, and then upside down put one's hands down on to the table, lower oneself down and crawl along under the swinging hammocks and the sleeping bodies to the nearest exit or gangway where it might be possible to stand up again.

They must have used a mathematician to work out exactly the number of troops that could be accommodated on each deck. During the day life was not too bad, but at night it was chaotic. We were so packed in that there were only a few inches between hammocks and they were slung head to foot in rows. It was almost necessary at night for someone to shout out 'all turn' and a whole row of men could turn over and ease their aching limbs. Often they were so tightly jammed together that it was impossible to move unless someone else did so first.

Curses were uttered as the men were woken by the bumping and pushing of those unlucky ones who were furthest from the gangways, and as they pushed and shoved and forced their way under and through the hammocks to get out, tempers would become frayed and fights break out, then things would quieten down for a while until another man had to relieve himself and the process would be repeated. It was not exactly luxury cruising, but the normal method of transporting troops around the Empire.

This particular journey was a six-week trip. In later years the troopers were larger and instead of hammocks, there were tiers of two or three steel sprung beds which could be folded up during daytime and let down at night. They were a marked improvement on the hammock. Later still the troopers were phased out; it was quicker, easier and cheaper to use aircraft.

Before the Second World War, troops serving abroad could expect to remain at their overseas station for ten years. They were shipped out as an entire regiment with wives and children, and none of them would see home at all during that period. Emphasis was on the interest of the army and not the men; they took second place. There were strict rules about marriage too and the single men had to stay single. The severe economic depression and mass unemployment ensured that there were plenty of volunteers for the regular army and working-class lads did not find conditions too difficult to handle. It was better than starving in civvy street.

To keep fit there were daily physical exercises and games. The boredom was relieved by quite unnecessary training and cleaning parades. First of all the ship had to be kept clean, everyone knew that, but the ship's officers were never satisfied with perfectly adequate cleaning, and the work had to be repeated several times over until the inspecting officer was satisfied. I believe it was a bit of come-upmanship, the navy had to impress on the army that their standards of cleanliness were higher, hence the necessity for repeated inspections.

Hammocks had to be precisely rolled a certain way, and stowed just so; the sight of one just not quite straight even if imagined, meant removal and re-stowing of the whole lot again. This work went on all over the ship and included the heads, accommodations and common rooms, and could last for several hours dependant on the ship's inspecting officer, who was always bloody minded and really never had any real reason to be as he was. But mostly they were dealing with old soldiers who knew the drill and who were in no way intimidated by the regime. They had seen it all before, so having done the cleaning properly once, and pretending to be suitably impressed and put in their place by the complaints of the inspecting officer, they would go through the motions of re-scrubbing and cleaning all over again, but in fact doing nothing, and the next inspection or the one thereafter would be satisfactory, thus proving that there had been no grounds for complaint in the first place. It is just not possible to fool the old soldier; he can seldom be fooled, he knows all the tricks and is far more cunning than is generally realised.

These troopers always sailed the same route calling at the same ports in different parts of the empire all over the world. The first stop on our way to the far east was Gibraltar and the troops were allowed off the ship for a few hours recreation. The local girls followed the men around until it seemed that everyone from the ship was congregated in two or three large bars, and most of the remainder were empty. Music, dancing, drinking and singing continued apace until it was time to return to the ship.

To turn a blind eye was the norm in the few cases of real drunkenness, as long as the friends of the men involved were in control of the situation and there were no serious incidents. Surplus steam had been released and the troops could now take a further period of close confinement for the next leg of the voyage.

The ship sailed through the pleasant waters of the Mediterranean and the next port of call was Malta. Again shore leave was granted and it was more or less a repeat of the activities at Gibraltar. The ship continued the voyage after a few hours and a few days later we anchored at Port Said. Shore leave was not allowed, but it was fascinating to watch the bum boats loaded to the gunwales and their occupants trying to sell us all kinds of goods, mostly leather ware, suitcases and wallets and handbags and a multitude of other items. The goods and payment for them were passed up and down the ship side by means of a rope with a basket attached.

Sometimes goods went missing and there was a lot of banter and some serious arguments as the traders tried to sell their wares, but things were usually sorted out to everyone's satisfaction in the end. On one occasion, we saw an Arab who was enamoured of the wife of a senior Warrant Officer (she had been watching the trading from the ship's rail) lift his shirt and bare his reproductive organ to her. It was of a size that produced immediate envy in all the men present, and it was also the main topic of conversation for a long time thereafter and the incident related for many a year.

He offered her a wonderful life if only she would come away with him and become one of his wives; he would transport her to the seventh heaven of delight, and as she could see, would be well satisfied because he was able to perform according to him, virtually non stop day and night.

She kept very calm despite her embarrassment, declined his offer with a firm 'no thank you', turned from the ship's rail, and walked away to the sound of cheering from the crowd of interested onlookers.

Chapter Nineteen

Port Said was the entry point of the Suez canal and we only stayed there long enough to arrange passage through it. The journey only took about one day if I remember correctly, and we emerged at the other end of the canal into the Red Sea and another British controlled port, Aden. What an awful place it is, just a collection of buildings, very hot, with a small garrison of army personnel; they had a Naafi canteen and little else. All water had to be imported, it had no supply of its own and I would have hated to be stationed there. To have nothing but sand to look at would drive most men crazy. The only reason for its existence was to guard one end of the canal, although I knew that most of the area was friendly to the British and we did give some military assistance to the Sultan of Oman and the Emirates.

We were allowed shore leave, but apart from the drinking there was little reason to leave the ship. There was no female company and fed up with nothing to do I returned early to the ship and passed the time leaning on the ship's rail and watching the small boats as they shuttled back and forth from ship to shore returning men.

One of the cooks came up on deck and threw a box of food scraps and leftovers from the evening meal over the side. I watched it as it slowly drifted along the hull of the anchored vessel and was surprised to see a large shark that came close to eat the food scraps. Startled is probably a better description for it was about twelve feet long and I had never been as close to one before; in fact it was the only one I had ever seen in real life and I shuddered to think what it could do to one; just looking down on it from the deck was frightening, what would happen if one came face to face with it in its own environment hardly bears thinking about.

There was an incident later that evening which I found quite amusing. A very drunken sailor was standing by the ship's rail, he had been separated from his mate somehow and had returned to the ship to find him. His just as drunk pal was at that moment returning from shore leave and was also trying to locate his friend. As the small boat carrying him approached the ship they spotted each other. Great was their joy as they shouted out, passing drunken incoherent messages to each other and in his excitement the one on the returning boat fell overboard and was splashing around, plainly a non swimmer and slowly drowning. His pal on the ship shouted to his mate, 'Hang on, Jim, I'll save you,' whereupon he clambered over the rail and jumped into the sea to save his friend. It was laughable because he could hardly stand let alone rescue anyone and it so happened that he was not able to swim either and there they were both splashing around and slowly drowning. Lucky that it occurred in full view of the boat crew who promptly pulled the pair of them out.

They staggered up the gangway with their arms wrapped around each other and made their way down to their bunks. It was a good thing that they were only passengers like the other troops; they were on their way to join a ship in Singapore. Had it occurred on their own ship they would have been severely punished. As it was, they had been so drunk that I doubt if they even remembered the incident.

The scorching searing heat in the Red Sea was intense. It was torture as we sweated our way through it; the old hands who had experienced a number of passages through said that summer or winter made no difference, the heat was always the same and one got no respite from it. We were given permission to sling our hammocks on deck to catch what air there was; for those still sleeping on the mess deck it must have been suffocating. It took three and a half days before we entered the cooler waters of the Indian Ocean.

I found the voyage quite pleasant now and I spent hours leaning over the rail near the bow, watching the flying fish as they left the water and sped along just above the waves sometimes for a hundred yards or more before diving back into the sea. I had heard that they leaped from the water because they were about to be eaten by larger fish that were chasing them and this was their means of escape. I don't know if that is true or not.

I enjoyed watching the dolphins, too, as they sped along in the bow wave of the ship, criss-crossing the bow and occasionally jumping three or four feet into the air, always in perfect unison with the others. It amazes me, there was never a collision and they would keep it up for hours. Then suddenly they were gone, and it might be several days before they returned again.

Once I saw a shoal of very large fish. It was a wonderful sight but they were just a little too far away for me to identify them. Someone suggested that they were killer whales, and they were of that same size but we could not be sure. It is a great shame that many species of these larger fish are being hunted to extinction and such sights will disappear forever. How stupid and short-sighted man is to destroy the very things that make life worthwhile. There must have been at least five hundred in that shoal and it really was a sight that I shall never forget.

Chapter Nineteen

We sailed on across the Indian Ocean for another three days and arrived in Colombo, Ceylon, now known as Sri Lanka. I wonder what was wrong with the old name. Again we were allowed a few hours ashore and almost everyone took advantage of it. There was not enough time to allow for much exploration, but what I did see was very interesting and quite pleasant.

One big problem was the beggars, street traders too were very persistent; we were constantly pestered, would we care to visit the brothels, did we want any dirty postcards, they were difficult to get rid of and rather spoilt what would have been a pleasant trip ashore.

The ship headed southeast toward Singapore, our next port of call. I recall having a discussion with a young conscript who had his life planned down to the finest detail. I tried to make the point that life did not always follow man-made plans and sometimes things went wrong, sometimes fate played a part in our lives that we had not foreseen. He could not accept that point of view, he knew exactly what was going to happen in his life, fate did not have anything to do with it. He was so cocksure and I knew that in about ten years it would be a safe bet that his life would be quite different to that which he had planned. It was one of many discussions I had with fellow travellers on our long voyage.

Sadly, it happened that this lad was involved in an accident on a level crossing; his vehicle had stalled and they were struck by a train. There were two fatalities and several casualties of which he was one. He had lost a kidney and had serious back injuries. Now permanently confined to a wheelchair he reminded me of our conversation some two years before on the troopship, and now accepted that life does not always turn out as planned. It is not a bad thing to plan ahead, but one needs to recognise the part that fate sometimes plays in our lives.

Singapore was the penultimate port of call in that long voyage. It is a beautiful place and the contrast in flora and vegetation with that of more temperate climes is very marked indeed. The vivid greens of different hues, and the brilliance of colours in the myriads of flowers and shrubs seemed to have a special beauty of their own and I enjoyed my short break there.

The reason for this luxurious plant growth is the tropical heat combined with the daily downpour of heavy rain which occurs regularly. The heavens open up to an hour's heavy rainstorm which created perfect growing conditions for food, fruit and flowers. The hot and humid conditions combined with the rain, made the climate almost like a greenhouse and everything grew rapidly. I would like to have seen more of this interesting place but it had to wait until I returned to England some years later.

The last part of the voyage passed quickly. We had listened to lectures on the history and customs of the people of Hong Kong, and after we arrived there I knew that I would enjoy my stay. The regiment was to be stationed at Fan Ling in the New Territories which was situated on the mainland of China, some miles from Hong Kong itself which is just a small island and part of a large group of islands off the coast. The British had leased Hong Kong together with a small part of the mainland. The border with China was at a small village called Sha Tau Kok about a further nine miles away from Fan Ling; there the British were one side of the street and the Chinese the other, everywhere else there were proper border crossing points.

Our camp at Fan Ling lay at the foot of Badge Hill, the whole face of it covered with large cut-out replicas of cap badges of the various regiments that had been stationed there. These were quite big and could be seen for miles because they stood out in contrast from the hill. I was reminded of the white horses carved on some of the hills in the west country back home.

The camp consisted of Quonset huts, lined half round buildings of corrugated iron, which were pinned to the ground with two steel cables which passed over the top of the huts and fixed firmly in the ground. The frequent typhoons could lift a building like a toy and carry it off if they were not fixed by the cables. One of these storms had lifted a large cruise liner and deposited it two miles inland such was its terrible power. Everything would grind to a halt at these times and people would just stay indoors and wait out the storm, for several days sometimes until the worst of it was over.

The advance party spent our time in preparing for the arrival of the regiment, and looking around the colony in our spare time. It was a beautiful place and had a thriving economy, but it was packed tight with people. The fact that the economy was booming and living conditions for the people were far better than in China, meant that the Chinese on the other side of the border were constantly trying to sneak into the New Territories and settle down and live the better life that was available there. The Police and border guards fought a continual battle to catch and return to China thousands of these poor people who were striving to get away from the bad conditions in their own country.

Chapter Nineteen

Inevitably quite a number made it through without detection and the population in the colony was increasing rapidly all the time. These poorer citizens would take up residence on the hillsides close to the town, building themselves ramshackle shelters out of bits of tin and wood or even cardboard. These during the rainy season would collapse and be washed away, sometimes with the loss of life. On occasions there have been disasters when the whole hillside has collapsed and been washed away by the tropical rain, and with an even heavier loss of life.

The authorities have built and are continuing to build more substantial and permanent housing where they can but it is an impossible task. There is a great shortage of building land and the population growth continually outstrips the capacity to provide suitable housing; it is a serious problem with overcrowding on a large scale and the serious health problems that it entails.

The fishing villages which are dotted about all over the colony could be located by their smell a fair distance away and long before one actually arrived. The overpowering stench was of fish in various stages of being dried, laid in rows on mats on the ground and also hung up in the air as if on a washing line; they were everywhere in sight. To western eyes it was an amazing sight, and I have never had my sense of smell so assaulted as it was on that first visit to such a village. Once dry, the fish was stored away, probably some for personal use and some for sale in one of the many markets.

There was also a considerable population of boat people. They lived on sampans of all sizes, whole families lived and slept on board boats some of which were quite small. I presumed they were fishermen, and when in harbour, one might see as many as two or three hundred sampans each tied to its neighbour. The people cooked their food in small cookers right on the open deck and mixed with the smell of drying fish and the countless meals being prepared at any one time the air was one terrible pong. I knew of no westerners that could stand it for any length of time.

In Kowloon, capital city of the New Territories, which lay across the bay from Hong Kong Island just half a mile or so away, lay a myriad of small sampans that acted as water taxis. Usually some old Chinese granny would do the work sculling with just one oar at the back; a lifetime of living and working in the busy harbour made them very skilful.

It was surprising how quickly they could get across. They had to weave in and out of other boats as they shuffled to and fro, and what with the wash from the larger motor vessels and the fierce current sweeping through the bay, these people made what seemed like a hazardous crossing more like a pleasant trip. No matter what time of the day or night it was one could always get a water taxi. The fares were very low and it seemed a hard life for such a small reward, yet they appeared to be satisfied with their lot. If one gave them a small tip extra to the fare, one would be rewarded with much kow towing and smiling thanks.

The shopping areas were very cosmopolitan and modern. The shops catered for all classes of people from the richest to the poorest. Almost anything could be purchased. Artefacts of ivory and jade beautifully carved into exquisite figures and shapes, jewellery, camphor wood chests and gorgeous silks catered for the most discerning customers, cameras, watches and more mundane goods were available in abundance for others. It was interesting to see the bargaining system at work. Most items on show were priced but these seldom had any relationship to the true value of the goods.

Customers were treated with great respect and shown the utmost consideration. A seat would be provided and a cold drink or some other refreshment pressed on them, but one had to be very careful when purchasing goods; many well known brands of cameras or watches might be on show but they could be fakes, just copies, and very good copies at that. It was just not possible to tell the difference with some goods. If one was buying any item of value it would be wise policy to take an expert along who knew and could verify genuine articles.

There was no Government duty to pay, and goods were much cheaper anyway, and there were some extremely good bargains to be had. The customer might show some interest in an item, and the trader would enter into a dialogue praising the quality and value of it and making a special offer just to you, of perhaps two thirds of the marked price.

One might be forgiven if one was a newcomer and not used to the ways of these Chinese or Indian traders, but if the price had been accepted straight away you could bet your bottom dollar that you would have been diddled, and the trader would have been delighted with the sale. There were many confidence tricks played on the unwary who arriving home frequently found that the charming piece of jade or ivory that they had obtained at a bargain price in Hong Kong was in fact a skilful imitation.

Old hands would not show much interest in the item they really wanted to buy. They would just browse around asking the price of one item then another. If he could make it appear that he was not really interested in buying anything so much the better, then when he did make an approach the trader would be keen to sell.

Having made sure that the item was genuine, and having fixed the price that one was prepared to pay for it clearly in the mind, an offer would be made of about one quarter of the true value or the price one was willing to pay. Of course the trader would be horrified and point out the price marked on the goods but he would reduce the price considerably. A shrug of the shoulders and a nonchalant attitude with an increased offer to half the true value would reduce the trader to tears: he had a wife and four children to support, they were all starving and he did not know how they would survive the coming weeks, surely the customer would not want the terrible responsibility of bringing such hardship on his poor family, after all, the customer was rich and he was just a poor trader, the sob story went on and on.

To be soft-hearted and succumb to his story would be fatal. It would not be true, if it were, how come that there were many thousands of pounds worth of stock in the shop? No, these traders were very practised in playing on the emotions. The spiel was always the same and identical to that from all the other traders.

The thing to do next was to make a final offer to the trader of around the final price that one had previously decided to pay which would mean that it was a genuine bargain for the customer. If the trader should decline the offer, one should promptly turn and walk out of the shop. In most instances this action will bring the trader running after the customer and agreeing the price. It would be a safe bet that the customer would have gotten a real bargain and the trader a satisfactory profit or he would not have sold the item. It was on the whole a very accurate system and seemed to work very well.

Child labour was used everywhere in the colony as it is throughout all Asia. One could order a suit of clothes in the morning and it could be picked up finished in every detail the following morning. It must have been very hard work to get it done in such a short time but it was exactly the same for the ladies: traders would actually visit the customer's address with samples of materials and a fashion catalogue. The customer selected the material and chose the style of dress she required from the catalogue, no special patterns were necessary, just the photograph in the catalogue of the style, even complicated evening wear or other special dresses could be ordered; the trader would take measurements and leave.

Within two or three days he would return with the completed garments, all faithfully reproduced as ordered. The customers were nearly always very satisfied and would build up large new wardrobes for themselves at a fraction of the price they would have had to pay at home in the UK. It did not finish there, the same principle applied to footwear; having chosen the style and colour, the feet were placed on paper and their outline drawn out with a pencil, the measurement of instep and toes were made and a few days later the finished shoes were delivered; male or female it was the same. They were very good shoes and whilst I was there, I got myself fitted out completely, as most long-stay residents did.

I found the Chinese people charming notwithstanding their strange beliefs and superstitions. Mind you they probably find western ways just as strange, but there are things that they do that I would not. As the weeks went by I was getting acclimatised and more used to the place. There were things happening that I found very strange indeed, for instance in the busy thoroughfares of Hong Kong and Kowloon the traffic was constantly on the move, and one could not help but notice the large numbers of road accidents and resultant casualties especially in the early mornings from eight to ten a.m. It seemed to be an inordinate number, and from my observations it was surprising that there were not far more.

As the buses, lorries and other traffic sped along the streets, pedestrians waiting to cross the road would wait until a vehicle was almost on top of them and then leap across the road in front of it; it was miraculous how they avoided being struck, frequently they missed death by just an inch or two. The crazy thing about it was that the pedestrians had ample time to make the crossing in absolute safety but instead would wait until the vehicle had almost reached them before they actually made their move.

Having gotten safely across, they would casually proceed on their way as if they never had a care in the world, which they didn't. I began to understand the logic behind these strange actions when some time later I broached the subject with my Chinese landlord. He was a school teacher by profession and spoke fluent English.

'Why do they do it?' I asked. 'You seem to be sensible and responsible people, why take these risks?' His answer flabbergasted me. He was quite serious as he told me that the people in the colony were very superstitious and when they went to sleep at night evil dragons would enter into their defenceless bodies so that when they woke up in the morning, these evil spirits would still be present in their bodies.

In order to have a normal day without bad things happening to them, these evil spirits had to be driven out. One of the best methods of doing this was to wait for a vehicle to approach and leap across the road in front of it. The spirit was cut off from the body because it was not quick enough to follow, and the actual leap allowed the car, bus or truck to cut the spirit off; it could not then re-enter the body until one slept again. The person who had followed this procedure was now able to continue with his day, secure in the knowledge that his evil spirit had been cut off, and he was very happy that this was so. I have no idea what the thoughts were of those that did not make it across the road, but there were a lot of them.

There were other customs that I found strange, weddings for instance. The bride was always chosen from a different village to that of the groom. Suitably dressed and prepared, she was hidden in a hand carried contraption very much like a sedan chair. It was completely enclosed and she was not visible. She could certainly be heard though; as men from her new family carried her to her new home and new husband, she would be wailing and crying so much that one wondered if it was worth it, and why was she doing it.

Having arrived at her new home the poor girl was put under the charge and care of the groom's mother. It was she that was responsible for the efficient running of her son's house. He might already have two or three wives, the number was controlled by the groom's wealth, more wealth, more wives. Obviously in this set-up there was a pecking order, and the groom's mother firmly controlled the way that the house was run and the way the work was done. Wife number 1 and number 2 and so forth would have priority and poor wife number 3, the latest acquisition, was at the bottom of the pile; she had the bulk of the work to do, and it was not an enviable position; perhaps that is why she wailed so much.

Funerals were on the other hand joyous occasions. I had a shock when I entered a house at the invitation of an acquaintance to find a party in full swing. The corpse, an old man, was seated at the head of the table and tied upright to his chair. He was dressed in his best clothes, and he was being fed by one of the women who was forcing rice down his throat. I was given to understand that the old man needed to have sufficient food in him to last the long journey he was about to make. Later in the midst of loud jollification and shouting by many relatives the old man was placed in a casket and made ready for the journey, wherever that was.

The very loud and noisy band arrived, and the casket was carried by slinging it under long bamboo poles which allowed it to swing and twist around unhindered in every direction; there were six carriers employed just for that particular job. Off they went with the band in front. Not being accustomed to the music I found it atrocious, it was certainly very loud, followed by the casket and it in turn by the relatives and mourners, about a hundred of them all singing and making much noise. It was a happy occasion. We then arrived at a road junction.

The band and the relatives continued noisily down the street but the casket party stealthily went down a side street following a different route. It was a case yet again of that old dragon, who tricked by the noise of the band and relatives of the funeral party, followed them instead of the casket, no way was that evil spirit going to get into that old man's body. By the time the party were reunited at the graveside, the body had already been buried and was safe.

I was told that many of these people practised ancestor worship; the body just buried remained in the grave for seven years and was then exhumed. The skeleton was cleaned and the bones placed in a large earthenware pot. I had seen them previously on the side of the road, sometimes in groups of three or four and occasionally as many as seven or eight. Curiosity compelled me to look into one of the pots, and it was a bit of a shock to see a skull staring up at me from the bottom. Displayed neatly around it were the larger bones of the limbs. At certain times of the year, the whole family of the deceased would hold some kind of celebratory picnic at the site of the pots, the bones would be removed and cleaned then reverently replaced and covered with a lid until the next visit, when the whole process would be repeated.

Chapter Twenty

THE CHINESE LOVED THEIR CHILDREN, especially the boys. Ancestor worship was perpetuated via the males; girls did not hold such an important place in the family and were considered to be inferior beings. Most of the manual labour was done by women and they worked in the rice paddy all day.

There were many old women who still had their feet bound in the age-old tradition. The barbaric practice of binding the feet of baby girls in linen bandages had been widespread. The tight bandages prevented the feet from growing and the bones became deformed. It was the fashion, small feet were supposed to be a thing of beauty, but from early middle age onward those women that had undergone such treatment suffered much pain. In later life they could not even walk. The practice became unlawful, but it was many years before it finally stopped and was generally accepted that it was a bad thing.

I discovered some interesting things about the Chinese men too: they liked to eat and drink and enjoy themselves but it was considered very bad taste if one became intoxicated. They would be very ashamed and lose face if it became obvious, but I never did actually see one drunk and out of control. The moment they realised that they were approaching anywhere near that state, their faces took on that oriental inscrutable blank expression and they became very proper and polite, they over emphasised everything they said and did so that people could see that they were in proper control of themselves. Even when they were stone cold sober they would always cover their mouths with a hand if they wanted to smile or laugh; it was not polite to show an open mouth.

Upon the hillsides around the border with China were many military defensive positions. Most had been constructed before the war by the troops that had been stationed in the colony at that time. Their effectiveness had not been properly tested because the Japanese attacks across Asia at the commencement of the Second World War were so successful that along with other British colonies in the far east, Hong Kong surrendered without any serious opposition having been offered.

However, as was the habit of military commanders everywhere there were frequent military exercises. Having in the imagination been attacked by a foreign power, we were required to take up defensive positions in the hills. Inevitably it became a matter of some urgency as to how long it took the battalion to prepare and get to them.

There would be a preparatory warning, followed at some time, usually several hours later, by the *stand to!* This received immediate priority; all other activities would cease and we would load up our personal equipment and set off into the hills. Most of the regiment marched. From the camp we would head across paddy fields of rice and other crops and wind our way up into the hills, I think the record time from camp to a state of readiness at our positions was about 1 hour 40 minutes. Once there we might stay several days and nights, making attacks on other regiments, and acting the part of an enemy, or we might be attacked ourselves, all part of the scenario that had been devised for the exercise. Once over, we marched back to camp and returned to normal camp duties. There we awaited the next inevitable imaginary attack on the colony which could be as soon as one week ahead, but was more likely to be in a month or six weeks.

Routine parades were held early every morning and normal duties continued until 1 p.m. The heat and humidity rapidly rose as the day progressed, so the afternoons were mostly spent pursuing leisure activities. This was the reason for the early start, the men could relax out of the heat when it was at its worse.

Normal dress in camp was *bare buff* or in other words shorts, boots and socks and a hat. Anyone on guard or other formal duty had to be dressed in full uniform of course, but a clean starched one would only remain dry for ten minutes before it became stained, limp, and soaked with sweat. We changed into clean dry uniforms four or five times a day, but after a few minutes they would be just as bad as the ones we had just changed out of.

There was only one way to stay cool and that was to sit under the large circulating fans that most of the huts were equipped with. These were working day and night non stop but of course it was not possible to remain under them for very long, there were other duties that entailed moving around the camp for much of the time, but it was nice to get under one, even for just a short while, the cooling air was so refreshing, but move away and one immediately began to start sweating again. Even after a shower the body started overheating and sweating within a few minutes.

The fans were also useful in blowing away the mosquitoes which constantly plagued us. Being very small and light the down-draught from the fans would blow them all over the place, but if one was further away, especially at dusk, we would be attacked from all sides as these vicious little flies homed in on any living flesh.

Malaria was rife at the time and it was mandatory to take one Paludrine tablet each day without fail which would prevent the disease from taking hold. In fact it was a chargeable offence to catch malaria, it being certain proof that one had missed taking the Paludrine that prevented it, so there were special parades each day, supervised by an NCO who had to sign a book as proof that he had supervised and overseen each man consume his anti-malarial tablet that day.

In camp we slept under individual mosquito proof nets, but if one or two of the little beasts got inside it, then a night of misery followed. They buzzed around our sweating bodies making a very high-pitched sound, searching for somewhere to have their evening meal. No amount of lashing out in the direction of the sound helped; one always missed. There would be silence for a minute followed by the start up of the exasperating buzz that drove some men to despair. It did not let up until dawn and one fell into a deep sleep just as it was time to get up; by then of course one had been almost turned into a suicidal wreck.

The continuous high temperature combined with the stifling humidity could produce an irritating rash all over the body. It was known as prickly heat and most people suffered from it especially the fair haired and lighter skinned individuals, but as the skin tanned and one did plenty of swimming it had less effect; some however suffered it constantly.

Married men who had brought their family lived either in married quarters near the camp, or in private accommodation which they rented in nearby towns and villages. Mosquitoes were less evident in built up areas, but the heat remained quite high late into the evening. It became dark quite early as it does in the tropics, but the families would socialise and sit in their rooms and on their verandas enjoying the cooler air of the open planned houses or flats.

The windows and doors were normally always open to allow what air there was to circulate freely, but the light would attract all manner of insects and moths very few of which were familiar to Europeans. Screams could frequently be heard from the wives as huge flying cockroaches, some two and a half inches long, would hurtle through the open windows and land with a loud thump onto the wall.

The oriental species are much larger than their European cousins and the wives would scream in terror at the sight of them. They were in fact quite harmless and the Chinese children played with them like toys, they were highly amused at the helpless antics of the army wives. Most families allowed one or two friendly chameleons to take up residence in the house, which would keep down most of the insects that got in.

The border patrols in the hills were constantly manned and guarded and changed over with fresh men every few days. Some positions could be reached with vehicles but most could not. Supplies to these positions were ferried back and forth by mule, teams of which were under the control of Gurkha troops. These sure footed animals were invaluable in carrying supplies up the narrow twisting tracks where no vehicle could go. It was one of the last mule sections in the British army and did sterling service in the colony.

In the New Territories there was a train from the border to Kowloon. If proceeding from the colony to China one had to change at the border, pass through a barrier and join another train. Now of course, the colony having reverted back to China, it is no longer necessary. Buses ran everywhere and carried not only people but market produce as well. Vegetables and livestock were also transported this way; chickens, even pigs were trussed up and fitted into a sort of woven basket still alive but unable to move. It would be carried, slung from a pole across their shoulders, by two men and lifted on and off the bus, and they would trot off to their final destination disappearing into the bustling crowd. Of course there were modern taxis, but these were too expensive for the local people; they were used by military personnel or businessmen.

Most of the locals travelled around on bicycles if they could afford one. Some enterprising individuals also used them as taxis; they had a seat fixed over the rear wheel on a carrier and the passenger sat on it and was pedalled to his destination, mostly just a short trip of a mile or so, but they did a good trade. Much use was made of them for carrying goods to the market, even the afore mentioned pig was often transported this way. It could not have been a very comfortable ride for it but I never saw anyone particularly concerned for the animals.

The authorities wanted to make a metalled road up the hill to one of the more inaccessible positions and negotiations commenced with the chief and elders of the village at the bottom of the hill. They came to a sticking point from which the villagers just would not budge, their point being that the road was too wide and would allow the dragon that lived on the hill easy access to the village at the bottom. They had enough trouble with him as it was without extending an open invitation.

The matter was finally solved to everyone's satisfaction: the road was to be narrowed to a single track, just wide enough for a jeep to pass up and down, and at several points along the track and at the bottom, heavy steel posts were to be erected opposite each other close to the track so that they looked like goal posts. Because the road was narrow, these posts would now be able to prevent the dragon from passing down the road to the village and he would not be able to do any harm, his wings would get hung up by the posts and everyone now felt safe. Another serious problem had been overcome.

It was somewhat confusing for us really, because dragons were very much in evidence at the many festivals and parades that frequently took place. Apparently there were friendly dragons as well as evil ones. Copies of both varieties were made from *papier mâché* and painted in brilliant colours. They all had different expressions on the faces and the bodies could be twenty or thirty yards long, made with a light cloth which was also highly decorated. The dragon would be held aloft by wooden poles carried by almost hidden dancers inside the body and head, the cloth almost completely enveloping the carriers.

They also constructed lions using the same process, and during the parade, these creatures would weave across the road in and out of the onlookers with great skill, zig-zagging as they progressed. The longer dragons carried by up to twenty men at one time, and it took training and practice to be a participant. There were a like number of relief carriers ready to take up the task as the other team tired; it was also I gather something of an honour to be chosen.

When viewed from a distance, it all seemed very lifelike as they bobbed up and down and wove around just like a caterpillar. All of this to the cacophony of noisy cheering crowds, and what was to most western ears the caterwauling of Chinese popular music. If a new shop or business was to be opened successfully, the proper ceremony had to be observed and one could be quite startled by the noise of a string of fire crackers sounding off.

Yes, it was that old dragon yet again; to keep him away and invite the good spirits in, a long string of fire crackers was required, the longer the explosions continued and the louder they were, the better. Special firms made these up, at a price of course; the very small business man might only be able to afford a small show, the crackers sounding off for only fifteen seconds, but large department stores and big firms would spend thousands of dollars and the loud explosions last a good five minutes to complete. In all cases, it was considered essential to start off on the right foot as it were, and guarantee a successful venture.

I had a small sailing boat built; it was in the Chinese style and looked what in fact it was, a small sampan. It was well built and sailed extremely well. It cost me exactly twenty pounds and had I been willing to pay a hundred I could probably have got myself an ocean going boat, but I was no sailor, I had no experience. I quickly learned though, and with my wife and friends spent many happy hours sailing around Tai Po bay.

Sometimes when becalmed, I could look across the bay to see boats sailing along at a prodigious rate of knots whilst I was stationary. I used to get angry, it always seemed to happen to me. How was it that whenever I was becalmed other boats managed to catch the wind? I had the sense of course to realise that the local fishermen were following centuries of tradition and local knowledge of tides and currents. I knew nothing.

So I kept my eyes open and whichever way out of the harbour the locals took, I followed, and thereafter everything was OK. I still had no idea how they knew which route to take. It wasn't a question of following the wind, that could be blowing as we started out and die down afterwards, no, there was some sort of trickery going on at times, and I never did find out how they did it. They would take one route out today, another tomorrow, and yet another on the third day with no apparent reason yet they always had wind. I guess they utilised the help of a friendly dragon.

We often sailed over to an island or an uninhabited shore where we would camp out for a day or two, swimming in the ocean and enjoying the sun. Much of the enjoyment was lost because there were many jellyfish in the sea. The small ones were not much trouble except that there were a large number of the stinging variety there and quite a lot of the poisonous ones too especially the Portuguese Man o' War which could be fatal.

The larger ones could be the size of a large dining table, at least six feet across. It was not pleasant to swim into one of these masses of jelly. There were a lot of them, and whilst most of them were harmless, if you happened to meet a stinger it was a very painful experience indeed and the horrible red weals they left on the body could take a week or two before they and the pain dissipated.

On the whole though the pleasure outweighed the unpleasant and it was a lovely time. There is something very special about the tropics especially at night. We could look across the hills and see the lights of distant villages twinkling away. The moon seems larger than it does at home, the tropical vegetation and the sounds of myriads of insects as they chirped, twittered and croaked, all combined with the smell of the plants, made it an experience never to be forgotten. Magic.

Mind you, I am referring to the quiet countryside and not the villages or towns. If you want peaceful nights, don't live in the towns, not even the small ones. Our stay in Tai Po wanted a great deal of getting used to. The people never seemed to sleep, tradesmen were shouting and selling their wares all night long; young children were clattering around in their clogs crying and playing, and people were living at night just as they did in the day time.

Being inveterate gamblers, the noisy game of Mah Jong continued all night long; the ivory gaming pieces were slapped down on the hard topped table with a noise like the loud crack of a whip, and every so often the pieces had to be shuffled which meant that all four players had to turn their pieces face down so that they could be dealt out again. Add to this the shouting and laughing and sometimes arguing, together with loud pop music of the eastern variety emanating from a dozen establishments and you will no doubt get the picture.

To sleep was an impossibility, but with time one did acquire some sort of troubled immunity to it all, eventually. Hearing the noise every night one kind of got used to it and could doze off for a while until a particularly loud noise would startle one into wakefulness again. This would be repeated throughout the night until with the approaching dawn, the noise gradually reduced in intensity and weary and exhausted one finally drifted into sleep only to be woken by the alarm clock giving notice that it was time to get up.

When the Chinese wanted to sleep they just put a blanket on the floor and lay down. Traders would close the doors of the business and lie down on a plank or bench in front of the shop; there were no set hours as far as I could see. Of course I am describing the life there that I experienced in the early nineteen fifties; whether it happens that way today I can not say but I expect it does, a permanent established way of life such as that would not be likely to have changed much and fifty years is not a long time when dealing with national traditions.

There was a lot of poverty and starvation amongst these millions in the colony. I was told by the local British Police Inspector that the authorities picked up seven or eight bodies every day, who had died in the night and were removed every morning early before the public started their day. This was in Tai Po which was quite a small village. In Hong Kong or Kowloon as many as a hundred bodies were likely to be found. Most of them succumbed to starvation, these were the unlucky ones that did not find their rainbow. Life always produces some losers as well as winners.

The Peak railway on Hong Kong Island was highly recommenced as being worth a visit, it travelled up and down to and from the peak. It was specially built for the one purpose and was very near to the vertical. It was a grand experience, and from the peak one got a breathtaking view of the harbour and the New Territories. It was well worth a visit and we went several times.

There was also the Tiger Balm Gardens, a kind of park full of oversize concrete beasts of all kinds, half hidden amongst the vegetation and very colourful. Children and adults alike loved it. The name 'Tiger Balm' also referred to a local ointment which was used as a kind of cure-all for almost any ailment. It had a pleasant sort of medical smell and was slightly perfumed. If a little was smeared on the forehead it had a cooling and soothing reaction, it was quite refreshing and was good for alleviating headache. Sold in small round tins, it was very popular with Chinese and Europeans alike.

There were two events every year that both the locals and the military could participate in. One was the swim from Kowloon to Hong Kong, the distance was about half to three quarters of a mile but I can not really remember. The problem was the current, which was so strong that it could carry one away and the actual distance swum could be four or five miles. Normal shipping business continued throughout the race and the swimmers had to avoid anchored cargo ships, cruise liners and sampans by the dozen. I finished somewhere in the middle of the pack but not at all ashamed by my efforts. The race was usually won by one of the professionals.

The other event was the Governor's Rifle meeting. I had long been a member of the regimental shooting team, we had been practising for about a month leading up to the meeting and the final team selections had been made when I was suddenly struck down with some bug. I had a fever and was admitted in to the hospital. The balance of the rifle team was upset, a replacement was made for me but the team was not as strong.

Chapter Twenty

It was a matter of some concern and regimental pride. We were competing against two other infantry regiments as well as numerous other ancillary units. Sadly the team did rather badly and had not won any event up to the last day of the meeting. That evening I was visited by the team officer who explained the situation and asked if I were well enough to discharge myself from hospital and partake in the final day's shooting.

I too had been concerned. It would not look at all well if the cream of the regiments which we considered ourselves to be came away from the meeting without a win. I had to agree that if I was on form we ought to win a match or two. I was still feeling a bit groggy and was advised by the doctor not to leave the hospital but I felt guilty about letting the team down so I agreed. I discharged myself that evening and went to the camp to prepare my rifle and settle in before the next day's shooting.

I have no wish to appear at all pompous, but I was one of the better shots and had been selected for the first team. We had trained to a high standard and would probably have won a number of events, to lose one member of the top team and replace him with another not quite as good meant that the average score for the team would quite naturally be lower by a few points. This would make the difference between winning and losing even though it might be only a few points, *a miss is as good as a mile,* as the saying goes and it is no consolation to lose even if it is only by a whisker. I felt sorry for the officer in charge of the team and fully understood how he felt, the team looked like a complete failure.

We had entered two competitions as a regimental team on that final day. The first was the falling plate, which took place at a range of two hundred yards. For the uninitiated, a plate of the kind used in these competitions was made of half inch steel and measured about sixteen inches by twelve. It was painted white and placed on the bank behind the butts so that they stood upright two feet apart in groups of four, the whole row of twelve spread over some thirty feet. If properly struck by a bullet the impact would knock it flat. The team consisted of four men who on the order to fire would attempt to knock down all the plates as quickly as possible. The team that did it in the shortest time was the winner.

We were the fifth team to fire. Our main rivals had put up a fair time of seventeen seconds, they were the ones we had to beat. I had a quiet word with the team: each of us would fire at his own plate, that is to say number one would fire at the first plate, number two at two and so on; having knocked down his first plate number one would then fire at plate number five, number two at plate six and so on. Having knocked down two plates each, eight plates in all, we would then concentrate on the last four.

Much of our practice during the training period had been rapid firing but at a controlled rate so that it was accurate. It is useless to fire rapidly if one did not hit the target; we had become very good at it and had the ability and the confidence. 'We must win this for the regiment,' I told the team. 'We can do it, we have well beaten this time of seventeen seconds many times before in practice, just concentrate.'

Then it was our turn. I made the team load slowly and get into comfortable positions before telling the firing point officer that we were ready. 'Fire!' came the order. Our first volley put down the first four plates, the second and the third volleys each knocking down four plates. We had completed the shoot in just ten seconds, a new record and well ahead of our nearest rivals. The huge grin on the face of our team officer said it all, he was over the moon. We had one more competition to participate in: let us hope we could do the same again.

The next shoot involved an obstacle course. It started at four hundred yards where we fired ten rounds at normal targets; we then had to run down the range to the three hundred yard firing point, jumping over and crawling under various obstacles on the way. Regardless of what the team did, from the moment we left the four hundred yard point the shoot became a timed event in that every five seconds one target was raised and by the time the team had cleared the obstacles and reached the three hundred yard firing positions there would probably be eight or ten targets up, each appearing at five seconds intervals.

However as each of these targets was fired on and hit, and only if they were hit, they were pulled down immediately so it was a race against time. If for instance five targets had been hit in twenty four seconds then the sixth target would not appear because it was not the twenty fifth second, the time it had to be exposed. The total time taken by the team was recorded and added to the scores of the shoot at four hundred yards and the winner declared.

Again it was a question of determination and confidence. We had practised the shoot many times and had reached a high standard, we only had to keep our cool and do what we had been trained to do. We were lucky again and had won by a handsome margin. It was a great pity that I had been taken ill at a critical time, our form was such that we would have undoubtedly won quite a number of events, but it was not to be and we had not disgraced ourselves.

Chapter Twenty-one

IT WAS MY UNFORTUNATE LOT to fall foul of my Regimental Sergeant Major. I have no idea why he disliked me so much. I was a good soldier and wanted to be a good soldier but for some reason he could not stand the sight of me and delighted in humiliating and persecuting me, and giving me a hard time. It was victimization of the worst kind, but I had too much pride to report it. I would not let him get me down whatever he did to me. I did not know him before I joined the regiment, and I did not know of any reason for his attitude.

As I moved around the camp performing normal duties, he would lie in wait behind some building ostensibly for the purpose of pouncing on me without warning. As I approached he would shout and scream and find fault with me. At one time he ordered me to get my shorts lengthened, they were too short, the next time he saw me I had to get them shortened again, they were too long; both times meant unnecessary visits to the camp tailor who must have thought I was crazy.

He missed no opportunity to bully, belittle, complain and rile at me without cause. My life became a hell and he did everything in his power to make life difficult for me. I remember very early one morning I was coming into camp for an early parade and was carrying a clean pressed uniform to wear on it. He spotted me in the distance and bellowed for me to double in to him. I stood to attention in front of him while he commenced shouting a tirade of abuse non stop for several minutes. I was at first very angry at this verbal attack on me, I had done nothing wrong and it was beginning to get me down.

Thinking the matter over some time later, I came to the opinion that he was out to get me somehow, and was trying to goad me into striking him. I do not know to this day why. It was a court martial offence to strike a superior officer, and he would have been delighted to have me sentenced to the glasshouse for punishment, but I was no fool and decided to bide my time. I would continue to take all he had to give and when the time was ripe, I would get my own back. Every dog has his day, and although I didn't know how, I felt sure that the time would come when I would repay his nasty attitude to me.

Physically, I could have flattened him, in a fair fight I could have beaten the daylights out of him, but he had the protection of his rank and what is more he used it to full advantage. He was a bully and delighted in making life difficult for those he disliked or could not get along with.

It is not a good situation to have in a regiment; a better team spirit and a better unit results from fair and proper treatment of men by their superior officers. I have known of young men driven almost to the point of committing suicide in despair as the result of victimization. One could accept a hard life, and verbal rollicking if one was making mistakes or failing to do a job properly, if one was scruffy and not clean, or guilty of unsoldierly conduct. But to have to take it without justification from those in positions of power because one's face did not fit, or worse, just for the hell of it was not fair.

I squirmed and had great difficulty in controlling my actions as it happened to me; often I was just a whisker away from losing physical control. Had I done so, I know I would have caused him serious injury I was so enraged at times and the feeling of wanting to have a go increased at every new encounter.

Despite every impediment he put forward, my ability to administrate and command a platoon brought promotion for me. My mortal enemy, for that is what he had now become, was privately furious, he could not prevent it and I had been reliably informed that he had fought against it making all kinds of false accusations about my abilities. Those who worked closest to me and knew my ability, including my platoon commander, were able to fight my corner with first hand knowledge. My enemy could only bluster away with hearsay and unconfirmed accusations. Our time in the colony was coming to a close; normally we would have served three years there instead of the two, but I had enjoyed every minute of it and would not have missed it for the world.

The Korean conflict was drawing to its close, there was an uneasy truce in the fighting and we had been earmarked to replace an infantry regiment that had served its time there. I was delighted, some more action at last. All the wives, sick and time served men were sent home on a trooper, whilst the regiment were kitted out with Arctic clothing and other necessities for our life in Korea.

We carried out one more training exercise in the New Territories, it was the last time we would move around these hills and valleys, fighting imaginary battles. There was every possibility that we would soon be doing it for real. We returned to camp and I spent several hours checking my stores and seeing that everything was in order. We had been ordered to attend a de-briefing on the exercise that same evening but I had become so engrossed in my work that I lost track of time. I realised that there were only a few minutes left before the meeting. Normally one washed and changed before attending but I had left it too late. Oh well, I thought, I can sit out of sight at the back somewhere and probably I won't be noticed, but I had not reckoned with the eagle eye of my arch enemy.

'Come here,' he roared. 'What the hell do you think you are doing, look at the state of you, you scruffy man?' On and on he went shouting and raving and making a huge song and dance about nothing. I tried to give him an explanation but as soon as I opened my mouth, he would interrupt, shouting and bellowing a further stream of abuse.

I knew I was in the wrong and should have changed my uniform, but what I was now on the receiving end of, was not warranted. I turned ice cold despite the high temperature both in reality and in the fever of the verbal attack. Something snapped inside my brain and I thought, this is it.

'You ignorant bastard!' I said. 'I'm fed up with your bloody-minded treatment of me and I won't take it any more, just you remember we are shortly going to Korea, and I'll make sure that you bloody well don't come back, and what is more, I will deny that this conversation ever took place if you try to do anything about it now.'

His face turned purple, never had he heard anything like it before. I remained stood to attention before him, my face set like granite but my eyes showing the hatred I felt for him. He knew that I meant every word I said and he was visibly shaken; he was used to servile compliance and a meek acceptance of his every word. This was pure insolence and a physical threat to his life.

I could see his mind racing for an answer, some reason to have me arrested, but there were now a lot of officers and NCOs hurrying in to the building to attend the conference. Had there been no witnesses, he might have accused me of striking him but there were too many people about now. Seemingly lost for words, he just turned away and left me standing there. I attended the meeting and when it concluded I left the camp and returned to my apartment in Tai Po.

I was half expecting to be called to his office. I remained on my guard expecting him to arrange some form of trickery with a couple of his

Author in Korea. Toc Chon, 38th Parallel.

cronies as witnesses, there is no doubt that his intention was to get me somehow and he would undoubtedly have thought up something nasty to make me pay. I was probably saved by the fact that we were shipped to Korea shortly after, and there was not sufficient time for him to dream up a plan. I briefly saw him from a distance after we arrived at Pusan, we were about to be moved up the line to relieve another regiment. Our eyes met; he was the one who looked away. The very next day he reported sick and was sent back to the UK, apparently suffering from a condition that prevented him sweating and that could be quite serious. However, I like to think that I was responsible and had got my own back. Would I have carried out my threat? I really have no idea; certainly if his persecution and victimization of me had continued, in all probability I would have been driven to it. It just goes to show that every man has a breaking point and that the old saying is probably true. The bully is a coward.

Korea had a climate that I had not experienced before. At the time we arrived there it was summer and quite hot. There were very few metalled roads, most of them being flattened earth packed down hard; it needed constant grading to fill in the potholes and make it a serviceable surface.

During the war, a constant stream of supplies was ferried forward to the front by heavy lorries; it was the only method available. They stirred up a dust cloud so thick that the second and all the other vehicles that followed could only see the road with great difficulty, and convoys would arrive at their destinations with the drivers covered in a white choking dust, with mouths, noses, ears and eyes gummed up with it, mostly American, because they were by far the largest contingent fighting there. They had a horrible task of making long daily runs re-supplying the forward troops with the necessities of war.

Being a United Nations force, there were troops from various nations all working together. One of the transport companies was from New Zealand. They were mostly all Maori drivers, and all carried a crate of beer in the cab with them and though they might arrive slightly the worse for wear in the sobriety stakes, they succeeded in damping down the dust in the cab considerably, and always made it to their destination. They were a great crowd and made beautiful music singing Maori songs whenever they got the opportunity.

There had been heavy fighting up and down the length of Korea and it had reached stalemate, the UN forces could not finish the job, neither were the North Koreans very successful despite all the help they had been getting from the Chinese army. A very uneasy temporary truce had been called whilst north and south negotiated a permanent border along the 38th parallel. All fighting ceased, and it was hoped that at last, a final solution was in sight.

In the meantime during the lull, everyone took advantage of the breather to make friendly visits to neighbouring units. We were very popular with the American army because we found that we had goods they wanted and vice versa. We were very surprised to see that the US Army food rations included what seemed to British eyes, great delicacies, for instance turkey and chicken were issued almost on demand, not canned but virtually oven-ready. Ice cream in all the various flavours was also in abundance; there were many other items of food commonplace to them but almost fairy tale and absolutely never ever seen by us.

If we had occasion to visit, and we made sure that we did, the friendly generous hospitality we always received at their hands was really something to experience. At meal times our men, quite naturally to the

Americans, were invited to partake in chow time. I have stated elsewhere, no nation looked after its forces better than the Americans, they had the best of everything. Their food was vastly superior to ours, indeed to any I had previously experienced, our men's eyes virtually popped out of their heads when they saw what was in front of them, a line of tables end to end about eighty feet or so long loaded with food of all kinds. Sections with different meats hot and cold, another with fish, a host of vegetarian dishes and innumerable others. Potatoes for instance were chipped, mashed, boiled, roast, sliced, fried and cooked in different ways and available hot or cold, salads and other foods quite unknown to us were on display to try or leave according to one's fancy; it was an Aladdin's cave of culinary delight. Desserts also in endless variety took up a whole section on their own.

Mostly it was a help yourself situation, but there were available a large number of clean white-coated chefs ready to offer help or advice if required, and serving up some dishes to help the queue along. And these were wartime conditions, albeit away from the front line, but it was quite normal for them and such a contrast from the good old British Compo rations of bully beef, stewed steak or meat and veg. together with a packet of Hard Tack (hard dry biscuits issued in place of bread). Oh, our rations were full of nutrition and plentiful enough, but one could only make a stew of it and our potatoes were vile, ask any serviceman what his thoughts on Pom were, that was the name it had. It was a dried sliced brownish grey substance, a bit like strips of rubbery plastic, reconstituted into potatoes by mixing it with boiling water, milk powder and adding butter and seasoning.

Some of our cooks did quite a good job and produced a fair imitation of mashed potatoes, but there were few that ate it. It had a smell and taste of its own and was generally disliked. In view of this, very little was prepared, and large piles of tins each about the size of a four gallon jerry can could be seen stacked up outside the cookhouse. Unwanted Pom.

Strange as it might seem, we discovered that the Americans wanted Pom and could not get enough of it; surely they did not use it for potatoes? I never did find out why they were so keen on it, but I think they used it in making cake. Anyway we didn't care, we had an abundant supply and when the word got round, truckloads of Pom were driven to our American friends and bartered for turkey, chicken, ice cream and other goodies. Both parties were well satisfied with the trade and it continued until we left Korea.

In the matter of hard liquor too, our Allies could not get enough. It was not issued to their forces on active service whereas we could get unlimited quantities and so that became a popular trading item too.

I rather liked the Americans, they have an inbuilt aggressive attitude to life that makes them appear in British eyes to be braggarts, but they are not really like that. Rather I tend to think they are extroverted optimists, their culture and way of life has instilled a need in them to prove that they are successful, whereas our culture has taught us a more unassuming and modest attitude. That is why, I believe, we get mistaken impressions of them.

I have to smile inwardly even now after all these years when I think about some of their camps in Korea. One could be driving along through open country and come upon perhaps a Transportation unit. The men would be sleeping in tents in a rough active service situation, vehicles would be drawn up in immaculate lines in a separate compound and parked in front of a marquee used for stores, and the whole camp would be surrounded by a barbed wire fence three metres high. The entrance however would have the appearance of the set of a Hollywood epic.

Built to a height of twenty feet, a huge board bridges the whole width of the entrance to the camp, colourfully decorated, resplendent as a sunrise, and boldly declaring to the world at large that this was the home of the 'FLYING 78th' or some such unit:

THE BEST GODDAMN TRANSPORTATION UNIT IN KOREA

The board would also state various things pertaining to the efficiency and combat readiness of the unit. A bit flamboyant to the British eye but quite normal to them. They were not backward in advertising themselves and I expect that they found the British reserve just as strange.

As time progressed, and there seemed there might be a likely solution to end the struggle, we set about making life more comfortable for ourselves. We acquired Quonset huts, a semicircular lined corrugated iron building that was infinitely better than a tent, and built them in our camps. We divided them into small compartments housing two senior NCOs and in we moved. All over the camp, the building continued until eventually everyone was housed in a Quonset.

Tents had their use of course and were fine in the summer, but with the onset of winter they were totally inadequate, heated by what was known as a Chuffer, a petrol fuelled and very dangerous form of heating where the petrol dropped on to a hot plate, was ignited and evaporated instantly as it did so. The ensuing heat would turn the body of the fire, and part of the chimney red hot which intensified or diminished according to how the fire was controlled. When running properly it would set up a peculiar chuffing noise, hence its name, but many a tent went up in flames when Chuffers went out of control. More sensible oil heaters were issued for use in the Quonset huts, they were much safer.

The problem was the weather. Summers were hot and dry, yet permafrost was ever present, and at a depth of six feet or so, items could be stored permanently as in a deep freezer that was always available and required no maintenance or power to run it.

The winter was a different matter. We had been issued with Arctic clothing consisting of woollen underwear over which one wore a string vest and fur lined trousers. Over this came the normal khaki shirt, blouse and trousers followed by wind-proofed jacket and trousers. On the feet we wore special oversized boots with insoles worn with two pairs of socks. On our hands we had three pairs of gloves, silk, wool and wind-proof. On top of it all, if the weather was at all bad, we wore a parka that came to below the knees with a hood that could be closed up to a small slit to see through. The clothes were bulky, how could it be otherwise? But it really was efficient and warm, it was first class. Orders were issued that no drinking was allowed in winter: if one fell down drunk and was unable to get up again, one would surely die from exposure.

One evening our Sergeants' mess was invited along to a neighbouring unit of the Black Watch of Canada for a social evening. They too had been building Quonset huts and their new mess was in one of them. As was the custom, we were plied with free drink and we spent a very pleasant evening. Two of our number, a Sergeant Major and a Sergeant were especially the worse for wear.

This particular Quonset had been built on a hill. Access to it was by means of a winding dirt road up which we had driven in our one-tonne truck. In front of the entrance to the Mess was an area of five feet by twenty. So five feet from the door was a 30 foot drop. The building really should have been erected at right angles to its present position, the drop would not have been a danger then.

Not that it proved to be much of a danger now because the Sergeant Major, in very good voice and much the worse for wear, staggered drunkenly out of the Mess singing away to his heart's content, continued forward and walked over the edge. Had a sober person done it he would have probably finished up with a broken leg at least. On this occasion the Sergeant Major landed on his feet still singing, and without any break in his song acted with no more surprise than as if he had stepped off a pavement. He never did believe he went over the edge when the event was later recalled.

What was really serious though was what followed. As the truck arrived back at our camp everyone jumped off and made straight for their beds. Oblivious to the plight of the Sergeant Major and his equally drunk companion, the more sober revellers forgot about the two left on the floor of the truck in the darkness, out for the count, and just continued back to their quarters.

The two men were found several hours later in the early morning by a passing sentry. He heard the sound of moaning coming from the truck, and investigating, discovered the two frozen stiff, and almost by now dead, bodies.

The guard commander walked and ran and pummelled the two men; he would not let them rest, pouring hot coffee down their throats and repeating the rough treatment, he eventually got some life back into their frozen bodies. They had been very lucky, had they not been discovered, there is no doubt that they would have frozen to death, only the prompt treatment given by the guard commander saved them. They had not even suffered any frostbite, toes, fingers, noses and ears were all OK. I reckon they were so pickled in drink that the cold had no effect on them.

Another very pleasant experience was when we were invited to spend a weekend on board HMS *Birmingham*, Flagship of the British fleet in Korea. A limited number of naval personnel exchanged places with an army unit. They stayed in our camp, and we went aboard ship in their place. I rather enjoyed the type of discipline used in the navy, it seemed to me that men were more responsible for their own way of life, everyone had a job to do, they knew what it was, and reported for duty at the right time; they were not supervised as much. Perhaps I should have joined the navy.

Extra rum rations appeared from somewhere: my word, what back-bracing stuff that navy rum is! Normal commercial stuff is like babies' gripe water when compared to the real stuff and our hosts were very generous with it; we had all that we could drink.

It seemed to me that after a certain amount had been consumed, the eyes rolled inward and became crossed for the duration of its influence. I have never actually proved that theory, perhaps I will one day, all I can say is that something strange happened and that it lasted a long while.

We watched the gun drill, Navy versus Royal Marines. Cool, efficient and fast, they handed the shells and explosives up to service the guns. These were quite heavy but they made the job seem effortless keeping up a steady rhythm. No wonder British Naval gunnery was the best in the world. Trafalgar, the River Plate, and all those countless battles were won with gunnery skills, and as I watched those gun teams I thought My God! I wouldn't like to be on the receiving end of this lot.

Back in camp after our brief respite, the normal time of first parade in the winter was 9.30 a.m. It was too cold to get up very early. We had wonderful sleeping bags filled with down and of excellent quality as indeed was all our kit. It was quite true that at the lower winter temperatures, well below freezing, a boiling mug of tea would become a block of ice in no time at all, fountain pens were useless because the ink in them froze. Life was almost brought to a standstill in such cold weather.

There was one bright spot that we looked forward to and that was R & R leave which was taken in Japan. Supposed to be for rest and recuperation, it was anything but that. Whilst many used the few days of their leave up in sight-seeing, and other such occupations, the vast majority, as soldiers have ever done, were intent on the high life, wine, women and song being their main interest. As the leave centre was in Tokyo, there was ample night life and entertainment of every kind to satisfy all tastes.

I wanted to see some of the sights, as I had my doubts that I would ever get to see Japan after we returned home, the expense would probably be beyond me: get around and see everything you can, I told myself. I visited the arena to watch the Sumo wrestling, I climbed up inside the great Kamakura Buddha, visited theatres and temples, saw where the Kamikaze pilots spent their last days before flying to death and everlasting glory. I looked upon the immaculate beauty of Mount Fuji, and I wondered how such a gentle and courteous race of people could show such savagery in wartime.

The answer of course is that people change under the leadership of ambitious men. They are constantly fed propaganda and lies about their enemies until fear becomes the dominant factor in their minds; combine that with the military traditions, so long a part of their history, their natural obedience to their king and authority, stoke up bad feelings about the enemy, and hatred will soon replace rational thinking. They are then easily led along the path required by their leaders. Hatred of the enemy is regularly fuelled, and the natural obedience to authority ensures that the population is compliant.

I had three leave periods in Japan, we flew from American air bases. It was a trip of two or three hours and I was very attracted by the country. The climate was mild and apart from the occasional earth tremors, sometimes actual quakes, it seemed a very pleasurable country. I would look down from the plane as it flew over villages and towns, the flights were usually made at night, and I would gaze at the twinkling lights of the habitations as we passed over. The effect was beautiful, especially if there happened to be a full moon.

Travelling around the country was very pleasurable. Everywhere the people took great care in the design of their gardens whatever size they were, large or small they were always beautifully maintained and a delight to the eye. Some of the customs were strange: they had a habit of nodding when they meant no, and shaking the head when they meant yes. There was also the polite bowing. They would meet up with an acquaintance and pass the time of day, there followed a continual spate of endless bowing to each other, which went on for several minutes until they parted. Apparently the superior being would receive the deeper and greater number of bows. To our eyes it could be quite comical, but to them the matter of custom and respect involved was all important. They are undoubtedly the cleanest people I have ever come across and seemed to take advantage of every spare moment to take hot baths. Every hotel and establishment had its own bath, they were the size of a small swimming pool. There were also public baths everywhere, and the whole family would attend and enjoy the occasion regularly.

Western modesty was entirely out of place, nudity had no effect on the bathers, and they took no notice of the nervous giggling of Europeans. Having stripped off, one went to a part of the baths where hot water was ladled over the body, one then soaped up and scrubbed oneself clean and then ladled more hot water over oneself from the same tub to rinse off the soap and lather. It was not allowed to enter the large main public bath until the scrubbing had been completed, and the dirty water and soap rinsed off.

Chapter Twenty-one

Most public baths employed several older grandmothers, who for a modest payment would actually do the scrubbing and rinsing down for you; it required very little effort, and because the water was so very hot, the feeling was one of relaxation and contentment. One could of course also have a massage, most of the boys had at least one complete treatment during their short leave; you hadn't lived until you had the complete bath and massage treatment, at least that was the general opinion, and a certain amount of barracking accompanied returnees from leave in Japan.

Chapter Twenty-two

PEACE FINALLY APPEARED TO BE HOLDING, life drifted into a series of military exercises to test readiness for the fighting should it recommence; there was also increased social activity in the number of invitations to attend neighbouring units for social evenings. A kind of rivalry sprang up between the various units as to who could put on the best show, and which regiment had the better entertainment etc. It was all interesting stuff and very popular.

The Dorset Regiment had the dubious honour to have been the first infantry regiment to serve in India back in the early days of the foundation of the Empire and it was on one of the voyages carrying the regiment to this new acquisition that a serious fire broke out on board. There were only sailing ships at this period in our history and a fire was a serious matter. The little ship was called the *Sarah Sands* and she carried the whole regiment and the wives and families. Such a fire could easily have destroyed the ship and her passengers as was frequently the case when serious fires took hold.

A Sergeant took charge of the fire fighting operations and managed to save the regimental colours and the ship; it burned for four days before the fire was finally extinguished and his name lives on in the history books. His bravery is celebrated annually by the regiment in the form of a parade, a holiday, and a social evening or some kind of mess function every year. It takes place in the Sergeants' mess, because the hero of the occasion had been an NCO. Normally it was nothing very grand, just a small buffet and a drink

This time however, a plan was devised to lay on a very special function. Invitations were to be forwarded to Allied units all over Korea. This was to be an occasion that no one would forget, our rival regiments were to be shown a function to be remembered which could not possibly be bettered. Out went specially printed invitations to hundreds of guests ranking from senior NCOs upward, including officers of Allied forces as well as all the British regiments, requesting their presence at a small soiree, celebrating the annual regimental holiday of the *Sarah Sands,* to be held in the Sergeants' Mess. If I remember correctly, an account of the heroic incident was also printed on the invitation. It would be the Cook Sergeant's job to prepare and produce the buffet ordinarily, but nothing would be allowed to stand in his way, and he would be given everything he required to produce a first-class table. He was a fine Chef anyway, but he would be able to call upon all the Chefs from the Officers' Mess and as many of the cooks as he needed.

A special committee was set up to discuss and plan the event and the menu. An officer with the right connections became the supplies chef, and would obtain all the turkeys, chicken, ham and other ingredients required by the chef. Ample time was allowed for the operation so that it would all go without a hitch. Extra marquees were erected and filled with tables and chairs obtained from who knows where, fine linen tablecloths and some of the best regimental silver pieces and tableware were used; it would be a magnificent sight and a magnificent buffet.

It was inevitable I suppose that somewhere along the line I would become involved. As the Assault Pioneer Sergeant I was in charge of the explosives, and the obvious choice for the job. With such a high powered committee, someone would be sure to have a bright idea and think of enhancing the evening by re-producing a replica of the burning *Sarah Sands* that would quietly stand outside in a prominent place, burning throughout the festivities. It was a fairly easy matter to reproduce a model of the ship, there were records of how she looked, but it was quite a different matter to set it on fire and keep it burning for some hours; it was likely to catch fire and destroy itself.

The idea having been mooted, I was ordered to take charge of this particular operation and devise the method to satisfy the requirements of the burning ship. Our Pioneer Sergeant produced a fine model of the ship, it was about five feet long and I asked him to keep the hold empty so that I could work out how best to control the fire.

Much thought and experimentation was carried out in the days leading up to the event; the ship had to burn continuously for four hours, but how to control it? That was the rub. Eventually we decided to use slow burning fuse. Critical lengths were cut and rolled and placed in a circular tin, one end of the fuse led from the tin and through a hole in the side of the model; we repeated this until the hold was filled with tins and a large number of fuse ends protruded out of one side of the ship.

Our experiments had shown that one fuse would burn for four minutes, but with a few holes in the tins, would continue to smoke for a further ten minutes at least. Hurrah! We had success, a fairly lifelike burning ship with smoke rising continuously.

The model was to be placed outside where the light was dim. It was positioned on a table close to thick bushes in which lurked my North Devon storeman. His job was to control the fire on board and light a new fuse when the smoke was in danger of dying out. He was supposed to light the fuse to a tin that was placed as far away as possible to the one that was burning at the moment, hopefully to allow the heat to die down. If two neighbouring tins had been lit one after the other the ensuing heat could really burn the ship out. It was a question of fine judgement and as I had promised the storeman I would keep his supply of ale coming, I wondered if his consumption might overtake his timing and a real fire start when his brain became fuddled. I also promised him a bonus payment if things went well, this being designed to prevent him from getting too drunk. As I occasionally went over to check how things were going, I would be met by a hiss from the bushes, and reminded that his ale supply was running low.

I have to say that it was a great success for most of the time but as the evening wore on, and with the lighting of each successive fuse, the heat generated in that small model increased to the point of instantaneous combustion and I was informed that the *Sarah Sands* was really on fire. It had done the job perfectly for most of the evening and I decided that its purpose had been met: the majority of our guests had seen it when it was doing exactly what we wanted, and nothing was to be gained at this late stage by attempting to save her.

Handing yet another two cans of beer to the storeman, I told him to let the model burn out, and when it was safe he could leave. It did not take long; he damped the embers down with water, and left with a distinct slur in his voice, saying that on the whole he had enjoyed the evening very much, and that he would always be available for duties like this if needed.

The evening was a great success. The guests had not been told beforehand that it was going to be such a grand affair, so their surprise at what they saw had a tremendous effect. The food had been prepared by experienced chefs, the quality was superb, and there was an endless supply of cakes and pastries and all the goodies one could wish to see, and it could not have been planned and executed better anywhere. Our foreign guests were dumbfounded and our rival regiments envious. There was no shortage of food and drink, we received many a compliment that night. I would bet that it was to be a never forgotten experience for most of those attending. It was well into the early hours of next morning before the last of the guests fell into their vehicles and made their way back to their units, still expressing compliments and thanks.

An uneasy peace had finally materialised, the eighth Parallel became the fixed border between North and South Korea, and we looked forward to the time when we would be ordered back home again. We had been away three years and that was the normal period for an overseas posting. We spent some time shooting pheasant but the damned birds persisted in living in the live minefields, so even if one got a good shot off, it would seem to struggle and arrange its demise just out of reach in the minefield itself, and we had to leave them more often than not.

Having outsmarted our best efforts to knobble them, I know that those birds (and they were magnificent specimens, none of your old scraggy, beaten up varieties here). Frequently, as many as five or six would parade up and down in the minefields near enough to torment us, but right at the edge of the distance inside the minefield beyond which it was prudent not to go. They could read our minds, and would not venture one inch our side of the safety line. They would call to us and taunt us and strut up and down with inflated chests as if to say, 'You can't get us here, pal, so up yours.' We were forced to accept final and humiliating defeat and seek some other form of recreation.

Our replacements arrived and we handed over stores and huts to the newcomers, a Scottish Regiment. There was a tragedy one night involving one of their senior NCOs who having drunk more than he should, thought he had put his portable oil fire out for the night but had not actually done so. The subsequent fire spread to his bedclothes and wooden partitions, and in nine minutes the whole building was a mass of flames; unfortunately he did not survive. There were good reasons for the strict fire precautions and the rigid rules. I think that it was sad that a life should have been lost that night, but the lesson learned was a vital one and greater care thereafter prevented other tragedies.

The dreary six week voyage finally got us home. It had not been as enjoyable as the outward journey because we had seen it all before and were retracing our steps. We were anxious to see our wives and families again, and enjoy the long leave that we knew was owed us.

Normally when a unit returned home from foreign service they would be sent straight away on leave for six to eight weeks after which they would report back to a depot or camp. At the time about which I am writing, Conscription was still in force, and there were quite a number of National Servicemen in the Regiment. Those that had finished their time were sent home, and others joined us from the training depots. Most of the senior ranks were posted off to units doing various jobs all over the country and it could be some years before one met up with old friends again.

There were literally dozens of jobs, PSIs to the Territorial army. Instructors at depots, working in store establishments and a host of others, all postings away from the Regiment for three years, some of which were plum jobs, given as a reward for good service. I was posted to Arborfield, a training establishment for Junior leaders. Here, boy soldiers learned all about army life, became trained soldiers and on reaching manhood would be inducted into the army proper. Many of them had received training in specialist careers, Engineers or Armourers, Radio or Radar specialists, Vehicle mechanics or one of the skilled trades; it was a good system, useful to the army and the soldier. The army built a continuous supply of future experts and the lads started out on a useful career; all the services had their own Junior training establishments.

There was not much wrong with Arborfield, except that the orderly room was run by a particularly unpleasant little Welsh corporal, who wielded his power in a small minded vicious little way. Having presented myself there for orders, he busied himself making inaudible mutterings and giving no indication as to where I should report, or what I should do. I patiently and politely waited for well over an hour without any word or gesture from him so I asked him again; he muttered something about waiting, and the ignorant man kept me hanging about for yet another hour. Now I realised that he was trying to humiliate me: I had to understand that he was the one with the power and I must learn to accept it. Once the penny had dropped, my blood boiled and I gave him the biggest rollicking he had ever had in his slimy little life. I was a regular serving soldier just back home from active service in Korea. How dare he treat me that way?

He had wormed his way into a favourable position over a number of years, in a quiet backwater where he could build his little empire and rule it from a fairly secure position. He ran the orderly room, the heart of the unit where he could learn all about the postings in and out, read all the files about everyone in the unit and manipulate others as he desired. Such units are run normally without interference from COs. Just as long as things went smoothly, such men make themselves indispensable to their superiors, who are normally happy to have what they believe is an efficient chief clerk able to run the unit virtually alone.

This clerk also had the dubious distinction of being the Band leader and Conductor to the very fifth rate and noisy drum and bugle band created by the junior leaders. It was horrible, it made up with excessive drum noise all it lacked in musical ability; to me it was rubbish and when I told him so I committed the unpardonable sin. Anyway, I told him that I would wait in my quarters, I was not going to stand around like a spare pratt at a wedding until he condescended to deal with me.

I knew that I would not be happy there and requested my Adjutant to remove me from the posting which he did. Instead, I was posted PSI to 'C' Co. The 4th Dorsets TA, their headquarters being in Wareham.

I had no idea what to expect or what I would have to do in this new job, but I found the officers and men very friendly. They had an attitude to life that reflected their status as volunteers, proud of their history and the fine record of service to their country that nearly all the Terriers had; after all, they had been among the first to be called to action in the war, and remembering the old adage, that one volunteer is worth ten pressed men, I soon realised that these were a special breed.

My first impression was that there was no discipline, or at least not very much. These ordinary working chaps would turn up on drill nights, wearing civilian clothes, go straight to the bar for a drink, call their NCOs Jack and Bill, seldom seemed to be military minded in any way, and yet there was something about them that demanded respect. It was a little while before I realised that they were of course civilians first, and soldiers only when on parade, whereas I was a soldier all the time.

My job entailed administration, recording attendances at parades, seeing to the pay, and preparing training programmes for the company. I had the help of a civilian storeman who cared for the weapons and the vehicles. Part of my duties included a weekly visit to Dorchester where I and all the instructors from the other companies assembled for conferences with the Quartermaster, Training Officer and the CO. All regular soldiers, of course. Here we received orders relating to the unit for future events.

The vehicles we were responsible for at our Drill Halls were a Bren gun carrier, a one-tonne truck, a motorcycle and a bicycle, all of which had to be frequently used and maintained in good working order; none of them were to be left idle for any long period. Needless to say the most used vehicle was the one-tonne truck which allowed some comfort and protection from the weather and it was with reluctance that we used the carrier or motorcycle, although one could have a very enjoyable afternoon taking the carrier over the rough tank training area nearby. It was tempered by the fact that it was necessary to spend some hours cleaning the blessed things afterwards. We all lied about the bicycle, it had no speedometer and therefore no way of recording the mileage. Mine hung in the garage and I don't recall it ever being moved during my stay at Wareham.

On one occasion when the one-tonner had to go back to the workshops for a major repair, it was replaced temporarily with a huge 10-ton vehicle. I was not used to driving such a large heavy lorry but I was forced to use it on my weekly visit to headquarters in Dorchester as I had stores to pick up. I drove to the compound and parked neatly behind the storeman's brand new moped right outside the stores.

I collected my kit and completed my work there and climbed back up into the cab of the lorry. It was about eight feet from the ground and the seating was set back from the windscreen, giving a first-class view of the road ahead, but unfortunately none at all of that brand new moped parked just forward of my front nearside wheel.

Not having it in view of course made me forget it was there, and as I pulled slowly away, I heard shouts and saw frantic gesturing from the storeman and several other people in the vicinity. Yes, I had mangled the moped into a semi-circular heap of metal suitable only for the scrap heap. Was my face red, and my friends did not let me forget the incident. However all was forgiven when some time later, the storeman produced a new replacement. I noticed that he never parked it on the road again, and who can blame him?

One other and more pleasurable event took place when the company rifle team went to a meeting at Bisley. They returned triumphantly, winners of a shooting event called 'The China Cup'. Never before had the regiment won such a magnificent trophy. Silver of course and beautifully chased and carved, looking like something from the Orient, it was huge, over four feet high and about three feet wide and very heavy. It was displayed in shop windows in every town where the regiment had a company, and caused much interest, admiration and comment amongst the local population. It really was huge for a trophy, and seemed to fill the whole of the window in the shops where it was displayed.

I rather enjoyed the three year period I spent with the Terriers, but

Chapter Twenty-two

I was not sorry when the time came for me to hand over my responsibilities to my replacement. I was returning to the Battalion which was serving overseas and I looked forward with anticipation, eager to see a new country that I had not previously visited.

I was given a splendid farewell party, everyone having contributed toward the costs. An artist who played the piano had been engaged for

The China Cup,
won by Author's Company TA, G. Co. Dorset Regt.

the evening. When later on, everyone having downed a few jars, I remember this artist making the announcement, 'I will now play the piano with my nose,' this was followed by an immediate reply from someone in the audience, quite plain and with considerable volume, 'I thought you had been playing with your nose all evening.' There were hoots of laughter from the audience but he took it in good part and laughed along with the rest of us.

We had a very enjoyable evening and having said my farewells, I left with mixed feelings leaving behind some new friends and an insight into a fine body of volunteers always ready to serve their country should the occasion arise.

During my posting with the TA, I had been ordered to attend a course to learn about signaling. Apparently the regiment had need of a Signal Staff Sergeant, and it was to be me. For eight weeks I attended the Signal school at Hythe in Kent, and crammed my head with new facts so that I could on completion of the course, not only take up my new appointment, but also instruct others in the mysteries and uses of all the equipment involved.

I started at a disadvantage: all personnel attending the course were already trained signallers and were supposed to have all the rudimentary skills and knowledge, and be of a certain standard sufficiently high enough to qualify for the course. I had no knowledge whatever of the subject and was promptly returned to my unit as not having the basic knowledge to be able to complete the course successfully. There ensued an argument between the School of Signals and my regiment which must have been won by the regiment because I was promptly posted back to the school having missed by now one whole week of instruction, not a very good start.

For some weeks thereafter whilst others on the course were taking in the delights of the surrounding countryside, and enjoying evenings out partaking of the local brew, I was forced to spend every spare moment, not only learning the Morse Code, but also having to practise receiving and sending it.

In three short weeks I had to pass a test of eight words a minute minimum, both sending and receiving, or suffer the indignity of once again being returned to my unit having failed to reach the required standard.

All of this was in addition to learning new unfamiliar subjects daily, as well as having to catch up on the first week's tuition that I had missed. It was nothing short of a miracle that I finished the course at all especially when one remembers that all the other students were fully conversant with and had a good knowledge of the subject before they took the course. I don't know how I did it but I did, and I was pleased with my efforts, I came to like and enjoy the subject and looked forward to my new job.

Shortly thereafter I received my posting and spent a pleasant ten day cruise on the *Dilwara*, another of those troopships which plied back and forth across the far flung posts of the empire. It was a much improved ship from the *Empire Pride* that I had made my first voyage in; it had real beds, and a respectable mess deck where one could eat meals in a civilised manner.

On arrival at the port of Limassol in Cyprus, there were no docks and we anchored offshore in the harbour. Our kit was off loaded on to small boats which ferried us ashore, and from there it was but a short distance to the camp.

I found the climate to be pleasant if a little on the hot side, but almost every day a cooling breeze swept in from the sea across the island. At that time, the mid fifties, the island was still united, but dominated by the Greeks and ruled by Archbishop Makarios with the help of anti-British revolutionaries Grivas and his henchmen who were fighting for the independence of the island and causing much trouble with a campaign of bombing and shooting not only of military targets and personnel, but also of British civilians, army wives, and other soft targets.

Cyprus did eventually get its independence, but not before Makarios had been removed and exiled for some time in the Seychelles. Their rejoicing was shortlived because the mainland Turks, fearful of the Greek dominance in the island, and mindful of a sizeable minority of Turkish descendants who had for centuries been the poor underdogs in the island economy, invaded it with airborne and naval forces and took control. They partitioned Cyprus into two, basically the north and south, set up a military border and moved all the Greeks to the southern area and the Turks to the north. Their military presence is a large thorn in the side of all Greeks.

Turkey had for centuries made claim to the island, but it is doubtful they would ever have invaded if the Greeks had treated the Turkish minority properly and fairly, instead of allowing the more businesslike and domineering section of their people to control the lives of the less aggressive Turkish inhabitants. They should have treated them fairly and recognised their right to be equal citizens.

All this happened after I had left the island, but I had discussed the history and present state of things when I was there with both Greek and Turkish Cypriots. There were many long standing grievances held by the Turks, and no effort had been made by the Greeks to put matters right.

I found that the Greek Cypriots were very pleasant and hospitable. I could not agree with some of the things they did however. For instance they would not harm an animal, and would never put to sleep any unwanted kittens or puppies, as their religion precluded killing, but it was perfectly all right to put five or six unwanted puppies in a cardboard box, and leave them on the side of the road miles from anywhere where their certain death was assured if not from the terrific heat of the day, then eventually from starvation. The onus was on God to save them if that was what he wanted; as for the perpetrators, they had only put the box out with the helpless animals in it, they had not killed them and their hands were clean, it must have been God's will if they died.

Survivors and the progeny of older abandoned animals, and I am referring mostly to dogs, would form packs of anything from twenty upwards, I have seen one of forty running wild; they were a great danger to people but the authorities did not seem to be concerned and I never saw any action taken to deal with the problem whilst I was there.

These packs could and did survive. The fully grown animals had learned once again to attack and kill sheep for food and I was glad that their natural hunting instincts had returned. It was not their fault that their human masters had allowed the situation to get out of hand, they had to survive, and they did.

I understand now that the position of strays and abandoned animals has improved considerably in the last forty years, neither would it be fair to tar all the people with the same brush. It goes without saying that there are good and bad in every race of people, but the situation then was appalling, and the majority of domestic pets had a very raw deal.

The first indication of friendship or kindness to a stray dog would to be an open invitation that the person was available for adoption. The animal would sit outside the door of the house for hours if not days waiting for an appearance of the one that had shown it kindness; one opened the door next morning to be greeted by a demented tail-wagging creature frantic for just a word or some indication of friendliness, and of course feeding the animal with a few left-over scraps was fatal; now it would never leave, and one became the owner of a dog.

I named one such dog Harry, he was a mongrel and had a body and head something like a spaniel. He just turned up one day and I gave him a pat, whereupon he just lay down by the back door and would not budge. Apart from the odd scrap, I never fed him and he lay there for days. My will power in the end was non existent; whenever I opened the door he was there waiting for me. One would have to be heartless to ignore him, his devotion and loyalty gradually wore my resistance down and unable to stand the situation any longer, I called him into the house and fed him.

He just went berserk, somehow he knew that he had acquired an owner and thereafter would not leave my side. I was often asked what method I had used to train my dog it was so obedient, and my reply to the astonished questioner was, 'I just feed him.' It was very amusing to see and hear him as I prepared his food. I would buy scraps of meat and cook the lot up together with vegetables; to this I added a proprietary brand of dog meal and biscuits. He knew of course that I was preparing food for him and he would sit beside me looking up and letting out heartrending whimpers and cries, and his teeth just chattered non-stop. One would have thought someone was playing castanets. He had never known food prepared for him before and in the past had probably existed on what scraps he could find. Certainly he had been starving when he found me. I would put his food down and he would ravenously devour the lot, he would lick the dish spotless pushing it all round the kitchen in his efforts to glean every last morsel.

I had put an old blanket in a box for his bed, and after thanking me by trying to lick my face all over, he would lie in his bed and sleep the rest of the day away, occasionally letting out huge sighs of contentment.

Most service personnel living in civilian accommodation as I was, did exactly the same as me and usually finished up with one or more pets. Quite a number paid to take their animals back to the UK after they had finished their tour of duty, these were the lucky ones. I was sorry to lose Harry; he had to be put to sleep, his former way of life had taken its toll and he became very ill. The vet advised me that he would not recover. At least I had given him food and happiness in his last few years, and I consoled myself with the thought that if I had not taken him in when I did, he could not have survived much longer.

Life in a foot regiment is very much the same whatever the regiment, and we like others carried out various exercises all over the island, training and maintaining outposts so that we would be prepared in the event of the troubles ever starting up again. However there was less chance of this ever recurring now that independence had been granted, and life gradually reverted to a more normal and peaceful existence. We still carried out exercises and manoeuvres but now in North Africa, in Libya in fact which was friendly to the British at the time. I took every opportunity to see the sights and enjoyed visiting the well preserved ruins of Cyrene, and the underwater city of Appolonia.

I was amazed at the knowledge and skills of the Ancient Romans who over 2,000 years before had during their occupation of the area, built a vast system of irrigation channels to carry water for hundreds of miles across this mostly barren part of North Africa adjacent to the Mediterranean, linking the towns and cities, and providing watering holes for the population, mostly wandering nomads and their animals, and including the ever inexhaustible camel trains and merchants of one kind or another. This water system was so well built that it is still in constant use today.

Chapter Twenty-three

THE GOVERNMENT OF THE DAY, in their wisdom, had decided to make drastic cuts in defence spending. This resulted in the amalgamation of many fine regiments and made a large number of serving servicemen redundant and surplus to requirement. I still had five years to serve in order to complete my contract. There followed, in my mind, a struggle and a problem: should I stay in the service which I loved, or should I come out?

As much as I hated the thought of civvy street, it seemed obvious that I would be infinitely better off leaving the army now. I would receive my full pension, and gain the benefit of a five year start in finding work and settling down. Obviously my chances of obtaining work as a younger man were far better, and there was one other factor: volunteers accepting redundancy would be eligible for a handy lump sum payment. There was an obvious favourable side to leaving with hardly anything to gain by staying and so I opted to leave.

My application for redundancy was accepted, and thinking that this might well be my last chance of any other real adventure in my life, I decided that I would like to drive my wife and myself back to the UK. Sort of a last fling. I planned to get to Greece and drive across Europe through Yugoslavia, Austria, Germany and then across the channel by ferry and home. I put no time limit on the journey and intended to play the whole thing by ear so I arranged shipment of my car, baggage and bodies to Greece. My wife and I then purchased the appropriate maps and spent some time planning our route home; we had a lot of fun preparing for the trip.

Having sought and obtained permission to make the journey home in this manner, I was required to get passports, and I needed a visa to travel through Yugoslavia so I went to the Yugoslav consulate in Nicosia where I was thoroughly questioned about my reasons for wanting to travel in their country. My answers must have satisfied the consulate because my passport and visa were stamped and we were all set to go.

There is no dockside in the port of Limassol; transfer of people and goods are effected by small boats ferrying from ship to shore and vice versa so my fully loaded car was driven on to a wooden platform fixed on top of the gunwales of a small boat. I was very fearful for its safety because it seemed precariously perched up above the gunwales and looked quite top heavy and unstable. It looked bad enough lying in the relatively still water close to the dock side, but what about when it headed out to the ship, it was a fair distance away and the sea was somewhat rougher out in the harbour? To put the cap on it, I was dismayed to see that the boat was powered by six oarsmen, there was no engine, the hazardous journey to the ship would take at least three quarters of an hour and even if it reached the ship safely, my car had to be off-loaded through a very small and inadequate looking hole in the side of the ship which was itself only a small one.

We were thankful to find that we were not expected to travel with the car, but went on ahead in another ferry where we boarded the ship. My wife went to our small cabin, and I waited at the side of the ship's rail anxiously watching my precious car and all our kit slowly approach the side. I almost had a heart attack and nervous breakdown simultaneously as the small boat was manoeuvred into position so that the car could be driven from the boat and through the opening on to the mother ship. Since the waves lifted the small boat up and down, and the larger vessel was not affected by the movement, considerable skill was required to time the exact moment for the car to be driven from the boat, through the opening and on to the mother ship. As the boat with my car lifted up and down with the waves, the size of the opening was reduced considerably and I had grave doubts if the transfer could be effected without the car sustaining some damage.

Reduced by now to a gibbering idiot, I watched with horror as the operation continued with much waving of arms and shouting, everyone seemed to be giving orders at the same time, and I could visualise disaster. I was quite unable to look any longer and turned my head away to await the crunch that I was sure would happen. I heard my car engine revving, and when I could bring myself to look again, there was the car safely parked in its position on the ship for the voyage, the transfer having been completed without serious mishap. There was a scratch or two on the car but nothing serious; however it was a severe and stressful time and I don't think I will ever use that mode of travel again.

The ship was very small and plied its trade around the Greek islands, into the sunny Mediterranean as far as Cyprus and back again. The Greek islands were beautiful, and we enjoyed the three day voyage it took to get us to Piraeus, except for the food. Not that there was anything wrong with it, but it was a Greek boat and served Greek food with which we were not particularly enamoured. The real problem was that we did not speak Greek, or the crew English, and so were unable to convey our requirements, however we managed very well and arrived without harm at this port nearest to Athens. The car and our gear were unloaded with far less trouble because we were tied up in harbour, and a crane transferred it straight to the dock side. At last we were now completely independent of the travel agent and could proceed at our own speed. We spent some time viewing the sights. The Acropolis and Parthenon looked exactly as they were in the photographs, but I hated the crowds and bustle of the city and headed north for the Greek border and Yugoslavia.

I had been warned that there really were bandits in the mountain regions, waiting to waylay tourists and unsuspecting travelers; although they seldom harmed anyone physically, they would and did rob every person they came across. To counteract this danger it was my intention to camp at suitable spots along the route I had chosen, stopping only when we felt tired or hungry and thus avoiding any semblance of a regular routine and denying any crook the chance to plan a mugging. On those occasions where we stopped for a brief rest in a town or village to partake of a coffee or take on petrol, I never disclosed my intended route, but let it be believed that we were just touring round the area and not heading for any particular town.

I carried a tent, but more often than not we would sleep in the car. I would choose a wooded area if possible where the car could be nicely tucked away and invisible from the road, such as it was.

I would stop where I fancied, having made sure that there were no other vehicles in sight and always in isolated or very thinly populated areas. I would be searching for such a spot maybe for an hour as I drove along and when I thought there were no villages or other habitation and having checked my map I would pull in off the road and out of sight, switch off my engine and wait for ten minutes or so. If I saw or heard anyone, I would drive off again and repeat the performance after a few miles until I was satisfied it was safe to stop. I would park the car so that I could drive away without any delay if necessary. It might seem to have been over cautious of me, but I knew that there was a real danger and always thought, better safe than sorry. I carried a pick helve with me in the car and was determined to give a good account of myself if we were ever threatened.

Eventually, I would get out of the car, unpack my trusty cooker which travelled everywhere with me, and light it up. It was very compact and would fit very easily into my pack and would boil a couple of pints of water in as many minutes almost. I very soon had a hot brew going, and would at the same time heat water for soup or a stew for the evening meal.

There was no need for a fire; it was summertime and the nights were warm. I always parked in the vicinity of a stream whenever possible, and we would strip off and bathe in the freezing water that was running straight off the mountains. It was a Spartan experience it was so cold but nevertheless very refreshing to soap and soak away the dust and grime of the long hot day. After drying and dressing it was marvellous, and we would know a wonderful feeling of peace and contentment as we lay in our sleeping bags gazing up at the early evening stars. I was very content with my lot, and we would drift into untroubled sleep.

Before I knew it I was wide awake; it seemed that I had only been asleep for a few minutes yet over eight hours had passed. It is very rare to experience such trouble-free nights, but they were quite frequent now and we would sleep the sleep of innocents, deep and refreshing. My internal alarm woke me at five a.m. It still does. I would rise, carry out my ablutions, make another hot brew, pack up and drive away still heading north. We spent three nights altogether in Greece and passed through the country without any problems at all. We saw no bandits, not even in the mountains, and those people we did come across were mostly very friendly peasants, interested and curious about us and generally pleased to see us. Mind you, we had not advertised our presence. Things might have been different if people knew of our route and plans and I had been careful to keep those to myself.

Friends of ours who had also decided to make their own way back to the UK did not camp out but preferred to spend their nights in hotels. One such night in central Greece they pulled into the yard of a hotel where they had booked accommodation for the night, and having been reassured by the hotel staff that their car and kit would be OK, and quite safe, they took a small overnight bag with them and left the bulk of their luggage on the car. As they were about to leave the next morning, they found that all their luggage was gone, and the car had been stripped of seats and wheels, all of their possessions were gone, and the car was not capable of being driven anywhere. The only response that the unfortunate owners could get from the hotel staff was a shrug of the shoulders and the word 'Bandits'.

Chapter Twenty-three

The police took statements, but it was apparent that nothing could or would be done. My friends made other transport arrangements, not without some difficulty I gather, but they never did recover any of their luggage, or any compensation from the hotel, who would not accept any liability for the loss. I was so pleased that I had taken the precautions I did.

I realised that we were nearing the Greek/Yugoslav border. The road deteriorated from a poor metalled fourth rate lane into an even poorer pot-holed track, the countryside became wilder and desolate, and we were astonished to see dozens of tortoises plodding up and down and across the track; it must have been their natural habitat. I don't know how they survived, there was hardly any vegetation and no water that I could see. They ranged in size from quite small, perhaps 6 inches long and 5 inches across the shell, up to huge animals bigger than a football, in fact they looked like a lot of moving footballs as they plodded around. I have never ever seen such a large number concentrated in one relatively small area before and most likely never will again. They were so thick on the ground that I had to drive very slowly and with great care so as not to run over them.

We turned a corner at the bottom of a hill and there was the Greek border post. At first I thought that it was not manned but there was a steel barrier across the road and we had to stop anyway. I collected my documents up together and walked over to the post; it was a small wooden hut and inside were a couple of officials playing cards. Smiling and greeting them with a good morning, I produced my documents and offered them a cigarette. One of them spoke a little English, I explained where we were from and where we were going, he stamped the passport and lifted the barrier and we drove on our way.

We bumped our way over four hundred yards of very bad track before we got to the Yugoslavian side. Here it was quite different and far more businesslike altogether. There were four guards who had a very good look over my vehicle, and they were very keen to know why I wanted to travel through their country. They seemed satisfied by my explanation and after a few more questions and yet another round of cigarettes, also stamped my passport and let us through.

There had been a bit of a problem when planning my route through Yugoslavia. First of all, the roads were mostly dirt, just glorified tracks, at least in the south of the country. Students were obliged to spend some time each year helping to build proper roads during their holiday periods. One could drive twenty or thirty miles over rough track full of ruts and pot-holes, then suddenly come upon a beautiful modern dual carriageway which would run for five miles and then just as suddenly end, reverting to the rough track again. It could be another thirty miles before the next bit of decent road. These tracks were shocking to drive on, full of holes and ruts; it would be a very easy thing to get a broken axle or prop shaft and one was forced to drive very slowly and with care around these dangerous obstacles, and glory be! We did not even get a puncture, the journey proceeded without a hitch. It did however wreak havoc with my timetable. In the end I completely ignored it, far better to get through without any problems than suffer god knows what in trying to get a major spare engine part delivered to such a remote area, and even if I could get one, it would have to be fitted. And there were so few garages. No I was determined to take my time, I had plenty of that, and slowly slowly catchee monkey was undoubtedly the best policy.

The other major problem was fuel. Petrol stations as westerners knew them were almost non existent in the south. The AA provided me with a list which on the face of it was not too bad, but they included a letter in which they informed me that it was by no means sure that the list was accurate. They covered themselves by adding that the traveller should themselves verify that petrol was available at some stations, and that the list did not mean that the AA actually knew that fuel was definitely available, or that supplies were guaranteed at some of the locations listed. Neither in fact was it; on several occasions I had almost emptied my tank and used my spare fuel before managing to locate new supplies. I heaved a huge sigh of relief when I managed to fill up.

I had decided to follow one of the main routes through Yugoslavia heading for Austria. The main towns would be more likely to have petrol points, and the roads should be better. It was not so in the south of the country but as soon as we reached Belgrade, the improvements were considerable, and when we reached the motorway running across the north of Yugoslavia from east to west, the level of comfort was back to normal and we had the feeling of assurance that we were now in an area of Europe where if things did go wrong we would have control over events. In any event we felt that the more difficult part of the trip was over. We had not come across any bandits here either; I had used the familiar pattern of travelling and camping as that in Greece. We had noticed the frequent appearance of policemen on horseback in the more remote parts of the country, but we were not approached or bothered in any way, and as we had no other intentions than passing through the country, I was not at all concerned. It took another three days to get to Belgrade where we treated ourselves to a wonderful Hungarian goulash in one of the many restaurants available, and splendid it was too after living rough for over a week.

Without wasting any more time, we drove on over the border into Austria and entered the lovely old town of Graz. I now considered myself to be on familiar ground, I spoke German and was able to relax more. We decided to make the best of this opportunity, take our time and enjoy life while we could.

We had a non eventful but very pleasant trip home thereafter and we spent some time touring Austria and Bavaria enjoying the many mountains and lakes and living the life of Riley, one of pleasure and leisure. I remember thinking, this is what it must be like if one was rich, able to afford without worry or problems, a life style that would take me round the world doing what I fancied. Alas, it was only a dream and the harsh realities of life soon brought me back down to earth. Finances were running at a dangerously low level, and the time was fast approaching when I had to report for demob. My God! What had I done?

I had volunteered to leave the life that I loved, and where I had been happy, to face the unknown in civvy street. What sort of work could I do, could I make a living at it? What a fool I was. With my mind in a whirl and a feeling of panic, I arrived back home in England. There were just a few weeks of leave left before I would leave the army for ever.

Part Three

Chapter Twenty-four

I WAS BORN IN SOMERSET and saw no reason why I should not take up residence again in my own county. My parents still lived there, and I had brothers and sisters also living in that area. I wanted to be independent and not live too near nor yet too far from them all. I chose a cottage on the Somerset levels. It was a beautiful spot and I was happy to be living as a civilian again, so with a few breeding sows and some chicken, I hoped to set up as a smallholder and I quickly settled into the routine of caring for the few animals I had.

I was quite content being a farmer although having only a few acres meant that it was farming in a small way indeed, and I suppose a real farmer would have laughed at the temerity I was displaying. I did not have the land or the experience to call myself a farmer, but I did have the cheek. I had all the confidence in the world. I loved and was very happy with all animals; breeding and caring for them is mostly a matter of common sense, house and feed them properly, and mother nature will do the rest.

What I did not know I taught myself, either by studying and reading up on the subject, or discussing matters with other knowledgeable neighbours. In any case I did not intend, nor indeed did I have sufficient land to grow crops, so arable farming was out of the question. I just maintained a kitchen garden large enough to supply all our wants for the home.

The Somerset Levels are one of the most beautiful areas I know; they are teeming with wildlife and the dawn chorus is really something to hear, a never to be forgotten experience. The ditches or rhines are almost always full of water and support fish and eels, and in the season when the eels swarmed in the river and pervaded the levels, my elderly neighbour would show me how to catch them. With a large bean stick about eight feet long, and a few earthworms tied on the end of it, she would plunge the stick into the ditch, hold it there for a minute then pull it out. Hanging on to the worms would be several eels who would not let go; she would knock them into a bucket and repeat the performance and in a very short time had enough for a good meal.

She prepared and cooked them in milk somehow and they were delicious, at certain times in the year, she informed me, elvers in their millions would swarm in the rhines and ditches having swum up the river Parrett, a tidal river, and to which all the rhines and ditches were connected of course.

This old neighbour of mine was quite a character. Already in her eighties when I met her, she was very active tending her garden and looking after her semi invalid and less active husband. She was a mine of information and had lived in the area all of her life. My cottage had been built by her parents, she had been born there and married the boy next door who inherited his parents' house after they died. She had never travelled more than a dozen miles from her home, and had brought up a family all of whom were married and living away.

The holding I now possessed had been her home and the orchard was full of different apple trees; many of the varieties were used for cider making. There were a large number of other individual trees that she told me about that had been planted by one or other of her family, either for a birthday or for some other special celebration. She was very fond of one tree that she had planted when she was a little girl, it was a very nice eating apple called Tom Pudd. She asked me not to cut it down whilst she was alive. I promised to respect her wishes and I did, the tree was still productive and still there when I sold the place.

There were many other fine varieties of apple there also, some of which I had never heard of or seen before. Most have now been lost forever as the modern trend of standardising everything seems to be the in thing. It is a great pity really but I suppose that is the price we have to pay for what is called progress.

I also had a wonderful walnut tree planted by my neighbour's father. It was a magnificent fully grown specimen. I had no idea what to do with it or how to harvest the nuts, but my mother who in her younger days had harvested the crop from trees on the farm where she had worked, was able to explain how it was done. Some of the crop was pickled in vinegar and stored for winter eating, the remainder was left to mature and ripen naturally. I had many good crops from that tree and was very amused to listen to the old Somerset advice given me by my neighbour, who produced the following rhyme:

Chapter Twenty-four

A woman, a dog
and a walnut tree,
The more you beat them,
the better they be.

Apparently, when beating the leaves and branches to bring down the nuts, the more damage that was done to the branches and foliage, the more vigorous was the growth of next year's harvest. It proved to be true and was I suppose a means of pruning the tree. Being so big and large made it difficult work though, but the resultant heavy crops made it worth while. The other problem was that it was necessary to wear gloves when picking up the nuts because the stain produced by the husks and the nuts was virtually impossible to remove. I never found any cleaner that could remove the stain, and was told by my mother that it would wear off with time. I have not put into practice the advice about the woman or the dog yet; I am not sure that the results would be quite as effective these days.

I was amazed at the variety of birds. I had only seen a kingfisher once or twice previously yet here they were in abundance. They were so fast when diving for fish that all that one ever saw was a flash of bright blue light streaking across one's line of vision, then back again just as fast to its perch beside the water, and it would have a fish in its beak. Herons too were everywhere, and barn owls would appear at dusk and quarter their territory, hunting for food which was plentiful. Another bird that I had heard of but never seen was the lesser spotted woodpecker, yet on most days right outside my back door, one hammered away like a pneumatic drill on the telephone pole, it was thrilling to see and hear it working away. I had thought that one required a hide in order to see these rare birds, but not so. I was constantly surprised to spot yet another as I worked on my land. The habitat must have been just right for the wildlife.

Plant life seemed to flourish too. The soil was thick black loam created by centuries of flooding and moor management by our forefathers. It was very fertile and whatever I planted grew in abundance and reproduced itself manifold. We were never short of vegetables or fruit and I was not surprised to learn that the levels were second to none in producing quality dairy products. The grass was excellent and nourishing and the animals fed well; the natural goodness of the soil was a great boon to those that farmed it.

I started off by purchasing fifty day-old chicks, Light Sussex and Rhode Island Red cross hen birds to rear for egg laying, and the same number of cock birds for meat. I had plenty of housing and when the birds were big enough, I intended to let them run free range. I was never happy with any of the intensive farming methods, and think it is cruel to enclose any creature for long periods; in any case, I always found that the quality of eggs and meat from birds and animals that were allowed the freedom to live in a natural way is so very much higher, and my flocks, both hen and cocks, separated of course, had plenty of room to live their lives in a natural way.

I had been advised, and in fact already knew from childhood that the breeds I had chosen were perfect for both eggs and meat. The hens were large and dark brown in colour. They did not produce as many eggs as some of the other breeds, but they were quite prolific, and what they did produce were top quality large eggs which were always in demand: none of your thin whites and pale yellow yolks, but a thick creamy white and a deep orange yolk that had a wonderful taste of its own; once having partaken of them, no other egg is ever good enough. As for the cocks, they would gain weight rapidly to seven pounds or so and were magnificent specimens. They were speckled white with black head and tail plumage, the Light Sussex strain of the cross being dominant in the cock birds. I had customers that drove fifty miles to purchase them, and I kept producing all the time I lived there without problems of any kind.

I also purchased two Large White breeding sows; they were a local breed and look exactly like their name, both large and white with no other markings. For some reason I was not particularly taken with another breed, the Wessex Saddleback. I do not know why because they too are very good animals, at the time I thought I would just start off with the Large Whites and perhaps later try the Saddlebacks. Then I bought yet another pair called Landrace which I believed originated in Denmark. They were long and slender but reputedly produced the best bacon pigs. I won an award for the best litter with one of them. Both breeds were very excellent mothers and good breeders, and I never did buy any Saddlebacks. So with my small herd I was very soon in production.

It was my intention to farrow two sows at a time as near together as possible, and the other two a couple of months later so that I would not have the problems of too many piglets at the same time. The sows had to be impregnated of course, and I arranged for them to be served at a nearby farm that had a good stock boar, and a good reputation. I was not disappointed. It is quite a normal thing, but I was tickled pink to learn that the gestation period for pigs was three months, three weeks and three days. I thought nature was wonderful in providing a time like that, how could anyone ever forget it?

Any farmer reading this must have a good laugh at my enterprise. I know that it was ridiculously small and would be unable to support a family on its own, but I had to start small, I did not have sufficient funds or indeed the land in which to create a business. In any case I was not seriously intent on making money, only a living, and I did think I would succeed at that. Also I had the sense to know that even though I had been brought up a country boy, I did not know it all, I had to get experience and that would take time. I found that I was not missing my former life in the army; rather I had taken to this new life style, it was interesting, and I was enjoying myself. So I put my back into the work of breeding chicken and pigs.

I was not completely ignorant about the livestock I had. We had always kept chickens at home and Father always kept two pigs for fattening at the bottom of the garden and I frequently had to clean them out and feed them. They are a much maligned animal, often described as filthy, noisy and stupid, whereas in fact they are none of these things. Of course if they are penned in and confined in a small area, they are forced to live in a way that is dictated by the farmer, and they will be very mucky. Yet for some unknown reason they have been given a bad reputation; those who think pigs are dirty creatures could not be more wrong, and they have not observed them first hand.

Cows, for instance, and by comparison are filthy beasts. They come into their stalls in the milking parlour, will defecate while they are being milked, and will willingly lie down in their own excrement, and the public drink the milk it produces. I am not suggesting that there is anything wrong with the milk; it is wonderful stuff, and the regulations laid down for its hygienic production are stringent. But it still is a filthy animal.

Yet the pig, if it is given the space, will never defecate near its bed or its food; it will find a spot as far away as possible and do it there. It is the only domestic animal that will make a fresh bed every day if given the straw. It is spotlessly clean if given the chance and shows affection to its owner similar to that of a dog. It can show devotion and loyalty and has an intelligence far greater than most other animals.

And finally, it is independent in its nature and actions. Anyone that has ever tried to move a pig from A to B will know that it is an impossibility to force them to move in any direction they do not wish to go; one has to outwit or trick the animal into thinking it is going where it wants to go, by blocking off any other avenue, and using food as the carrot to encourage it along. To attempt to force it will only end up in frustration and exhaustion with the pig anywhere except where you want it. No, it is not the stupid or dirty animal that many think it is.

When all my sows were pregnant, or 'in pig' as it was locally called, and I was awaiting the first farrowing, they had been running free during the day and returning to their warm comfortable sties at night. I had prepared two farrowing pens and because I had heard a great deal about sows lying on their young and suffocating some of them, quite unintentionally of course, I followed the advice given by many breeders and inserted a strong metal bar across the farrowing pen, leaving a space between it and the wall. It was wide enough to allow room for the piglets to escape if they were in danger of being lain on by their mother. I also built in an additional small chamber adjacent and close to the farrowing pen, put in plenty of bedding straw and installed an infra red lamp over it. The sow would be able to see her offspring but be unable to reach them.

Within twenty four hours of birth, the piglets had learned to make their way into the warm chamber, and I would find them cuddled up in an untidy pile under the warm lamp. They only left their warm bed when the sow called them for feeding. I found that the lamp prevented them from catching a chill and also helped to keep them safe. I never lost one piglet from chill or lying on in the ten years that I was breeding. As the piglets grew, I gradually decreased the length of time the lamp was on until it was no longer required and the piglets were big and strong enough to do without the extra warmth. One could easily discern when farrowing time drew near, the sow would become agitated and start building a nest, her teats would begin to drop milk and it was time to bring the sow into the farrowing pen. If left out in the field they would carry mouthfuls of grass and straw and build a huge circular nest with a large hole in the centre. I made sure that I got the sow into her sty in plenty of time where she and her offspring would be protected from the weather and nice and warm with clean bedding that she quickly made into her nest. Near her time I would feed a light meal and warm drink, put on a low level light and leave her to get on with it.

Chapter Twenty-four

My wife had given all the sows a name to which they answered. I can honestly say that when the first sow, Mirabel, farrowed I was not one bit worried. I was naturally very interested and curious, and I intended to be present during the farrowing. The sows knew and trusted me implicitly, I fed and cared for them and they knew I would not harm them or the piglets in any way; I would just stay and talk to the sow keeping her relaxed and calm. Very shortly, and with no apparent distress, Mirabel lay on her side, gave a little grunt and produced her firstborn. There followed a repeat performance every few minutes until a grand total of twelve beautiful piglets had arrived, and it seemed that it was all over.

It is amazing but quite natural I suppose, that straight after birth, still with closed eyes, the baby struggles from the back end of the sow, through or over her back legs, up her middle and fastens on to one of the sow's teats, the firstborn choosing the one giving the most milk, those following on in decreasing order of birth, choosing the next best place at the milk bar. The last piglet, the runt, and also the smallest, has to be content with what is left; they do survive as long as the sow has plenty of milk, but they never grow fast enough to catch up with their brothers and sisters in size. Being smaller, they had to fight harder for their share and were far more aggressive. I suppose it was nature's way of making up for their size. They usually managed to hold their own amongst their larger kin.

Another very interesting fact is that having chosen its place at the milk bar, it keeps that place for life, and whenever the sow calls her brood at feeding times, she lies down and there is a mad mix up of grunting and squealing piglets for about two minutes, until each one has found its proper place, when there is an absolute stillness as twelve little piglets suckle noisily to the soft grunts of satisfaction from a proud and contented mum. And I can think of no sight that gives greater pleasure.

After the first two or three farrowings, I would stay with the sows for a while, and if everything was OK, I would leave them to get on with it. They did not need me there anyway and thereafter I would go down to the sties early the next morning to find yet another litter safely in residence. They always seemed to time their arrival at night and I came to believe that as long as the sows were healthy and happy, there was very little to worry about, nature would take better care of them than I could at such times. As a precaution though, I always informed the vet and asked him to be prepared to attend in the event of something going wrong. But I never did have occasion to call him out, at least not during the time any of my sows were farrowing.

The only unpleasant task that needed to be done was the castrating of the male piglets. This had to be done otherwise the meat would not be fit to eat; many breeders did the job themselves and it was not difficult to do. However, big softie that I was, I just could not, and I would call for the vet to do the job, and ask my friend to assist him. I would keep well away. It is not a painful operation for the piglet, and if performed at an early age they hardly noticed it and they got over the shock quite quickly. One had to ensure that the sow was out of earshot and well out of the way because nothing is more dangerous than a sow in the business of protecting her young.

She is quite capable of killing a person if she imagines they are hurting her babies; the problem is that just handling a piglet, even if you are not hurting it in any way, causes the most horrendous squealing, loud and non stop it continues until the pig is released, the decibels hit the roof and the noise is far out of proportion to its size.

On one occasion one of my sows demolished three sty doors to defend her babies from the person she thought was harming them. The vet vaulted over one wall and my friend over another as the sow smashed her way out of one sty and in to another where her offspring were. Boy was she mad! Nothing more could be done that day, she tore after the vet with those coughing snarls of rage and heaven help him if she had caught him. I managed to calm her down eventually by feeding and talking to her but she remained very wary and started up at any unusual noise. She never forgot the vet because whenever he was on the premises she seemed to know, maybe she could smell him and she would pace to and fro and get very agitated until he left.

I was quite happy with the way things were going. I was making profit, but not enough to call it a viable business, in fact I was busy discovering what most pig and poultry breeders already knew, you would never get rich at it. Both projects were the poor relations of the farming world, it had been like that for many years and it did not look as if things would change very much in the future. I needed a part time job to top up my income, one that would give me time to tend to the animals as well as help keep the wolf from the door.

I happened to read in the local paper that British Cellophane were looking for process workers in their factory at Bridgwater. It was not what I wanted, but it was shift work which gave me sufficient free time to look after the holding, and the pay would take care of the other problems. I was accepted and started training on a machine which coated cellophane film with a waterproof finish, which kept all kinds of food and other items fresh and dry. I soon learnt the job and was given a machine of my own to work on. It was not difficult once one had learnt the complicated roller system through which the film had to pass; when the machine was running correctly it only required an eye to be kept on it, and new rolls of film loaded as old ones ran out. The film was coated with a dispersion that dried as it passed through the machine and the finished roll was inspected and graded, then removed to another part of the factory for preparation and packing for distribution to customers.

We worked in three shifts which ran from 6 a.m. to 2 p.m., 2 p.m. to 10 p.m., and 10 p.m. to 6 a.m. The shifts were worked for ten days, then there was a break for five days, then one started back on the next shift. Workers were rotated on to a new shift every fifteen days. I was used to the outdoor life and I found the work tedious and boring. I looked forward to the five free days that followed the ten day shifts but there was no way that I could foresee this becoming permanent. I could not come to terms with it and constantly kept my eye open for a more suitable job.

My patience was eventually rewarded when I saw an advert for a part time Bailiff in the local County Court. It offered employment for three days a week, the pay was much less but the hours of work ideal. I duly applied for the job and was appointed; it proved to be just right for my purposes.

I had no idea what the job entailed, the dictionary told me that a Bailiff was a servant of the Court and nothing else. I reported to the court office and was put under the wing of Charlie. He was a Bailiff of many years standing and he set about explaining my duties, and training me for my new job. I found it fascinating and was keen to learn all about it. I wanted to prove to my employers that they had made the right decision in choosing me for the job.

Charlie was into his sixties when I first knew him. He was quite a character, he had served in the army during the Second World War and would frequently reminisce about his experiences, but prior to and at the conclusion of hostilities he had been the Warden of the Workhouse Institution at Langport in Somerset. I was just old enough to remember them, or rather I remember hearing about them, but the stories he could tell were really fascinating.

In England before 1600, the poor and destitute had to exist as best they could, and many starved and died as they struggled to live in an uncaring world. The authorities were not interested, and the better off mostly thought that paupers and other such people were themselves responsible for their situation: they were too idle to work, or were thieves and scoundrels and did not deserve a better life.

With the introduction of the Poor Law in 1601, it was at last recognised that this section of humanity were in some need of sustenance and shelter and the Parishes should be made responsible for the poor and unfortunate living within their jurisdiction. They built the first workhouses to employ paupers and the needy in profitable work. The workhouse became the last resort for the starving who were forced to accept this only alternative. Unfortunately it became very difficult to make any profit in these establishments and in order to discourage the poor from relying on parish relief the regime in the workhouse was made harsh and degrading; families were split up, the males housed in separate accommodation from the women and children.

It also became the norm to house criminals and the infirm, young or old, and even the insane in these workhouses and they became an evil hotchpotch of humanity living at the absolute lowest level of poverty and completely under the thumb of the wardens who literally held the power of life and death in their hands. The workhouses improved somewhat over the years and were still in existence when I was a boy. My parents frequently spoke of people they knew who had been forced to enter the workhouse, and my own mother-in-law when a young woman with three children and destitute after the loss of her husband was offered a place in the workhouse. She had the strength and dignity to refuse, and worked ceaselessly to provide food and shelter for her family. Anything was better than having to accept the only charity offered by the parish councils, the workhouse. They had earned an awesome and terrible reputation, once entered, one was unlikely to come out alive, and the weak and undernourished had no opportunity to regain their health and strength in the harsh regime that ruled inside.

As the years passed the institutions evolved and were no longer required, as social security systems supplanted their use by the early twentieth century. They were used as hostel type accommodation when Charlie was a warden, the idea being that anyone wanting to seek occupation in other towns or cities would tramp the roads. Obviously, not able to afford any transport they were obliged to use Shank's Pony. They could obtain accommodation for the night at one of these institutions for a very small fee. If they were penniless, they could still stay without charge in return for some light work. They were only able to stay one night at a time, but could return at a later date if they were passing through the same area.

The schedule according to Charlie was that the customers had to book in by 6 p.m. Latecomers were not admitted. Immediately following registration, everyone was issued with a towel and soap and ordered to bath. This was followed by a meal, usually soup and bread with a large mug of tea, and then they were issued with a straw pillow and a blanket. Lights out was at 9 p.m. It was a strict, almost military type discipline.

Everyone had to be up at 6 a.m. and all the inmates were obliged to scrub floors and clean up generally, return their bedding to the store, and after a breakfast of porridge, or bread and jam and another mug of tea, wash up their own utensils and dishes. Not until the warden was absolutely sure that the work was done to his satisfaction, did he unlock the doors and allow the men to go on their way.

I have no idea how the service was financed, but one would imagine it was by the local council who probably had to make up any shortfall, the whole idea being to help the poor and needy. The warden had supreme authority and could refuse admission to tramps and vagrants who could not answer his questions or satisfy him of their need for accommodation that night. No drinking was tolerated, but there were frequent quarrels and fights. The warden was expected to maintain peace and order, and often had to resort to fisticuffs himself to sort matters out. Charlie had acquired a reputation as a strict and hard taskmaster, and the nickname of Bridgwater to go with it. One had to behave at his establishment.

As with many other early charitable arrangements for the poor and needy, the institutions became obsolete; the Second World War had changed everything for ever. Charlie lost his job in the institution and became a County Court bailiff for the last twenty years of his working life. He had many interesting memories of the legal practice concerning debt recovery in the early part of the twentieth century. They were unique, tough, and extremely hard on those unfortunate citizens who got themselves into debt.

When a warrant (known as a Distress warrant) for the recovery of money owed by one person to another had been obtained in the Court, the debtor was visited by the bailiff and payment of the debt was demanded; costs were included in the total figure of course. If the debtor paid up, all well and good, he would be given a receipt for the money and that would be the end of the matter. But if he did not or could not pay, the law allowed any of the debtor's goods and chattels to be seized and sold in order to recover the money owed. There were some goods that could not be taken, bedding or clothing for instance; a debtor was also allowed to keep his working tools so that he could continue to earn his living, but almost everything else could be seized.

That practice for want of any other practical system is still in use today. The method of carrying out, or execution of the warrant, was far more brutal in past times. For instance, when a small trader or shopkeeper was unable to pay his debt, the shop would be immediately closed, and preparation for an auction of any goods on the premises, to take place that same day. Unemployed men could earn a little hard cash running around the streets advertising the fact that the bailiff was holding a sale of goods seized by order of the Court at 2 p.m. and many people turned up in the hope of getting a bargain. There is no reserve placed on the value of goods held under distress and the bailiff would auction off the debtor's goods to the highest bidder regardless of the true value of those goods, and he would continue with the sale until, if and when he had realised sufficient money to pay off the amount owing including the costs. The auction was then stopped and things returned back to normality. Charlie had personally held many such sales in his early days as a bailiff.

In later years the debtor was given five days and on some occasions longer in which to pay the debt before such drastic action was taken. It was also very embarrassing for the debtor because although as always there were a lot of poor people around, and consequently a great deal of debt, it was not considered to be respectable to be in that category oneself, and every effort was made to conceal it, and give the appearance of being a sound, upright and virtuous citizen. Much use was made of the numerous pawnshops which flourished at the time; there the best Sunday suit, or the bed sheets of the householder would be pawned for a few shillings on Monday and redeemed again on Friday after pay day.

Chapter Twenty-five

IN EARLIER DAYS much use was made of the possession man and Charlie would recall some of his experiences. Instructions for the use of possession men were still printed on warrants up to the time that I retired from the service in 1983, but I never had occasion to use one, at least not in the manner for which they had originally been intended, and the practice had gradually fallen into disrepute; the bailiff was still happy to have the instructions for their use printed on the warrant though and with its forbidding undertones and old legal language, would use it as a formidable weapon in impressing on the debtor the very serious nature of his predicament.

Charlie himself had frequently been given the job before he became a bailiff, and told me once he had been ordered into a debtor's house to take possession and remain there until the debt had been paid. The reason for this was because the debtor was on his death bed and every effort had to be made to recover what he owed before he died. Charlie received his instructions in the presence of the relatives of the dying man.

'You will remain on the property until you are paid in full, the amount of eight pounds six shillings and threepence, or until you receive other instructions from me. Whilst you are here you may use for your own consumption, any food that may be in the larder or on the premises. You may kill and cook a chicken if necessary and use any vegetables in the garden or in the house to provide yourself with a cooked meal. You may also find a bed to sleep in if you have to stay overnight but you will not leave the premises.'

In this particular instance Charlie related how the local Vicar was called and told of the situation, then having failed to dislodge Charlie by making him feel bad about it all, went away and returned later with the money, angry and disgusted at the cold-hearted treatment of his dying parishioner and very distressed relatives. However it was a lawful thing to do and it was effective even if it was hard. Charlie received the princely sum of three shillings per day or part of a day thereof for his services, not bad pay then.

In the case of evictions, mostly for non payment of rent, the debtor was given one week's notice of eviction, then promptly evicted on the time and day notified. Poverty was not considered to be an excuse for non payment of rent, and more often than not, the next stop for the family was the workhouse and possibly prison for the husband. Bailiffs were ruthless in carrying out their instructions to the letter, the Courts rarely showed any leniency to these poor unfortunate people; in fact, they were more likely to be treated as if they were criminals. They were warned of the dire consequences if they attempted to re-enter the premises later, and the bailiffs would pull tiles off the roof to discourage that possibility. Things have improved since then, and most of those early practices are gone. Thank goodness.

I learned a great deal from Charlie, and not just the basics of the job either. One's mental attitude and demeanour and a quiet confidence frequently determined whether the outcome of any particular job would be difficult or easy. Humour too was much in evidence in his dealings, and in fact he was a very reasonable and helpful man. He could also be very firm especially in the face of insult or abuse. I recall one very angry farmer who was shouting and swearing at us, making abusive remarks, threatening violence and refusing to pay the debt for which we had a warrant. Charlie was very patient and repeatedly tried to talk to the farmer, trying to explain and discuss the debt but the man just would not listen, and ordered us off the premises. Charlie gave him plenty of warning but eventually grew weary of the stream of abuse and insults coming from the farmer.

Speaking quietly, Charlie said to him, 'Mr —. You owe this money, the judge has ordered that you pay it, and I have a warrant from the Court ordering me to recover it. If you will not pay it voluntarily now, I shall have to make you pay it.' Interruption and more abuse from the farmer. 'What is more,' Charlie interjected, 'there will be considerable extra costs you will have to pay.'

'I don't bloody well care, you will get bugger all here, sod off, you can't make me pay,' etc., etc. Another tirade of invective and abuse aimed at Charlie. Still in the process of learning, I remained silent, wondering what was going to happen next.

'For the last time of asking,' Charlie said, 'are you going to pay?'

'No, I bloody well won't,' the farmer replied. Charlie's final words were, 'Well, you will pay, and what is more, before we are finished here today, you will beg me to take you.'

Chapter Twenty-five

The events that followed were an object lesson in debt recovery. This very proud and haughty farmer was about to be humbled and humiliated in a way that he had never experienced before, and what is more, in front of his neighbours, and just as predicted, ended up later, begging for Charlie to allow him to pay.

Leaving the angry and still remonstrating farmer at the farmhouse, Charlie called me away to the edge of the property. He told me not to leave the premises or the warrant would no longer be valid, he was going away for half an hour, first to get the police, and also to arrange help for what he had to do, I only had to remain there until he returned. Being new to the job, I had no idea of what was about to happen. I was very interested though and sat down on the stump of a tree to await his return.

He was as good as his word. He returned shortly after accompanied by the farmer's neighbour driving a tractor; they drove in to the farm entrance and up the track to the farm buildings and parked in front of the barn. About ten minutes later, a police car with a Sergeant and three policemen arrived; they had been briefed by Charlie that they might be required to prevent a breach of the peace. The farmer had reappeared and was warned by the police sergeant that he must not act aggressively, or make any attempt to prevent the bailiff from carrying out his duty: if he did, he would be arrested. He was certainly not prepared for what was about to happen next.

The debt was for £700, a fair amount in the sixties, and Charlie was about to increase that figure because there were now costs being incurred which would have to be added. Without another word to the farmer he opened the barn door to reveal about twenty tons of hay which half filled the barn; in front of this was a tractor and trailer, mowing machinery, ploughs, seed drill, baler and a number of other farming implements.

'Now let me see,' Charlie mused, yet I knew that his murmurings were loud enough for the farmer to hear, 'the tractor will only be worth about two hundred pounds.'

'What do you bloody well mean?' shouted the farmer, 'I paid two thousand for it just a short time ago.'

'Please do not interrupt,' Charlie said, 'otherwise I will be forced to ask the police to arrest you.' Then resuming his thoughtful mumbling, still purposely loud enough for the farmer to hear, and having produced his notebook, he painstakingly entered the item. 'Oh! Just a minute, what make is it? Ah yes a Ford, registration number ...' He was being deliberately slow and a little vague and I realised his purpose was to get the farmer to comprehend just what he was going to lose.

Turning to the neighbour who had been employed by Charlie for the job, he said, 'Now Mr Jones, will you please drive this tractor away and store it safely until I can arrange for the sale, which will probably be in a week or two.'

The farmer was visibly shaken and white faced with anger; he had not realised the power of the law and was very upset to see his neighbour driving the tractor away. 'Come straight back,' Charlie called out, 'there is a lot more stuff to be moved yet.'

As we waited for him to return, Charlie continued to enter and appraise all the implements in the barn calculating their value. The farmer was frantic and trying to remonstrate, but was restrained by the police and totally ignored by Charlie. The neighbour returned, and methodically all the implements were removed. Charlie still talking to himself was adding up the total value of all the goods seized. 'Well, that should cover the debt, but there will be considerable costs, so I will need more goods yet, let me see, ah! We could sell the hay, and possibly some of the livestock.'

'Oh no!' the visibly shaken, and by now utterly demoralised farmer was witnessing the decimation of all his assets, he was now silenced and had been forced to accept the powers that bailiffs could employ when executing a warrant, realising that he had lost his implements, which was bad enough; if he also lost his hay and some of his cattle he would be ruined and made bankrupt. Gone was the arrogance, the threatening behaviour and the insults now replaced by whining subservience and humility. 'Please stop, I will do whatever you want, please, please.'

'Well,' Charlie finally condescended to speak to the farmer, 'I suppose we can talk about it. I don't really feel inclined to, how can I be sure that you will not start acting up again as you did before I had to get the police, and will you promise to keep calm and not offer any violence?'

'Yes, yes, I promise.'

'In that case I think we can let the police go. Thank you very much for your assistance, gentlemen, and I will inform your superiors of your prompt and efficient action in preventing a serious breach of the peace.'

The policemen left in their car and Charlie suggested to the farmer that we might discuss matters over a cup of tea, we would return later to finish our business. The farmer entreated us to come into the farmhouse, we could have tea there, he was very distressed and was eager to get back what he had lost and was anxious to talk about it. Charlie replied that he did not think it would be quite proper for us to accept his tea really because after all we were on duty.

There followed some discussion for a few minutes after which Charlie allowed himself to be persuaded to stay, pretending to be very reluctant; he had of course planned everything that way. Leading us into the farmhouse, the farmer requested us to be seated in the parlour, the tea would be ready just as soon as his wife could make it. In the interim, we chatted away just like normal visitors, talking about the weather and other various subjects, everything else, but not mentioning the warrant.

When the tea arrived and had been poured, the farmer implored Charlie to return his goods; he would now pay the warrant in full.

'I don't know about that,' Charlie said, 'after all you said you would not pay, I asked you politely a number of times, I warned you a number of times, and in return received nothing but insults and abuse, and you threatened us with violence, I even had to get the police for protection.'

'Yes and I am very sorry about everything.' The farmer was now begging to pay and almost in tears as Charlie extracted every crumb of revenge: he thought it was now too late to stop the sale, there were the costs of removing and returning the goods, the neighbour too had to be paid, the Court's time had been wasted, we had been there several hours, the police had to be called. On and on he went, like a schoolmaster admonishing a little boy.

Utterly spent and beaten, the farmer now in tears continued begging and asking for mercy. After a second pot of tea and another twenty minutes discussion, Charlie relented, and having achieved the desired effect, worked out the costs of the whole operation.

'Well now, you have to pay an extra £180, and I must have the cash now as well as the money owing on the warrant.'

'If you will give me just half an hour, I will go and get it from the bank.' The farmer dashed off, relieved at last that he was going to get his goods back. He returned shortly with the money and paid up in full. Charlie arranged the return of everything taken and paid all the costs of the removal and storage as well as the wages for the neighbour; we then adjourned to the local pub for a well earned pint.

The reader might wonder why such a low valuation is made on goods seized by the bailiff. It is because the law only allows one bite of the cherry. Having seized goods to cover the costs of removal and sale, the amount of money realised by it invalidates the warrant. If too much money is raised, the debtor receives the balance remaining after payment of the warrant plus costs. If however the goods sold do not cover the amount required, the bailiff has no power to return to the debtor to seize another lot of goods. The general public have to be notified when there is a sale of goods seized by order of the Court; they have to be sold to the highest bidder and there can be no reserve put on the value of such goods. Those in the know exploit this situation to the full, the bids are always low and seldom anywhere near the true value of the goods; they have to be sold whatever the bid. The money realised by the sale has to cover the warrant and costs because there is no second chance to return to the debtor. It was quite important therefore to ensure a correct seizure and appraisal the first time.

There was a purpose behind everything Charlie had said and done; it was standard practice and whenever hostile debtors were encountered he used this same method. I had many occasions to do the same in future years, it humbled the proud and troublesome, it taught them to respect the law and made those who thought they could avoid having to pay their debts, realise that they would be forced to pay in the end.

Charlie had an awesome reputation amongst all the regular debtors and was well respected by them all. He knew everyone and could tell me about most of the people we dealt with: where they worked, what pub they used, whether they were trying to pull a fast one or not, or were they just ordinary hard working people that had got themselves foolishly into debt more by ignorance than by design.

He would be very helpful and kind and give sound advice where he thought it was needed, and would approach the authorities to suggest that some people needed help; on the other hand he would be firm and unyielding to those he called professional debtors, those who knew all the tricks of how to avoid paying what they owed. He was a mine of information and I learned much from him. I was sorry when he retired because I had lost a good friend and teacher, there were few bailiffs with his knowledge and experience and he was a loss to the service. When I learned that he had died some years later I felt that the world was a poorer place.

And so I adapted to my new work. It was really a very interesting job: when serving different kinds of summonses for instance, there were strict rules that had to be observed and some were quite different than for others. One kind of summons could be handed to a relative or any other adult person residing at the address, to be handed later that same day to the named person on it, for others it was imperative that they were served personally. The bailiff had to sign a form of affidavit stating how he had served each process because later it might influence the judge in the way he made his judgement; everything had to be done correctly and properly. There were different kinds of warrant too, not least were those that ordered the arrest and imprisonment of the debtor.

This was not always the harsh treatment it seemed as I will explain later, I had quickly learned that the majority of debtors were the same people; as soon as one debt was cleared, I was very quickly back with another, they seemed to follow along as if there was a never ending pipeline. Most of the average debtors had been living that way all of their lives, as had their parents before them, it was a way of life. There could be no doubt that the children learned from their parents, and the various tricks of the trade were passed down through the generations. So it was the same people over and over again. To them and their relatives the bailiff was a familiar figure, just as the rent man, or the insurance man, a weekly visitor, and there developed a kind of rapport and mostly friendly relationship between them. This was evident when the auditor visited the court; he was now himself at the point of retirement but as a young man, had worked in this very court some thirty years before. He came across the name of one of our debtors in documents that he was auditing and told me that this was a particularly well known family that he had dealt with all those years ago. They were the grandparents of the present debtors.

When a Commitment Warrant had been issued for non payment of a debt, I would visit the debtor at his home to acquaint him of the facts and explain that if the debt was not paid, I had to arrest him and convey him to prison. In my area that was Horfield prison, Bristol for males and Exeter for females. More often than not, the debtor having been in the same predicament many times before was perfectly familiar with the procedure, having been informed of the amount owing. A number of debtors would work out whether it was more in their interest to go to prison, or pay the warrant. There was good reason for them to consider these facts as I will presently explain.

It was the practice in our court in the sixties for the judge to award one day's sentence in prison for every pound of the debt that was owed, or thereabouts. So for a debt of twelve to twenty pounds the sentence would probably be fourteen days. It just so happened that one pound at that time was about the rate of pay for one day's employment too. Now according to the law in force at that time, a person could only be committed to prison once for any particular debt, so that to all intent and purposes the debt was effectively cleared once the prison sentence had been served.

Our crafty debtor then would work out whether it was to his advantage to go to prison. If the amount owed was fairly high and the sentence fairly low, prison would be the best choice, because the debt would be cleared, he would not be too long inside and could not be imprisoned again for that debt. He would be well fed and probably have a reasonable time there; though most prisoners disliked being locked in a cell for long periods, it was tolerable. If the debtor was unemployed he would jump at the opportunity to go, often men on very low pay would also choose to go. In many cases it was looked on as a short break, in fact almost a holiday. I was frequently invited to sit down and discuss the options over a cup of tea.

When the decision had been arrived at, and if it was to go to prison, I would discuss the timing of the arrest and arrange perhaps for two or three debtors to meet at a certain spot on the day and at a fixed time, and off we would go in my car to Horfield. On one occasion I took five prisoners. I was considered to be a tough bailiff because I frequently took more than one prisoner at a time to prison. But I was not being tough at all; they were all volunteer prisoners and never presented me with any difficulties, they knew that I was sympathetic to them in most cases because many of their problems were not of their own making. The old hands, as I called them, were not worried in any way, they had done it all before and would be quite cheerful and helpful in putting to rest the minds of any new first timer who would be forearmed with the knowledge of what to expect and do when he arrived at the prison. We would stop for a cup of tea on the way, and we would have a sing song as we travelled north just as if we were on an outing rather than a visit to prison. I encouraged it, it was a means of keeping their minds off the unpleasant time ahead.

This type of prisoner bore no animosity or hard feelings, in fact I was considered to be OK. Because of my considerate attitude, I always made sure that the families left behind knew exactly when they would see their husbands again, and I would write a letter to the Welfare Dept. so that the wife and family could obtain help and not starve whilst the breadwinner was away. Not all prisoners were so compliant however and there were occasions when it was necessary to take a colleague along for additional security and to prevent escapes. Such men caused a lot of trouble and we were required to put on our thinking caps and plan a course of action to achieve success.

I never let a debtor beat me in this game of trickery and deceit and always got my man even if it took a little time. The word would get around that I was after someone and the debtor would be alerted and on his guard and actively avoid any form of contact with me. I just used to wait for the time when the debtor felt he was safe, and it might be in a pub, or the very early morning, but sooner or later he would make the fatal mistake I was waiting for, and I would quickly arrest him and take him to prison. I never let them feel they were safe, or were going to get away with anything. The debt, the law, the court and my reputation were things they had to learn to respect, and by and large I believe they did.

There was one very poor man who was also very hardworking. He cut withies for a living, which were used to make baskets and furniture. His pay was atrocious and he was never out of debt. He lived a life of sheer misery because he had a shrew of a wife who constantly nagged him and gave him a hard time; she was unfaithful to him and demanded every penny he earned. I really do not know how he put up with her or his lifestyle, I certainly would not have stayed for one minute, but he seemed to accept his lot without question. I reckon he had been driven down and kept at such a low level of degradation for so long, that he did not have any will left. He frequently served time in prison because there was no way he could pay the debt, he just had no money. It was his wife who had got into debt and who did not care that her husband had to pay, and she was not particularly worried about him having to pay by serving time in prison.

The amusing thing about it, and unknown to his wife, was that the man wanted to go to prison; he confided in me that he got a lovely rest from his nagging wife, three very good meals every day and companionship, things he never got at home. Our circuit judge would always ask us to use our discretion at Christmas time. He would suggest that we might go easy over the holiday period and not arrest anyone at a time that might entail their absence from home and their families on Christmas day, but rather we should wait a few days until after the festive season. Obviously, this did not apply to the withy cutter who would beg me to arrange things so that he would be in prison for

Christmas thus ensuring that he got a good Christmas dinner, and all the companionship and goodwill that went with it, something unheard of at his home.

The judge would remark that it was inconceivable there could be such people living such miserable lives in these modern times.

There were of course, all kinds of people who found themselves in financial difficulties and put themselves in a position that threatened immediate arrest and imprisonment. Many could pay the debt off and did so as the threat became imminent, they were holding off the evil day as long as possible, and were released immediately after payment, but there were others who felt that they should not be in that position; they would deny owing money, deny receiving a summons, or argue that they had not been treated fairly, every conceivable excuse under the sun would be produced and I had heard them all. 'My Grandmother has just died and her burial is in two days.' I got that one regularly, often from the same person. The problem if you are a habitual liar is that you need to have a good memory also and the debtor had forgotten that the same excuse had been used before.

'But this is the third time you have told me that your grandmother has died,' I would reply and he would just shrug his shoulders and admit defeat. I always did my homework before any of these visits and always had an answer for all excuses. I usually closed all discussion on the subject by producing the warrant and showing the debtor his name and address, and then reading the instructions written on it. I would then add that His Honour the judge had signed the warrant but I would take the debtor to appear before him if that was what he wanted, but of course it was the last thing they wanted; any sign of contempt could make the judge increase the sentence, and so unless the debtor paid, it would mean another trip to Horfield.

When I had to deal with known violent or hostile debtors, another method had to be adopted. Sometimes one knocked on the front door and the quick witted debtor would make his escape out the back door, so I had to be more crafty than they were. Enquiries into the life style and habits of the debtor were recorded: did they work? Where? What pubs if any did they frequent? Were they married? Did they have any children? As much information as possible was compiled and a plan made to apprehend the wanted person. If they were unemployed for instance I would be at the Unemployment Office on pay out day hidden away in a back room and only making my appearance when the debtor arrived to sign on and pick up his money. He would turn away from the counter to find me waiting at his shoulder to arrest him.

If on the other hand if he was employed, I would go to his place of work, speak to the manager and have the man brought to me. Quite often the employer would be willing to pay the debt after making an agreement with the employee to deduct a small amount from the man's pay every week until the debt was repaid. Generally speaking, employers were reluctant to lose an employee; many of them were good workers. As my old partner Charlie used to say, 'Most of these chaps are likeable rogues, they are not criminals. It is easy to pay your bills if you have a good job, but if you don't earn enough to make ends meet you must live the best way you can.' I agreed with him in principle, but there were some very hard criminal types also who would sometimes give us a run for our money and who became violent; in these cases we were backed up by the police, the sight of whom would take all the fight out of the hard men.

Probably only about one in ten were like this, what I would call hardened debtors, the vast majority were ordinary men and women forced by circumstance to live at or just below the poverty level.

I recall entering the home of one chap; I had been chasing him for a couple of weeks but he had eluded me, 'Where is Fred?' I asked his wife, 'I know he is here somewhere.'

'I think he went out,' she said, 'he doesn't tell me where he is going.'

I quickly searched through the house but did not find him, he was not in the bedrooms and the beds were not made but he was not there and I was forced to withdraw. Several days later, Fred called at the court office to pay his debt. He was grinning and acting like a dog with two tails and pleased as punch that he had outwitted me.

'I was in the house all the time you were there,' he said, 'The one thing that you didn't do was feel the bed. If you had you would have realised that I must have just jumped out when I heard you come into the house, it was still warm and I had enough time to get up into the attic before you got to the bedroom.'

He was tickled pink to have got one over on me, and I have no doubt that the tale passed around all of my regular customers and was repeated many times. I didn't mind though, I could see the funny side of the situation.

I was not fooled very often, but I vividly recall holding a Commitment warrant against an operative who worked at the Nuclear Power Station at Hinkley Point, the building of which was very near to completion at the time, and this person who worked for the Electricity Generating Board was preparing for the time when the station came into full production; they were rehearsing for the big day. It was a very skilled job and the pay was very good indeed when compared to the average rates at the time. There was no reason at all why anyone employed on that particular job could not have paid their way and still have money to spare. There certainly was no reason why they could not stay out of debt. I called at his home and informed him that he would be arrested unless he could pay the warrant.

I was then subjected to a catalogue of woe, the likes of which I had never heard before: his wife had run away with a friend leaving behind a mountain of debt which he had to pay, both of his parents had been killed in a car accident quite recently, and he being the only living relative had to pay the burial costs. He had suffered a serious mental breakdown and was only now beginning to recover and get his life back into some sort of meaning. Of course he wanted to pay his debts and was endeavouring to do so, but there was no way that he could pay this additional debt which had come as a surprise to him, yes, he admitted to owing the money but with all the worry and trouble it had slipped his memory.

With that he burst into tears, and fell sobbing bitterly on to his sofa just like a child. I was quite embarrassed to witness a grown man brought down to such awful circumstances through no fault of his own. We were granted the means of using our discretion if we thought that circumstances were particularly hard on a debtor, and on this occasion I felt that I should bring the matter to the notice of the Registrar who could order that he could pay a monthly amount rather than be committed to prison. I made the man a cup of tea, and managed to quieten him down by explaining what I intended to do to help him. He agreed that he could pay a monthly order and thanked me profusely for helping him. He said he was near to suicide, and if the Registrar would make such an order, he would be eternally grateful.

In due course a new order was made suspending the warrant as long as the monthly payment was made. I impressed on him that it was imperative that he should make his payments regularly and on time; any deviation from this would mean an immediate re-issue of the warrant and resultant imprisonment.

The man paid the first month but missed the second, the warrant was duly re-issued and I went hot-foot to his home to confront him. He was very sorry but said that in the week the money was due he had been forced to take to his bed with a mystery illness and he had been unable to get to the court. There followed another breakdown, tears flowed and sincere apologies rendered, he had the payment there and would I please take it, this would never happen again, etc. etc.

Oh well, I thought, this poor fellow is certainly having more than his fair share of bad luck. I will accept the payment even though I ought not. 'Don't let me down again,' I warned him, 'I will have to arrest you if it happens again.' The following month, no payment was forthcoming and I visited the debtor yet again. Immediately he set eyes on me he broke down again, sobbing bitterly, the tears streaming down his face.

'You will never guess what has happened, someone stole my pay packet. I could no pay the court, and I have not had any money to buy groceries, the firm has given me a little to see me through to next pay day, but I can't pay the court until then.'

I was by now getting very suspicious of this person, yet he seemed genuine enough, his tears and remorse were really strong evidence of the truth of his situation and helped to confirm that he did need help.

'Look,' I said, 'I will give you the benefit of the doubt just this last time. Come what may, if this non payment occurs again I shall take you to prison, I will not accept any excuse whatever.'

'I understand,' he said, 'and I promise to pay on time, thank you very much for your understanding.' He mopped up his tears and smiled weakly, showing me to the door.

I was mad with anger when a month later yet again there was no payment received from the debtor. I was now fairly certain that the man was taking advantage, it was beyond the realms of possibility that such continuous bad luck took place at exactly the same specific time when payments were due, and this time I was determined to arrest him. I went to his home early in the morning so that after the arrest I could get in to Bristol and back early. I had wasted enough time on this man. I knocked on the door, and the debtor opened it straight away. 'There has been a mix up with my wages,' he said, 'I haven't been paid, but I am expecting things to be sorted out this morning and I will come into the court office later today and pay.'

'No you won't, you are now under arrest and I am taking you to prison straight away. I warned you that I would not accept any more excuses from you, so lock up your house and get in my car.'

'Oh! Please no, give me another chance, it won't happen again I promise'. There followed the usual tears, sobbing, pleading and begging, but I had made up my mind not to give way to him and I ordered him again to come peaceably or I would have to use force. I was sure he would come quietly once he realised he had no other choice. Grim faced, I assumed the stern attitude of authority that I used on such occasions, and I ordered him once more to lock up and come with me.

The realisation that this was the end of the line finally dawned on him: I meant what I said, there was no other way out of the predicament. His personality seemed to change and he shrugged his shoulders. 'Never mind, I will go and get the money and pay you.' He then laughingly informed me that he had thought he had got away with not having to pay the debt, or at least spinning payment out over quite a few months, it had worked before in other cases and he had every confidence that it would work with me.

'Are you telling me that all this sobbing and crying was put on in the hope of getting away with not paying the debt?' I asked. The man had the ability to cry and sob at will, even to the extent of producing actual tears. 'That's right,' he smiled, 'I have done it many times before.' I was very angry but I did not show it. 'OK, get the money and let us get it over with.' Off he went in to another room and returned a few moments later with the missing payment. 'Here you are.' The debtor was all chirpy and bright now, just the opposite of the weary sad demeanour of a few minutes earlier. 'I'll see you with another payment next month.'

'Is that all the money you have?' I asked, 'because I want the full amount of the warrant, not just one payment.' I gave him a receipt for the money. 'You will have to wait for the bank to open then,' he said, 'Come back at eleven o'clock.'

'Not bloody likely,' I exploded. 'You must be joking, for the last two or three months you have been lying and pulling the wool over my eyes, fraudulently got me to persuade the Registrar to get you special terms in order to help you pay by monthly instalments, I have had to run back and forth like a yo-yo, and now you have the effrontery to order me to go away and return at your convenience. No way.'

I must teach this man a lesson, I thought, he will not try to bamboozle me again ever. Holding his arm firmly, I allowed him to lock his house up then walking him to my car, I sat him in the passenger seat beside me and we set off to drive the hour and a half it would take to get to the prison. He moaned and complained throughout the journey but I had no sympathy for him and ignored his protests. I could have waited for the banks to open so that he could pay the debt in full, but I chose to teach him that I was not a person to be trifled with. I told him that I was not prepared to believe that he had the money in the bank, he had lied so much that even he was not sure what the truth was any more.

We arrived at Horfield and I handed my prisoner over to the duty warder for registration. When I got my live body receipt, I told him about the debtor and how he had tricked me, and warned the warder that he might try the same tricks on him.

It was normal practice for the police and bailiffs to inform the prison warders if a prisoner was particularly nasty or violent or obstreperous in any way, or had made life difficult for them so that forewarned with this knowledge, the warders would be prepared to deal with any problems that might arise. It goes without saying that any such prisoner was treated correctly within the rules of the establishment, but in a way that made him wish he was not there. There was a completely different attitude taken toward the moderate and cooperative prisoner. The warder seemed more like a friendly father figure, than the stern, barking, authoritative officer that my debtor was now confronted with. I also omitted to inform him that he could get out of prison that same day if he knew how to go about it. Instead he had to suffer the system in force and it was three days later before he was able to obtain his release.

He never tried his tricks on me again and I was treated with the utmost respect in my future dealings with him. This was the only time that I had been hoodwinked by a debtor and I never trusted one again, at least not without careful and complete enquiries into his background.

Chapter Twenty-six

WELL, ACTUALLY, THERE WAS ONE OTHER TIME when a particular lady who was a regular customer of ours, lied to me, and to everyone else for that matter. In my job one got used to the frequent white lies we were told at the door, 'Mum says she's not at home', or 'Can you come back next week, Mum has gone shopping.' This from young children sent out to meet me by the beleaguered wife who was trying to eke out her housekeeping money. 'I have to pay the Tally man, or the Rent man, or the Gas bill.' It was human nature in the raw, and I soon learned that the majority of what I would describe as working-class debtors just did not have sufficient money to pay their way.

The main problem in most cases was that the man brought home his pay packet having already deducted his beer and cigarette money, this would have been a sizeable proportion of the pay. The balance was given to the wife who had to manage as best she could on what was left. Inevitably this meant that someone would not get paid and the skilful wife would somehow avoid having to pay me one week, and the rent man the next, and the tally man or the butcher or someone else the following week, and we the collectors were shuffled around like a pack of cards, and, dependant on the seriousness of the debt, were sooner or later paid off. The bailiff was quite high in the pecking order because of the warrants he held and the power of the law backing him up, but some less important debts were left unpaid for weeks, sometimes for months, and some were never paid at all.

On Friday evenings then, winter and summer, the normal pay day for the majority of working-class men, there would be a frenzied dashing from house to house of regular debt collectors of one kind or another, criss-crossing each other and attempting to beat the other collector to the door. They all knew that only the first two or three would be successful and get their money, so a kind of rivalry existed and much planning done on how to beat the opposition. However since one only had one pair of legs and a large number of clients to visit, there was a limit to the success or otherwise of one's endeavours.

Frequently debtors lived close together, there might be as many as a dozen in a few terraces in the same street and two collectors might arrive on the same doorstep at the same time. One would have to give way and the loser would dash on to the next call, probably only a few doors away. But I digress, and referring back to the lady that was such a good liar, I did not think she was a poor person unable to make ends meet, rather, she was a professional debtor and an outright criminal. She was known by all her friends and neighbours as a lovely woman. When one of these had a birthday or wedding anniversary to celebrate, they would receive a gift from her. Not one of your old ordinary kinds of gifts though, but an expensive item such as a cooker or washing machine, quality cutlery, or perhaps some beautiful bone china dinner service. Whatever it might be it was always the best money could buy.

Whatever goods they were, they would have been purchased from a mail order catalogue. She did not just use one, but every catalogue available, she acted as an agent for them all. Fictional customers would be ordering goods continuously. When they arrived, and if they were not actually required as a gift to someone there would be an advertisement in several local papers describing these goods for sale, new and unused and at a fraction of the actual new price. There were various reasons given as to why they were for sale, perhaps an unwanted gift, a prize from some competition, or she had been asked to dispose of it for a friend, there was always a good reason why it was no longer required. The seller could always manage to allay any fears that the goods were not genuine; the price too was so very reasonable that she inevitably finished up selling them. Of course I did not know of her wheeling and dealing at the time, and only learned about it much later.

The goods always sold well, mainly because the price was so low and they were such a good bargain. The purchasers left well satisfied with their efforts, and our debtor was also doing quite well thank you. From the money she received she would pay to the various clubs the minimum payment required, supposedly from all the fictional customers for whom she acted as agent. The catalogue proprietors always gave their customers twenty weeks to pay, a form of credit sale, and our debtor could manage to pay sufficient money to enable her to keep in business, but in fact she owed hundreds if not thousands of pounds. Eventually the time must come when her fraudulent activity would be discovered as the overall amount of debt increased to a point where she would not have sufficient money to pay her creditors, but it did not seem to worry her unduly at the time.

In the 1960s the law held that the husband was responsible for his wife's debts, that is except for furs and jewellery, and so when eventually she was unable to pay off the ever increasing debt, a summons would be issued against the husband for the recovery of the money. It would be a Judgement summons which had to be served on him personally and in most cases it would be the first time that he would learn that his wife had got him into debt. She would incur them without his knowledge and the deeper into debt she sank, the more frightened she would be that her husband would find out.

I have to say in defence of these women that in my opinion the amount of money given to them by their husbands was pitifully inadequate and insufficient to cover all the living expenses. Not only the rent, gas and electricity bills had to be paid, but food and clothing also. Very few wives were allowed to work to augment the family income, and the majority of the husbands would withhold sufficient money from their wages for their own beer and cigarettes regardless of whether the wife had sufficient money or not.

There are very few mothers that will allow their children to suffer or go without, and it was asking too much to expect them to ignore the Tally man or the catalogues, when by paying a few shillings a week these women could buy household necessities and clothes and at least give the appearance of having a reasonable standard of living for their families. Of course the amount of the debt increased over a period of time, until it reached the point where it became a struggle to pay everything, and repaying the debt which by now had become a greater amount than the family income, would be a choice of selecting who or who not to pay that particular week.

It was inevitable that firms who were owed considerable amounts of money became impatient and resorted to the law to get their money when it was impossible to get it in the normal way from the housewives, and the terrified wives would lie and plead and do anything to avoid the husband learning about the debts. When he did become involved, probably only when confronted by a Bailiff with a Judgement summons informing him that he had to show why he should not be imprisoned for not paying his debts, his reaction was understandable. In the majority of cases the wife would be severely beaten up and become even more terrified than ever of repeating her folly. I have seen wives beaten black and blue and even suffering broken bones by enraged husbands who had been forced to pay quite serious debts on occasions. It was not just the money of course, but the ignominy of facing imprisonment, and his neighbours and friends knowing his personal business. If the debt was large, and if the husband managed to get a court order to pay it off over a period of months or even years, it meant that his visits to the pub would have to be seriously curtailed and he would not be able to afford the pleasures he had been used to for some considerable time in the future. Not all husbands were the same. There were those who recognised their own shortcomings in not giving the wives sufficient money to manage the house on; these would at least come to an amicable arrangement with their spouse and peace would reign in the home, but they were in the minority.

The wives remained mostly loyal to their men despite not being able to show their faces because of the bruising and other injuries, the general excuse was that they had fallen down, but it happened time after time and some of them never learned.

Returning to the wife in question, she had by this time reached the position where she was unable to keep up with her payments, and several judgements had been issued against her husband. I would call at her address in the morning perhaps. I usually had one or two warrants against her, and she would come to the door with her finger to her lips, shushing me and explaining that she had her granddaughter asleep inside and she was rather poorly. 'I haven't had my money yet, but can you call tomorrow evening and I will pay you then?' She usually kept her word and did pay when she promised so I fell in with her wishes; however, Judgement summonses against her husband were a different matter. I had to see him and serve them personally.

At first she would ask me what the debt was for, and knowing that she was responsible for it I would tell her. She would admit that it was her debt and not her husband's and that if he found out about it he would kill her, however if I could hold it for a few days she would come in to the office and pay it in full. In any case, her husband was in a Sanatorium in Scotland so I could not serve the summons on him anyway.

I would leave the matter pending for a few days and on a number of occasions she would appear at the Court office and pay the outstanding debts thereby nullifying the summons, but her difficulties were rapidly increasing and the time came when I had a number of Judgement summonses against her husband.

'I'm sorry, Mrs A.,' I said, 'but as your husband is not here I shall have to return these summonses to the office and report his address, in any case it is not fair that you should carry this burden of debt on your own.'

'Oh but it is my debt,' she replied, 'and in any case my husband is so near death that the knowledge would probably kill him. Please leave it with me, I will be able to sort it out.'

'I am very sorry, Mrs A. but I am not allowed to do that. I want you to come to the Court office in the morning and we can discuss the matter with the Chief Clerk.'

Having extracted a promise from her that she would come, I left and continued with my other work. True to her word, she arrived at the Court office next morning. I explained her situation to the Chief clerk, and she produced to him the address of the sanatorium where her husband was recuperating; it was several hundred miles away in Scotland. Having explained the serious nature of her husband's illness, and according to her account he was virtually at death's door, she persuaded him that she could pay the debts given a little time, and she produced a substantial amount of money from her purse saying that she would pay that amount now, and the same amount each week until the debts were cleared.

He accepted her offer, after all there were special circumstances in this case and as long as she kept up the payments there would be no serious problems. In fact however, new debts were being incurred all the time until they rose above the amounts she was able to repay, and as the number of judgements increased it became obvious that there was no way that she could continue with this arrangement. The law was quite clear, the husband would have to be served with the summonses regardless of his state of health. The Chief Clerk set in motion the action required in such cases and was awaiting a reply to his letter. In the meantime Mrs A. continued paying what money she could into the office.

Shortly thereafter I was working in the vicinity of this debtor's home when I met up with the local council rent collector; we were acquainted and our paths crossed frequently.

'Have you been visiting Mrs A.?' he asked, 'and has she told you that her husband is dying in some sanatorium up in Scotland?'

'Yes, that's correct,' I answered.

'Yes, that is what she told me too, she owes God knows how much back rent, and I have just discovered that she is a bloody liar. Her husband is not ill, neither is he in Scotland, he is living here at home and is working on the permanent afternoon shift at British Cellophane.'

When we compared notes the reason why we had not caught up with Mr A. became apparent. When we called at his house in the evening he would be at work of course, and when we called in the mornings he would be in the house but Mrs A. would always come out shushing everyone up because she had her sick grand-daughter asleep inside whom she did not want disturbed. It was her husband she did not want disturbed of course and when I gave it some thought I realised that it was not possible for the grand-daughter to be sick and asleep every time I called in the mornings. She had bamboozled everyone for months.

Returning to my office, I repeated the story to the Chief Clerk, we gathered together all the summonses issued against Mr A., and I would call that very afternoon at British Cellophane and have a little chat with him.

I spoke to the Personnel officer who kindly arranged for Mr A. to come out of work to meet me and he provided an empty room where we could discuss the matter. I knew that what I had to say would come as a great shock to Mr A. and I quietly explained and gave him all the facts in as gentle a way as I could. I had seen men go berserk when faced with similar situations, but I knew that if I kept a calm and quiet profile myself, it would help to lower the temperature of the inevitable outburst as realisation of his position began to sink in.

It must be a tremendous shock to the system to be informed suddenly that you owe a lot of money and are in immediate danger of being committed to prison if you cannot pay the debts. And if you have been giving your wife the rent and housekeeping expenses regularly to pay all the bills it must be even worse.

He took the information and the summonses very well considering the enormity of his wife's actions. He was of course an innocent party, but when I told him that the reason I had not been able to contact him before was because his wife had told me he was supposed to be dying in a sanatorium in Scotland, he exploded in a rage.

'I will bloody well swing for her, the cow, I have never kept her short of money and paid her regularly every week and she has done this to me.'

I attempted to calm him down; had his wife been present he would have throttled her, I could only hope that he would cool down before he got home, I knew that Mrs A. was in for a rough time when they met. He was stocky and a powerfully built Scot and quite capable of doing his wife serious injury in his rage; only time might lessen his anger.

Mrs A. was not seen in public for almost two months. When she did appear, the evidence of her husband's violence could be seen in the bruising on her face, the chastising must have been severe for it still to show after such a long time; her arm was still in a sling, it had been broken. But never again did she get into debt, I think he would have killed her had she done so. He asked me to let him know if she ever started to do the same thing again so that he could nip it in the bud. He cleared his debts finally and I never had occasion to meet him again.

Another time when I finally managed to meet a husband, having to serve process on him due to his wife's disastrous financial mis-management, I would rather not have been present, but I was already in the house and had no other choice than to watch as he bodily lifted his wife till her feet were off the floor, then pounding her against the wall he cursed and blasphemed, repeating the actions and emphasising every word with another thump against the wall. Her body might have taken the punishment, but with every thump, her head snapped back and struck the wall with considerable force.

I feared for her life and managed to placate and persuade him that he would be much worse off if he murdered her. He stopped beating her up but it would be a long time, if ever, before she would be forgiven. Certainly she would not be allowed to forget and would have to account for every penny her husband gave her. I experienced many of these situations and used to marvel how the wives of these violent men could take the beatings and ill treatment and yet remain living with their husbands.

Most of the wives remained loyal to their men. I can only surmise that they were aware of their responsibility, they had done wrong, it was their fault that the husband had to face the music and they must have felt very guilty about getting him into debt, because of this it was natural for them to be punished. Of one thing I am sure, women would not accept such treatment as readily today and there would be Divorce petitions galore at the first sign of trouble. Perhaps it is just as well that the law no longer considers the husband to be responsible for his wife's debts; she has to sort out her own problems now.

I was not in the habit of interfering between husband and wife in normal circumstances, and I got my fingers severely burnt on the one occasion I did.

I knew of one regular debtor, a small time criminal who was seldom at home. He spent most of his time detained in prison at Her Majesty's pleasure. Whenever their happened to be a burglary, house breaking, or other similar crime, the local police would make a bee line for Mr C. Ninety nine times out of a hundred, he was the culprit and when confronted would cheerfully confess his guilt and inevitably end up doing another term of imprisonment.

When I called at his home I was very surprised to find him there during one of his rare spells of freedom. His wife answered the door as usual and answered my query, yes her husband was at home, and yes she would call him. She was heavily pregnant and looked as if the baby was due at any minute. It was a very cheerful and happy man who appeared a few moments later, at least until I presented him with two Judgement summonses for quite a fair amount of debt. With the realisation of the part his wife had played in putting him into this position, his face clouded over and he angrily called her to the door.

'Look,' I said, 'I don't want to talk out here where your neighbours can hear your business.'

'Well come inside then.' The husband ushered me into the living room and invited me to explain what the debt was all about. I went into my usual routine for these occasions and told him that when the wife got seriously into debt and could not pay it off, the husband being responsible for her actions was the person who had to pay. She interjected several times as I was talking in an attempt to justify what she had done and in the hope of pacifying her husband, but his rage intensified almost with every second as he listened and the understanding sank in.

'You f—ing bastard!' he cried, and he punched her in the face. It was a severe blow that felled her immediately to the floor and he started kicking her in the body. It had happened so quickly and the violence was so intense as to take me by surprise; quite a few seconds elapsed before my brain started working normally again and I had recovered my wits.

Grabbing him and wrapping my arms around him thereby pinning his arms to his body, I pulled him away from her and shouted at him to calm down.

'You will kill the baby and her too,' I cried, 'It must be due any time now, and that will not solve the problems you have, will it?'

I held him firmly until I felt him relax. 'It's not the end of the world,' I said, 'and I will show you how to deal with this matter, you really must not abuse your wife like that again, you could cause her serious injury as well as the baby.'

The wife, who was slowly getting to her feet looked up at me and said, 'You mind your own f—ing business and f— off.'

You could have knocked me down with a feather. Here I was, risking injury to my own body in defending her from a vicious and dangerous attack, being told to mind my own business and go away. I could only surmise that she was quite used to being physically abused on a regular basis, and what is more she must have enjoyed it. I promised myself that I would never again interfere between a husband and wife whatever the circumstances. I came across many cases of similar violence, and found it very difficult to understand why it was accepted by so many wives.

Can there still be some strange form of love still existing between a couple who are constantly fighting and arguing with one another? I can only conclude that there is, and it is far more common than one would suppose. Frequently I came across cases where the wife was more violent than the husband.

I came across a different kind of violence once; many would smile at this kind of situation, but I don't suppose it would be so funny if one was personally involved.

This poor chap seemed to be very down in the mouth, so much so that I asked him if he was OK. He was very thin and weakly, his face was drawn and haggard, and I thought he was quite ill. Thinking perhaps I might be able to help him in some way, I persisted in my efforts to get him to confide in me and get his problems off his chest.

'My wife is a nymphomaniac' he explained. 'I didn't know when we got married and everything was fine for a while anyway, but I can't keep up with her now, she demands sex all the time, after almost every meal, and then she wants it three or four times every night. I am completely knackered and have a job to keep my eyes open at work I am that tired.'

The poor fellow had tears in his eyes and was pretty much at the end of his tether.

'You will have to insist on her being more reasonable,' I said, 'I don't know of any man capable of such a sustained effort, it might be all right now and again, but it would be impossible for most men to perform seven or eight times every twenty four hours day after day.' I had managed not to smile as he told me of his predicament. Most men would have been rolling in the aisles with laughter by now and chivvying the unfortunate man unmercifully, wishing they could be so lucky. The fact that I was sympathetic and serious about it made him feel that at least someone understood.

'Yes but she tells everyone that I am useless in bed; not only that, she comes from a big family and has several large brothers, they threaten to beat me up if I don't do what she wants, what am I going to do?'

I could not think of any sensible answer. 'You can either find a good friend willing to help you out by taking on some of your duties, or failing that you will have to leave her and disappear forever before you drop dead with exhaustion.'

I never saw him again and I have no idea how he solved the problem, but I thought, I am experiencing life in all its strange facets. I would not have cared to be in his shoes for a fortune. What a life to be sure, easy for some and hard for others. What force I wonder, directs who is to suffer, or who is to be rich or poor. Why do some suffer, and yet others have comfortable and uncomplicated lives, and will man ever know the answers to those questions? I doubt it somehow.

I was finding much interest and satisfaction with my new job, and as time passed and the opportunity came to become full time I had little hesitation in accepting it. My employers were very happy with my work, and I knew I was good at it. The fact that it was impossible to make a decent living from my holding without enlarging and increasing stock to a much bigger operation was the crucial point. I did not have the land or the capital to expand even if I had wanted to, but I did not, I really wanted to be independent and self sufficient in a small way without having to work day and night like a lunatic, or having to commit myself to a big and expensive business venture which might or might not succeed. And there was the rub.

Oh, I could have managed and lived as I wished to, I would have been independent, but only at the expense of a very poor and lacklustre life; this I would not accept.

When considering all aspects of the situation there was also the possibility of promotion which I felt I could achieve. I set about learning my job with a thoroughness that was to stand me in good stead in future years. It would mean giving up the holding probably but it could be worth it in the long run. Anyway it would be some years before I got

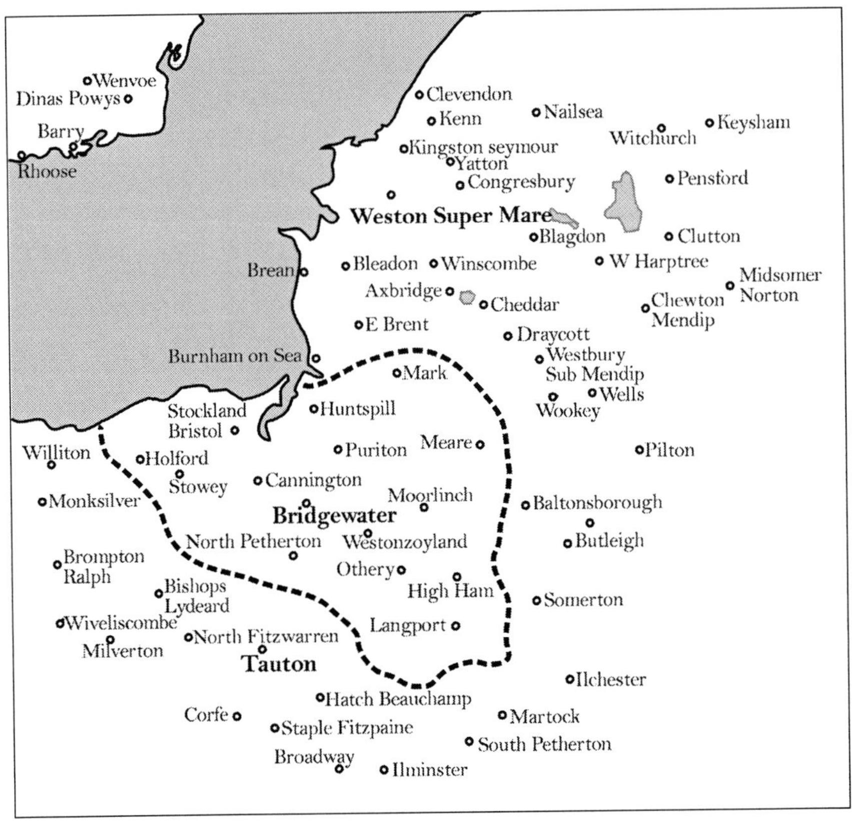

Bridgewater County Court, 1963 to 1970.

promotion and be required to move to another area, and so, having decided to pursue a career in the Civil Service I concentrated more on that side of my life, and kept the holding just ticking over.

The main Court was in Bridgwater, Somerset, jurisdiction was exercised from there east as far as the village of Ashcott, north to the Huntspills and the edge of Highbridge, east to Hinkley Point, Nether Stowey and that part of the Quantock hills and south to Langport, from there across country to within two miles of Taunton. An imaginary circle drawn around these villages and towns would enclose all of the court area. In later years there was a great deal of alteration to the boundaries and the numbers of Bailiffs required to operate within them in an effort to modernise and reduce the costs of the service.

There were two Bailiffs allocated for Bridgwater. Charlie and I divided the area in two and each of us worked one area for six months after which we changed over. It was a good arrangement, the type of work being what it was made it impossible to be exactly in half, but if one of us had more work than usual, then the other was willing to assist by taking a few processes from the overworked Bailiff to help even up the work. There were also many occasions when we were obliged to work together, when we had awkward evictions to deal with, or perhaps a particularly violent man to arrest.

I particularly remember when one particular farmer threatened to loose the bull on us if we did not go away, and a pretty vicious looking beast he was too. Charlie picked up a pitchfork and said, 'Let him loose, I'm not afraid of him, but I tell you this, I don't know how much he is worth at the moment, but he will only be good for meat when I have finished with him, he certainly won't do any more breeding.'

Needless to say the farmer never carried out his threat. Charlie had a reputation and would have carried out his promise.

We frequently worked together, it was prudent at times. One was open to all kinds of accusations when working alone and without any independent witnesses. I have been accused of making improper suggestions, improper advances, homosexual actions, and at one time attempted rape. None of the accusations were true, and no action was ever taken against me in pursuit of any of these allegations. The shoe was frequently on the other foot though, and I was often invited into the bedroom whilst the husband was at work in the forlorn hope that the wife could settle her debts in a way that did not involve parting with money.

I quickly learned where the dangers lay, and whenever I felt that things were tricky I would ask my colleague to accompany me. I felt vulnerable at times for I knew that some women who in a financial sense were at the end of their tether and could not see any other way out of their problems, would make almost any accusation in the hope of gaining sympathy and avoid having to pay their debts. Some would phone or write to the court with various complaints. Charlie's answer to such accusations was to tell the wife that he was going to tell the husband all about her debts (something they were all anxious to avoid), and also have her brought to court to face the Judge to answer to her lies. This remedy usually worked and the threat to have them brought before the Judge was enough to prevent them causing mischief.

One's integrity could be challenged in other ways too. Quite frequently Judgement Summonses had to be served by meeting and handing to the individual named in the process, it was known as personal service. The

Bailiff had to serve that named person, it could not be given to any other party and the Bailiff swore on oath that he had performed this duty correctly. He could not even give it to the wife who might promise to give it to her husband; she could, of course, be lying and not give it to her husband; the obvious reason being that she herself had incurred the debt and did not want him to know about it.

This was a requirement of the law, and it was really the same as an order to appear before the Judge to answer personally why the debt had not been paid, judgement against the debtor having been given some time before. It was also important in that it was the start of the Commitment process; from here on in, debtors were in the dangerous situation where there was a real possibility that they might be ordered to prison, and they were required to appear before the Judge to show just cause why they should not be committed to prison for non payment of a debt.

Unfortunately for them, there are snobs in the world who feel that they are superior beings.

Perhaps because of family position, maybe wealth or education or just old fashioned class, their attitude towards anyone of the lower orders of humanity was that they needed to be kept in their place in society and constantly reminded of it. They were looked down on with disdain, and only when absolutely necessary would the snob condescend to meet, talk, or listen to them.

So it was on those occasions when I had to serve a Judgement Summons on such a person. I was just the Bailiff and could be snubbed, insulted, looked down on, reviled and argued with and was often ordered to leave the premises. I had more problems with this type of person, the so called better class, than with all the working-class debtors put together. Not only the poor get themselves in financial trouble, but the better off, better educated, and those who should know better were also frequently in debt.

Many of these people would refuse to accept the summons from me, arguing that they did not owe any money, or, 'Go away or I will call the police, you have no right to come to my house!'

I had learned to let insults run off me. I was inured to abuse and could remain calm under most situations and because of the serious nature of the summons I would explain its significance to everyone, but to the snob I had great difficulty in not being sarcastic. The name that follows is of course a fictitious one, but is typical.

'I beg your pardon, sir, but you are Mr John Warrington Neville Percival Smythe-Fitzwarren, are you not?' I would wait for affirmation, then on receiving it would add, 'Then I'm afraid I can't go away, I am obliged to serve this summons on you, sir, and it is my duty to point out to you that you are ordered to attend court at the time and day stated. If you do not attend, His Honour the Judge could send you to prison in due course for contempt.'

'If you don't go away, you horrible man, I will call the police and have you arrested, I do not owe any money, and I am not going to accept the summons from you.'

'Well I'm sorry about that, sir, but if you will not take the summons from me, I shall drop it here at your feet. That still constitutes proper service.' I would hold out the summons offering it to the debtor.

'You can do what you bloody well like, I am not taking it so go away.'

On this retort I would drop the summons and leave.

Many of the debts were paid of course before any further action had to be taken, but some were not. The Judge would frequently ask me about the debtor and I would give him any information I might have including the debtor's attitude to the debt and to me. His Honour might issue an order for the debtor to attend court and it would definitely mean a prison sentence if the order went unheeded, and I would return to the same person hoping that he still might have the same haughty attitude as before and ignore this order too. 'Sir, I have another order here, and if you will not accept it I shall drop it on the ground as I did the last one.'

He did ignore the order, and I took great pleasure in arresting him and delivering him to Horfield Prison in Bristol where he served fourteen days for contempt and still had to pay the debt when he was released. He learned the biggest lesson in his life; he never again insulted me, and showed me the utmost respect thereafter. It is good to know we are living in a country where all citizens are treated equally regardless of position or wealth.

Chapter Twenty-seven

THERE WERE OF COURSE others who were gentlemanly enough to accept the inevitable without making a huge fuss about it all. One, an elderly Colonel (retired), had tried very hard to persuade me not to proceed with the execution of the warrant I held against him; he needed more time to complete a deal that he was convinced would end all of his financial problems. Being ex-army, as indeed he himself was, I explained that I was under orders to carry out my duty just as if I was still in the army, and there was nothing that I personally could do to help him. He understood perfectly what my position was and did not attempt to make life difficult for me. I was glad to see him later overcome his problems and turn his affairs around making his business profitable again.

The average debtor was working class and I could often see the humorous side of many of the situations I faced. I recall Ron and Eff, so named by me because of their similarity to an engaged couple of lovers who were part of a weekly radio show at the time. Having visited Eff a couple of weeks earlier to warn her that she was in imminent danger of losing her cooker to the Gas Board if she never paid them some of the arrears, and again just a few days before to give her the removal time and date, I turned up early one evening with the gas fitters to remove the cooker.

The usual argument started with her shouting and swearing and wasting time until I would have no more of it and I ordered the fitters to move the cooker.

At that moment Ron her partner arrived back home, and Eff opened the cooker oven door, produced Ron's dinner and placed it on the table before him, 'Now you can take it away,' she said. She had been holding off the removal just to keep Ron's dinner hot for him, that was far more important than losing the cooker.

In fact at that time the nationalised Electricity and Gas Boards were very lenient with the customers who were seriously indebted to them, and payment of a few shillings with the promise of a continued effort to pay off arrears would be sufficient to let them off the hook until the arrears accrued once again to an unacceptable level, until even the Gas or Electricity Boards would no longer allow the situation to continue. The comical thing about it all was that after the removal of the cookers or whatever appliance it might be, the payment of a small deposit by a different partner, in other words by using a different name, one or other of the utilities would immediately install a new or as good a new cooker to replace the old one, thus making a nonsense of the system, and doing nothing to recover the debt. Social Services would immediately replace any cooker that had been seized more especially if there were children in the house. Naturally, seasoned debtors were familiar with the system and took every advantage. Ron and Eff were professional debtors and Ron was one of those who could work out the profitability or loss of serving a week or ten days in prison as opposed to paying the debt. If he found it in his interest to serve time rather than pay the debt, he would always present himself at our rendezvous in good time and ready to jump in the car to go to prison, he was never any trouble. His fourteen-year-old daughter was already well versed in the tricks of the trade and could lie like a trooper as well as plying the same trade as her mother, prostitution.

There was another poor chap that I felt rather sorry for, he lived in a small almost derelict cottage on the moors with his wife and daughter. He barely scraped a living doing odd jobs for farmers and trying to support a few animals on his tiny bit of land. He was not a great deal in debt but I always had a summons or other document for him. I often wondered why he was never at home when I called. In time I discovered that whenever he heard or saw a vehicle approaching, he dived for the nearest ditch and stayed there until his visitor had left. He lived in crisis from one debt to another. He died of pneumonia one severe winter and I could not help but think it was a blessed release from his problems.

I also learned not to make assumptions, things are not always what they seem. I used to visit one farmer on a regular basis, always having to collect debts or serve some process or other. It seemed that this fellow was also living close to poverty. He had four or five young children and I became a little concerned for their welfare especially when I had to look through his home for items that I could levy on as security against a debt. The home was very poor and the children's bedroom floor was covered with bricks; apparently the farmer had been doing some building work there and it was still unfinished. I noticed that the beds had no mattresses and the bedclothes were just old coats, no proper sheets or blankets. Then when I got outside I could see that the children were dressed virtually in rags.

I determined that this was a case for the RSPCC. These poor kids should not be living in such obvious hardship so I made a report to that authority and forgot all about it. It was not until several weeks later that I received a phone call from an inspector, wishing to discuss my report. He thanked me for my vigilance and then enquired if I had actually looked at the children during my visit to the farm. I told him that it seemed obvious to me that they were deprived because of their poor clothing and lack of bedding.

He then explained to me that the children were not hungry or neglected, in fact they were all healthy well adjusted kids and perfectly happy. It was not his purpose to criticise the way people lived, and the fact that they were poor and not well clothed, or had no bed linen was neither here nor there, but there was no case of child neglect. I had assumed that poverty meant neglect and it was not always so, I had learned another lesson.

Because we were a small Court, the bailiff also acted as Court Usher and Charlie and I would take turns for this job several times a month for the Registrar's Court, and once a month for the Judge. Many of the cases were dull and seemed never ending, but occasionally there would be something more interesting and also entertaining. Our own Judge seemed to find cases involving farmers and their cattle something to be enjoyed far more than mundane business cases, and he would go into great detail with the evidence of both parties, I am sure he liked to listen to the broad Somerset accent that emanated from the protagonists as they put forward their arguments. The failure of a prize bull to perform his duty on a farmer's cow was a frequent source of litigation which he particularly enjoyed hearing. Of course he lived in the countryside himself and no doubt was involved in village affairs.

During my service in the Bridgwater area I experienced a rare situation. I have written elsewhere that the vast majority of our debtors or as I liked to call them, clients, were from what was commonly known as the working classes. But I did have a titled Lady whom I will refer to as Lady B. She lived in an old house in the country where she spent her time riding and caring for a few horses. She was quite elderly at the time, in her seventies I would imagine, and she was married to a wealthy business man who was the principal owner of a well known chain of fashion shops.

Chapter Twenty-seven

They were happily married, but he lived and worked in Scotland most of the time, and she remained at home in the west country. He returned home for short spells on occasions and they had an amicable life style. The home was beautifully furnished and full of quality furniture and antiques, and the house stood in about ten acres of lovely wooded countryside.

I was a regular visitor to Lady B. usually because a warrant had been issued against her by some trader or other for non payment of a bill. She could be seen in Taunton or one or other of the major towns in the area every few weeks, beautifully dressed and bejewelled, shopping in the better-class establishments and always buying on credit. She would spend the whole day out, taking her lunch and tea in a good hotel before returning home. The problem was that she could never pay her bills and I would be forced to levy against one of her horses as security against the debt. I did that specifically because she so loved her horses and would do anything rather than have any of them sold.

Yet inevitably she would arrive at the court office just at the last minute prior to the sale and pay her debt together with the costs, and thereby save yet again her precious horses. I had great difficulty in understanding her actions. She was so obviously wealthy, whatever reason did she have for not paying her debts? They were not unduly large, usually six or seven hundred pounds, and why did she always wait to pay at the last minute? When I got to know her I asked how it was she got herself into such a pickle every time she owed a little money.

On the previous occasion that she had been in trouble I visited her with a warrant for seven hundred pounds. She must have been expecting me because she had taken the trouble to remove her horses and in so doing, prevent me from levying on them. She told me that she did not like me taking her horses away and I was not going to do it.

I told her that it did not matter because her house was full of splendid furnishings and I would levy on something else.

With that she went into her bedroom and returned with two necklaces of beads which she handed to me saying that she was sure they would cover her debt. We normally did not levy on jewellery, but I knew she always paid up in the end, and it was less time consuming than arranging the removal of furniture. I slipped the necklaces into my coat pocket and returned to the office and explained to the chief clerk what I had done.

He was not too happy with my actions but told me to take them down to the jewellers who valued items for the court prior to them being entered in a sale. I entered the shop and asked the owner if he would value the necklaces for the court.

'Yes of course, sir, if you would care to wait a few minutes.' With that I sat down. I had not up to now given any thought to the necklaces, I did not know if they were valuable, they could have been cheap beads from Woolworths for all I knew, but if they were not worth anything, Lady B would have made a mug out of me. Back came the jeweller,

'I am sorry, sir, but I cannot give a valuation on these necklaces.'

'Can't you give me any idea at all, I only need to know if they are worth putting in the sale or not?'

'Well sir, one of these necklaces is a perfectly matched set of opals, and the other a perfectly matched set of jade, and I am not qualified to value them, each necklace must be worth at least fifty thousand pounds.'

Almost struck dumb with shock, I took the necklaces, mumbled my thanks and tore back to my chief clerk with the news. We had committed an offence and over levied.

'Get them straight back to her now and get a receipt before we get into trouble,' he said.

I told him that I did not think she realised the true value of them, and in any case she was the one that had insisted I take them as security, we could not be expected to know the value. I was fairly sure she did not realise we were in breach of regulations and I did not think there would be any repercussions. I returned the necklaces and Lady B cleared her debt shortly thereafter.

When I got the opportunity to talk with her, she explained her situation to me. As a young debutante she had become a lady in waiting to Her Majesty Queen Mary. She produced photographs taken when she was very young together with Her Majesty. Her father was a very rich and titled member of the aristocracy, and had seen his daughter married off successfully to her present husband. It had been a good match and they had been very happy, they still were. Her problem was that she had never handled money in her whole life, she had been born with a silver spoon in her mouth and completely spoiled.

Daddy handled all the finances before she got married; if there was anything at all that she required, a new dress perhaps or maybe shoes, everything was put on his account. She just did not need or have any use for money. Even after her marriage the same arrangement continued and her husband paid the bills. It was only since their present arrangement started, with him working and living most of his time in Scotland, and she did not think it important enough to bother him about such unimportant matters, so he was unaware that his wife was not handling the finances at home and having difficulties.

It was on one of the rare occasions when he was visiting home that I met him. I had yet another process against Lady B. that I needed to see her about. He was sitting in the garden reading the newspaper, and I introduced myself and asked to see Lady B. He in turn told me who he was and wanted to know what a bailiff required of his wife? I explained everything to him, and suggested that his wife needed some help in managing her affairs. He was astonished to hear what had been happening, and had no idea that she had been in such trouble. The outcome of it all was that he immediately gave me a cheque to settle the debt. He also gave me his card and requested that if anything similar occurred again I should contact him and he would forward me payment by return. I think we both were quite happy with the outcome and I never saw Lady B. again.

Divorce in the 60s was on the increase too and there were many times when I had to smile at hearing evidence. One case was brought by a wife who had four children by her first marriage, against her husband who also had four children by a previous marriage. They were all happily living together in a house on one of the estates until there was an argument and the wife locked her husband out one night. He went boozing down the pub and returned home some time after midnight well and truly intoxicated to find the door bolted against him.

The wife's evidence went something like this: 'He was shouting at me through the letterbox, he said he loved me and that I should let him in. I told him to go away, but he said he would kill me if I did not open the door, he would kick it in. I would not open the door and he urinated through the letterbox and then kicked the door in and he came in and punched me.' Back and forth the accusations passed until the Judge threw the case out of court. Both of them had been lying through their teeth and it was a case of six of one, and half a dozen of the other. The amusing thing was that they left the court arm in arm, perfectly reconciled.

There were a lot of women who tried to use the court as a means of controlling their husbands, by getting an order preventing them or ex-husbands from visiting their children by accusing them of violence in the home even if were not true. They would try to force the husband to comply with their wishes. It was my experience that the majority of husbands were not willing to attend court or argue out the actual evidence; they frequently got an order issued against them by default, that is to say they were not present at the hearing to put their side of the matter and so everything the wife said even if it was a tissue of lies, was accepted by the court as the truth without question.

It follows from the issue of an order against the husband that he was a violent man who beat up on his wife because everyone knew that the wife had got a court order restraining him from doing certain things, one of which could well be visiting his children. I knew of one vindictive woman who built up such a case against her ex-husband, that he was forbidden ever to see his little girl again; his wife had made accusations that he would interfere with his daughter if he got to her.

He was a quiet unassuming man who idolised his little girl. The order so depressed him that he committed suicide. Everyone acquainted with the couple knew the truth of the matter: there is much truth in the old saying, 'Hell hath no fury like a woman scorned.' In general, the Judge would be aware of these situations and took them into account in his deliberations.

It was in 1970 that I was promoted to Supervising Bailiff. It meant that at last I had decided to make a career out of my job rather than continue with the smallholding; it also meant that I would have to move, there were no other vacancies except the one at Barrow-in-Furness which at that time was in Lancashire; when County lines were re-drawn it became part of Cumberland. My first wife and I separated and were divorced that same year. I had always been of the opinion that if people could no longer get along and live in harmony, what is the point in trying to prolong the agony.

My promotion meant that I would be supervising all the bailiffs in a group of County courts, which included the Whitehaven and Kendal courts, each one covering fairly large areas. I was confident that I could do a good job and given time to settle down would probably enjoy the Lake District which was included in the group area. After a couple of years, the Lancaster Court was added to my area of responsibility making the overall group of courts the largest in area in the UK. I had to drive considerable distances, and occasionally spend a night away from my base at Barrow since the greater amount of work was done in the evenings when the debtors are home, and I needed to be present with the bailiffs when they made their visits in order to assess their work.

Lancaster Group Courts, Kendal, Barrow-in-Furness, Whitehaven 1970 to 1978.

In this respect I knew that I had been accepted by most of those I was now in charge of. Most bailiffs were recruited from retired police officers or ex-army personnel; some of them had been quite high ranking officers, and since I was new and the youngest of them all, and also that I had been promoted over the heads of the lot of them, it must have been annoying and irksome to have to take orders from a jumped up nobody who seemed intent on altering their comfortable established arrangements. I was faced with near rebellion by a couple of the bailiffs, and one in particular was intent on ousting me if he could.

I had been promoted for the purpose of improving efficiency and that is what I was going to do. There were a number of things I was sure of, I was good at administration and had the ability to identify problem areas in the way work was performed, and I could produce and execute any plan I devised to remedy the situation. I was also experienced in handling men. I had also known for many years that to earn respect from one's men, one had to show them that one could do the job better than they could; also, I would never ask a man to do a job that I could not do myself. I set out in my new job to prove that I could not only do it, but I would also have the respect and friendship of my men. I would ask each bailiff I accompanied, which warrants were his most difficult ones; these we would visit and I would demonstrate my methods in the art of debt collecting. I was usually very successful and made quite an impression on the men, one of whom was heard to make the comment that I was definitely first division. Thereafter when they had a problem I could rely on the bailiff to approach me for advice or help, and even the one who had given me the most problems finally accepted me and made it evident by inviting me to tea at his home; thereafter we got along fine.

There were many different situations in which we had to work, and to do the job well required a deal of experience. One needed to quickly assess the situation, and then take action, not too tough nor yet too soft. It did not do any good to antagonise the debtor. If it was possible to get them to understand that it was only fair after all that the Plaintiff or trader should be entitled to their money, the debtor would reluctantly agree and this would often produce the desired effect, then by giving them a little time to pay, the bailiff was not forced to remove any of the debtor's furniture and the threat of a sale of their goods was avoided.

It was not always so. A debtor could become so incensed that he could turn violent and lose all control of himself. I had a case in Whitehaven where the debtor had bought furniture on Hire Purchase and almost paid for it and then lost his job. Because he was not at fault he believed that the balance of his debt could be paid at a rate to suit himself. The trader disagreed but the debtor still would not pay at the required rate and the trader issued an Execution warrant to seize the furniture.

I could see the problem and I could sense trouble, so I accompanied the bailiff to the debtor's house hoping against hope to take the heat out of the situation. Unfortunately the debtor would not listen, and I could not calm him down, events took their course and as he became more and more enraged he shouted out that we could all go to hell.

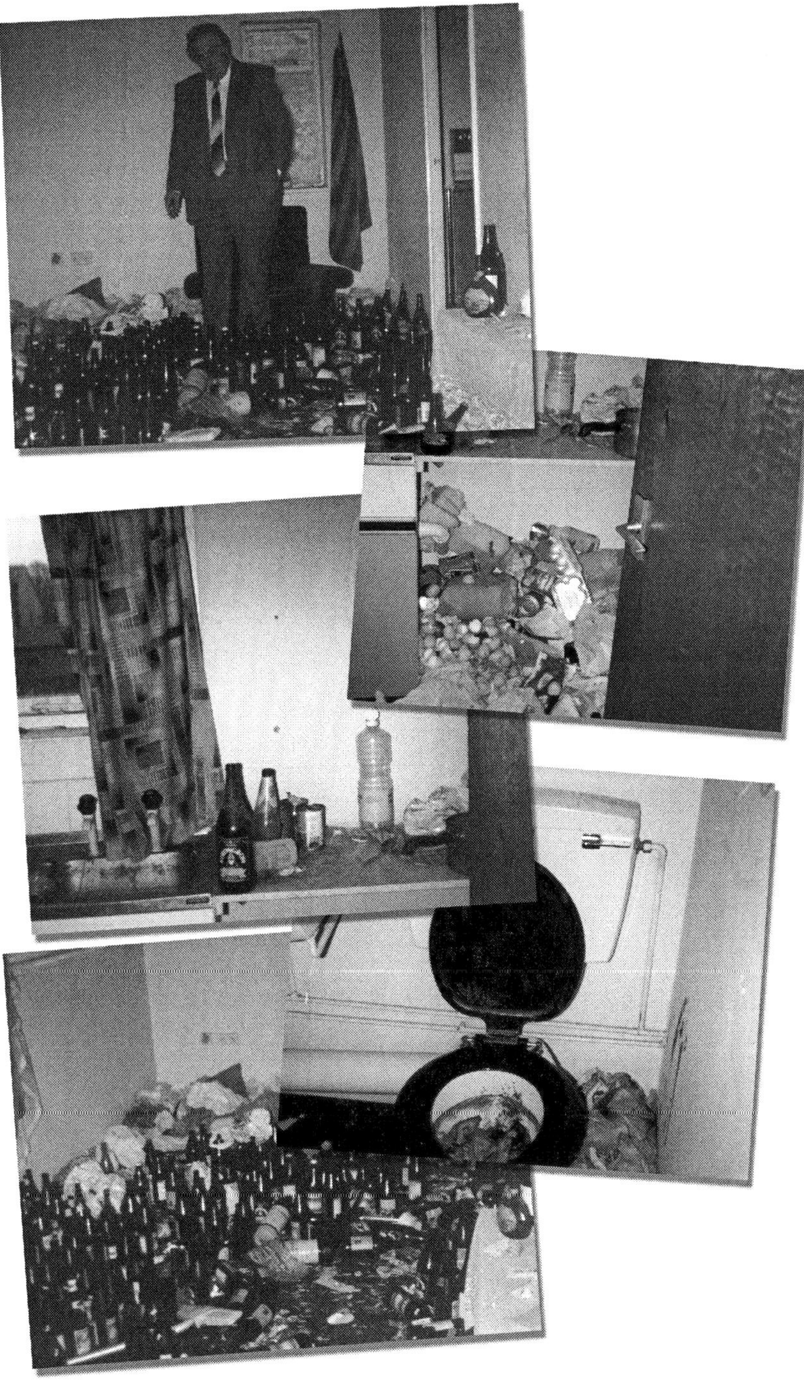

Author inspecting premises left by an alcoholic after eviction.

With that he ran to his garden shed and returned with a full sized woodman's axe and proceeded to smash and chop up every item of furniture in the room. His wife fled from the house, and my colleague and I stood back in the corner as the wild eyed and uncontrolled debtor destroyed everything. His rage was such that I feared he was going insane and we felt he might turn his attention to us; he continued slashing and chopping at what was now only small bits of wood until he became exhausted and could no longer swing the axe. 'Now you can take the furniture back,' he said.

I had to make a report of course, and the debtor was brought before the judge who sent him to prison for a short term to teach him that he could not ignore the court without incurring the wrath of the judge. He was put under supervision but he did apologise to me for his actions when I saw him again some time later.

There was also a great deal of trouble and unrest with farmers all over the country. The Government in its wisdom had arranged training courses for agricultural workers. These courses were voluntary, farmers were not required to attend or send their workers for training. The problem arose because, regardless of whether anyone from the farm had attended a course or not, the cost of these courses had to be borne by every farmer in the country. They had been ordered to pay even if they did not require the services.

The farmers would not pay and the Government created the Agriculture Training Levy Board in order to enforce payment, and all over the country, bailiffs were serving summonses on farmers for the costs of the system for which they did not want, create, nor in the majority of cases, use. The farmers were very angry and there was great difficulty in enforcing the orders. In an attempt to carry out the job, I think many a bailiff was put into an impossible situation and frequently only just managed to avoid physical violence by the skin of his teeth. Those officials who had been responsible for the idea should have been the ones to visit the farmers, they would have had to face the anger of those being forced to pay an unjust levy. There had been so much trouble that finally these charges were wisely withdrawn, and the attempt to make farmers pay gradually phased out.

There had been in Barrow-in-Furness in the seventies, a formidable sales campaign to persuade people to purchase the latest state of the art 26-inch TV. After payment of a small instalment the householder would get their set installed in the home and everything in the garden

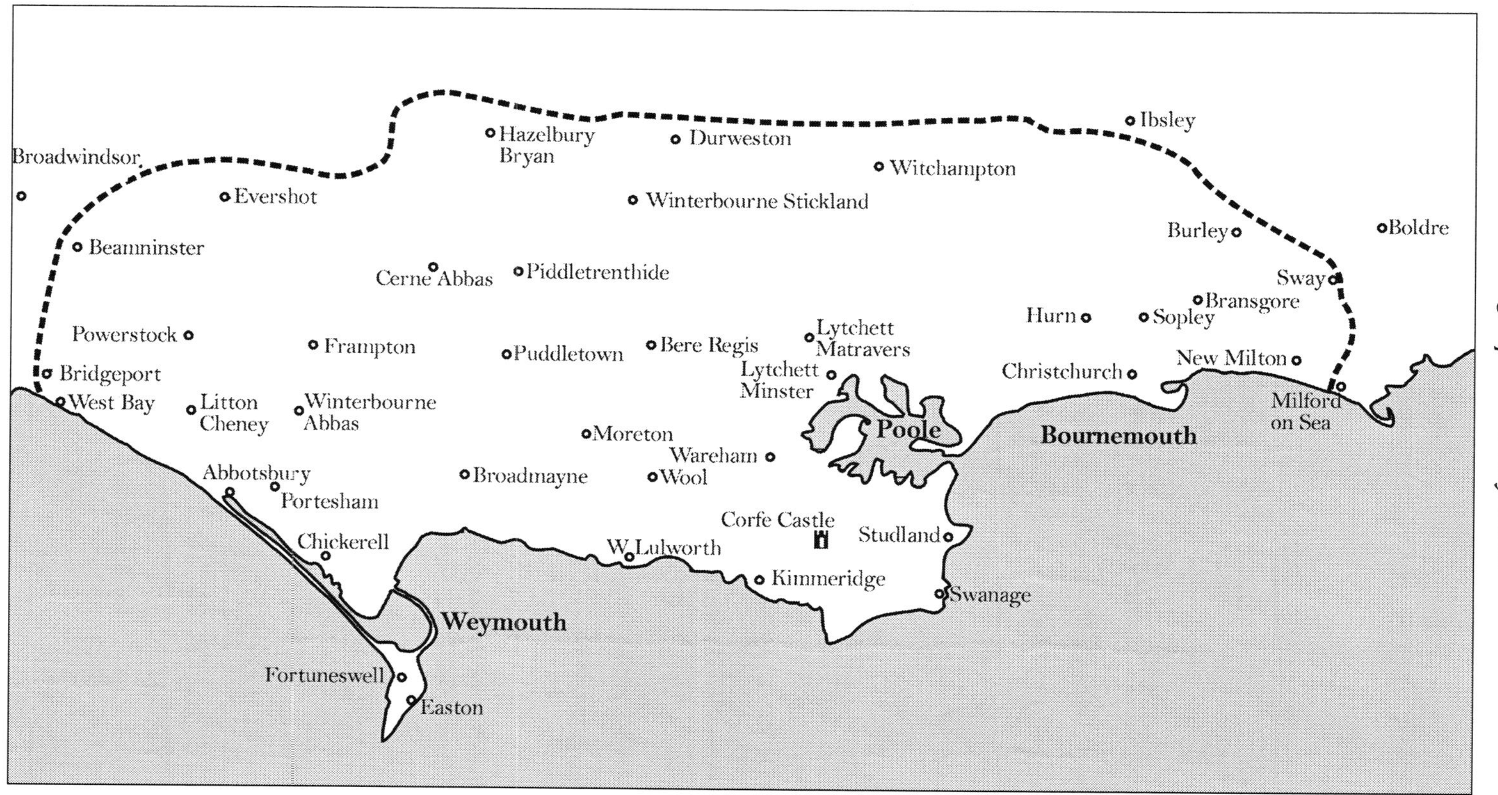

Bournemouth group of courts, Poole, Weymouth and areas inside dotted line 1978 to 1982.

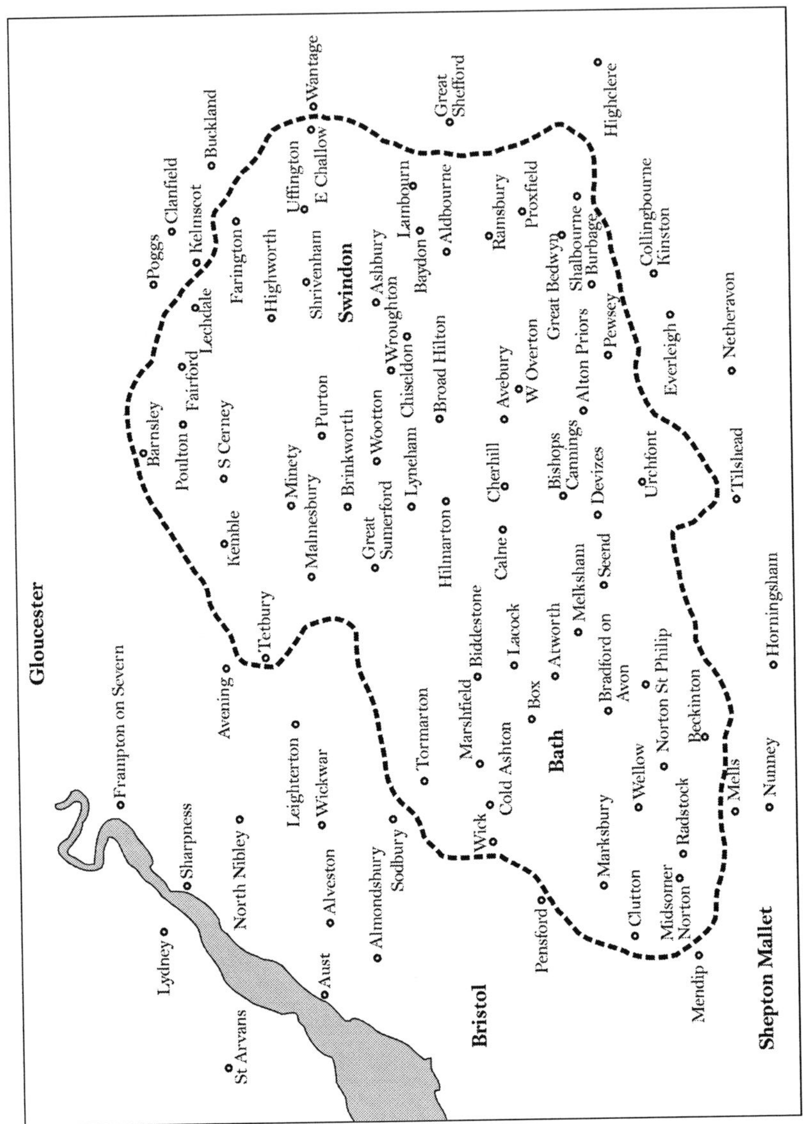

Swindon Group Courts, Bath, Trowbridge, Chippenham, 1982 to 1984.

was lovely. The problem arose when dozens of our regular debtors failed to pay the monthly rentals and the court was flooded with orders for Delivery Warrants to collect the sets and return them to the owners. I well remember that the total cost of one of these sets was four hundred pounds; they were very nice sets too, albeit perhaps a little expensive.

I accompanied one of the bailiffs to a small terrace house to recover one of these sets. We knocked on the door and entered the house. In one of the rooms a number of chairs had been arranged in rows just like the cinema, and seated in them were fifteen or twenty neighbours and friends all watching a programme on the TV. With a mumbled apology to the debtor, the bailiff and I unplugged the set and carried it out of the house to the waiting car leaving the audience still seated and gazing at the vacant space where the set had been. It seemed a very humorous situation indeed to me, and I cannot but wonder what explanation the debtor gave to the obviously disappointed assembly.

The Company had lost money on the campaign because for every set actually purchased, there must have been three returned and of course they were now second hand and of little value and there was no way they could have recouped their losses. The Company must have been very inexperienced to have been so lax in allowing known debtors to purchase goods that they could not afford. It would have taught them a valuable lesson no doubt.

Evictions were one of the most difficult assignments we had to carry out because frequently children were involved. I have to say however that I never experienced an unjust eviction during my years of service; always, the tenant would have been given plenty of opportunities to take some action that would alleviate their problems. Inevitably the eviction would take place as a result of failure by the tenant to do what had been ordered. Ignorance, lethargy, uncaring mentality and a reliance on the Social Services to provide an answer to their problems all played a part. The Social Service officers would frequently ask me not to carry out evictions even though they knew we were under court orders and were obliged to comply with the law. I always referred them to the Judge, 'He made the order,' I would tell them, 'And only he can rescind it.'

Frequently there would be animals of one kind or another on the property and it would be necessary to call in the RSPCA to deal with them. One eviction I did had 23 cats on the premises; you can imagine the problems in catching and housing that number of animals. At other times the children might have to be taken into care. It could be quite harrowing emotionally and very demanding physically to carry out some evictions and quite out of proportion in respect of the cost and subsequent benefit to both landlord and tenant.

I remember a case where a particularly rough family almost destroyed their home and made it virtually uninhabitable. The windows and doors were broken in, there were holes in the walls and the garden fences had been used for fuel. They had not paid any rent and owed about two years money. The authorities finally evicted them but the Social Services immediately put them in a new council house. I had already made it quite clear that within three months the new house would look exactly as the old one did when they were evicted. My words were proved true, I used to be annoyed at the way these useless layabouts were looked after and provided for at the expense of the responsible majority of decent people. And yet the authorities and those that I call do-gooders could not see that they were being taken for a ride. These scavengers would not work, yet they could wrap their Social case workers around their fingers. They were well versed in how to obtain every perk and allowance there was, and they lived and scrounged their way through life, managing quite well thank you, whilst the gullible, trusting and unsuspecting do-gooders feel sorry for them. They still do, yet most of this poor, destitute, deprived and hard done by class of citizens, who spend most of their lives sponging and being supported by the honest tax paying members of society, never ever contribute one penny to the public purse. And what is more, in spite of all their numerous social problems, there does not seem to be anything wrong with their drinking apparatus, or their breeding apparatus either.

Squatters on the other hand were even worse in my opinion because they would actually break into an empty property then claim that it was open and they just happened to walk in and take possession; they too would destroy perfectly good and well maintained homes, often pulling up the floor boards to burn as well, illegally connecting the electricity supply and doing all kinds of damage for which they would deny responsibility. The poor owners, arriving back from a holiday or sojourn away from home would be unable to get back into their own house without a protracted court hearing sometimes lasting for weeks, and they would then find there was no recompense or compensation, all repairs would have to be paid for by themselves. I strongly disagreed with some of the law dealing with squatters' rights since it was not intended to be used in the way most young hooligans had taken advantage of it and not for a genuine purpose. In my opinion the law should be far tougher when dealing with the useless undesirable and anti-social parasites that live in our country.

I also felt a strong sense of outrage when I had to deal with so called foreign students and all the other varieties of the same ilk who would rent a flat or apartment and then not pay the rent. By the time the matter had been through the legal system, the unfortunate landlord could lose hundreds of pounds and the perpetrator of the fraud live rent free for several months, then move to another area and repeat the same confidence trick. Time after time, the foreign visitor would carry in his pocket, clear instructions in how to approach the authorities and take advantage of the free benefits available in the UK. The first item printed on the leaflet was telling the visitor that he should first of all make his way to the Social Services and claim what was available. How stupid we British are to offer our hard earned money without any strings attached to all and sundry just for the asking; no wonder the country is flooded with asylum seekers. It is a heaven-sent paradise for them and it will continue until someone finally stops it, and that will probably be when it is too late and we have run out of resources.

Chapter Twenty-eight

THE JUDGES THAT I SERVED WITH were wise and just and extremely conversant with the law and all matters legal as, of course, they should be; they also seemed to possess an insight into the workings of human nature. There was one elderly mother trying to get her middle aged son evicted from her home because he drank and was doubly incontinent in the house. This resulted in repeated arguments and extra unnecessary work for her.

A few relevant questions from the judge quickly revealed that the man was an alcoholic. No one had realised the real problem during the several months it had taken to bring the case to court, yet the judge brought it to light almost immediately. Naturally he had the man admitted to the hospital for treatment, and refused to hear the case until the man was very much improved in health, and was able to speak in his own defence. Freedom of the individual and their rights is enshrined in our legal system and I never ever saw that abused by any judge. Every one I served under took great pains to protect defendants, and ensure that they understood their rights under the law.

I have known Judges visit locations without the knowledge of either parties in litigation, just to see for himself the place where certain allegations might have been made by either party.

He might have wanted to clarify some point or other, or even make a decision where there appeared to be conflicting evidence, but I witnessed many a person caught out by 'His Honour', embroidering their own particular version of events and attempting to influence the judge. Not realising that the Judge had popped out to view the situation for himself during the last adjournment, they would be left with egg on their faces when they realised that he was fully conversant with the situation. I remember one case that the Judge visited in this way. It concerned two neighbours, both elderly lady pensioners, who had fallen out with each other. The dominant one was continually harassing the other, knocking on her door at odd hours, pulling bricks from the foundation walls of her shed and throwing them at her door and making a real nuisance of herself, so much so that the poor old dear was terrified and afraid to leave her home for fear of abuse from her neighbour. Eventually she decided to bring a court action in an attempt to stop it.

The defendant causing the trouble denied everything on oath, putting the blame on the other party, and herself made wild accusations against her neighbour. Unknown to either party, the judge visited their homes during the lunch hour adjournment and saw for himself all the loose bricks still lying around the door where they had been thrown; he also noted that the bricks had been prised from the foundation wall thus undermining the shed which was now dropping lower on the side where the bricks had been removed. It was obvious who was lying. When the case reopened after lunch, the judge made very short work of the matter and committed the old lady to prison for a week at Risley. The experience cured her. It was subsequently realised that her real problem was one of loneliness, her husband had only been deceased a few months, her son and daughter both pursuing professional careers did not have much time to spare for her, and her mind led her into the vandalising behaviour that eventually got her noticed. She later became involved with charitable work which seemed to provide her with an interest in life; this seemed to cure her problem. Many and varied are the ways of the world, and during my service in the courts I have seen my share of them. The saying 'There is nowt as queer as folk' is also very true and I have found people to be as different as the stars in the sky. Human problems may be the same for many folk, but there are a myriad ways those same problems may be solved and one can never be sure just how a person might react.

I have experienced many assaults on my person. I have been chased by an enraged man brandishing a meat cleaver (which I have no doubt he would have used had he caught me). One person attempted to set fire to me, once I was attacked with an axe. I had many, many physical punch ups, and enough verbal abuse to fill a volume of *Encyclopaedia Britannica*. But I survived by being all things to all men: where sympathy was called for I sympathised, where a firm hand was required I used that too and in the main I gave respect where it was due, and received it back in abundance. It must be recognized however that the work of the bailiff is not an easy thing, there are not many who have the ability or the stamina to face up to the job.

One does not have many friends, and it takes quite a bit of backbone to face an irate family who are constantly shouting and verbally abusing you and where the thin line between verbal and physical violence is only maintained by quick thinking. It can be on occasions a very dangerous occupation and in some respects similar to that of a police officer, except of course that the bailiff is usually on his own, and the police work in pairs.

Now that I am getting on in years and approaching the end of my life, I would not have changed anything. I have lived life to the full, I have not been better or worse than my contemporaries and I have always held to the belief that one has a place in the order of things.

I constantly recall that little ditty my parents taught me as a young boy: 'Shine like a glow-worm if you can't like a star.' If you cannot be the best, be the best you can. No amount of striving will get you to that top position or job, if it is not meant to be. There can only be one boss, it is very unlikely that he will be you. If you cannot be the driver, then be the best wheel greaser there is, accept your place in life, do your best at the best job you can get, you will be far happier.

I believe that this is the greatest problem of our modern world. Parents are so busy urging their children to greater and harder studies, higher and even more academic achievement, putting more and more pressure on the kids, forcing them on and on. And in the process of this they fail to see that maybe Johnny or Mary are not able to cope. The kids get depressed and not knowing which way to turn, frequently attempt suicide. The parents are shocked and have no idea that their child was in such a mental state. There are hundreds of children that do away with themselves unable to take the stress and pressure forced on them unwittingly by their parents. Is it so important to be the top dog?

Crime by the young is rife in our society. Once we were a nation of practising Christians, families went to Church, kids were brought up to respect their parents and other people; if a child was naughty he or she received a smack from a parent and quickly learned that there was a right and a wrong; one was always punished for doing wrong. If a child received the cane for bad behaviour at school, the parent would admonish the child, thus backing up the authority of the teacher. Subsequently the children grew up to respect authority and other members of the community and there was far less crime.

Along come the do-gooders. Oh! One must not smack children, it will harm them mentally; let them act and behave as they wish, let them punch and kick and abuse their parents, let them cheek their elders, mug and rob pensioners, break into homes and steal other people's property, gang up and beat up people on the streets until old people are afraid to leave their homes and live in fear of their lives. Let them vandalise and cause havoc, and let the innocent citizen pay.

There was a case of a young thirteen year old who had a history of burglary, mugging, and a host of other crimes committed by him. His punishment for all this crime was to be sent on a £6000 holiday; the do-gooders felt he had been deprived as a child and would benefit from the holiday. Needless to say, he committed an offence at the holiday residence and continued with his former behaviour when he arrived back home. Are they blind or stupid or both, these people who think they know it all?

One frequently hears of prisoners complaining of the difficulties they have to put up with in overcrowded prisons. 'How awful!' cry the do-gooders. We should upgrade the prisons so that those undergoing punishment can live in five-star luxury.

From what I see of the prisons, they are far too luxurious as it is. How on earth does it profit society to make life so much like a holiday camp for offenders? If life is so good inside, the crook is never going to be afraid to return to his holiday address when he re-offends. He can laze around, read, play games and sports and do all the things one does when on holiday. Are we mad? I think that life in prison should be so horrible and hard, that anyone experiencing it should never ever want to go to prison for a second term. I remember talking to a man who had been punished with the birch for an offence when he was young. He told me that he would never ever want a second beating. We should bring it back, it did work, society is far better served if criminal offenders are not allowed to have any say in the manner or matter of how they are punished. I believe all punishment should be sufficiently severe to persuade the offender that it is just not worth the pain and suffering they will undergo if they break the law.

It is a load of twaddle to reason that a bad or an impoverished childhood causes a person to vandalise or steal. There are many thousands of citizens in the UK who suffered poverty and hardship as children, but the vast majority turned out to be law abiding. What is more, many thousands voluntarily laid down their lives in two world wars so that freedom and democracy would survive in this country. To treat young criminals with kid gloves instead of the severest punishment is an offence to those millions who died to uphold the law so that the rest of us could live without fear of young thugs that are allowed to do what they like and get away with it.

It is the parents and those in authority that are the real criminals, they have allowed little Jimmy to grow up without any discipline and without that there is no respect for anything or anyone, least of all the law.

Young Jimmy then, who has been allowed to do what he likes all of his young life, and is now thoroughly selfish, reaches his teens and begins to want more and more of the goodies in life. Up to now his parents have spoiled him and provided everything he has wanted or demanded but now are probably unable to do so any longer. He has probably been roaming the streets in a gang for some time, vandalising, and stealing. He sees no wrong in drug dealing, or other anti-social activities. He does not work, he has not been taught to earn a living, and as he attempts to enrich his life he can only do it by following the criminal trail.

Neither does he see any need to respect anyone. Why should he? All his life he has gotten his own way: shout, scream, make a fuss, be violent and smash things up, you will not be punished, at least not in any meaningful way. By the time he has to leave school he will have been indoctrinated to believe he can act and behave just as he pleases without consequence.

I fear for the future of society if we do not rectify these problems. It is a fine line between order and disorder and without a serious attempt to reinstate democracy we could see this country decline slowly into an insignificant third rate nation. Already there exists a whole section of society (our old age pensioners) who are afraid to leave their homes for fear of attack by gangs; no longer are they able to go out, they sit behind locked doors at night listening to hooligans rampaging through the estates at night, terrified that their home may be attacked. One can hardly believe it but it is a fact. The police do not have the power any longer to take the action they know is required to correct matters. It has been corroded by the lack of backing of the authorities. Government is afraid to act in any way for fear of losing support. The country needs new radical thinking backed up with firm action, only then will Great Britain retain its power and independent validity.

And so I come to the end of my tale. I hope it will have been of interest.